Cuba before Castro

Cuba before Castro

A Century of Family Memoirs

Jorge J. E. Gracia

Hamilton Books
Lanham • Boulder • New York • Toronto • London

Published by Hamilton Books
An imprint of The Rowman & Littlefield Publishing Group, Inc.
4501 Forbes Boulevard, Suite 200, Lanham, Maryland 20706
Hamilton Books Acquisitions Department (301) 459-3366

6 Tinworth Street, London SE11 5AL, United Kingdom

Copyright © 2020 by The Rowman & Littlefield Publishing Group, Inc.

All rights reserved. No part of this book may be produced in any form or by any electronic means, including information storage and retrieval systems, without written permission from the publisher, except by a reviewer who may quote passages in a review.

British Library Cataloguing in Publication Information Available

Library of Congress Control Number: 2020941497

ISBN: 978-0-7618-7213-9 (pbk.)
ISBN: 978-0-7618-7214-6 (electronic)

For my family and other Cubans in exile. A recollection of
a Cuba that no longer exists, except as memories
in the minds of Cuban refugees scattered throughout the world.

Contents

Preface		xi
1	Names and Identity. What's in a Name?	1
2	*"Je Suis Française!"*	7
3	Escaping Mexican Wrath	9
4	The Jesuits Stole My Inheritance	13
5	Poetry, Spirits, and Flair	15
6	Treasure Trove for Christmas	19
7	Promising Future Comes to Naught	23
8	*Una Señora Muy Aseñorada*	27
9	Unexpected Success	33
10	The Storyteller	37
11	Bedroom Suite for a Pompadour	41
12	*"¡España Es Nuestra Madre Patria!"*	45
13	Better Marry Than Burn	47
14	The Marquis' Mistress	49
15	Ruined by a Hurricane and Resentment Against Spaniards	53
16	Tears from a "Bileless Dove"	57
17	Murdered by the Guardia Civil	63
18	*La Dolorosa's* Miracle	67
19	Promising Beginning and Sad End	69
20	Is Having to Work Punishment for Sin?	73

21	Broken Promise	77
22	A Twenty-Five Year Engagement	81
23	Romance on a Scale	87
24	*"Te Voy a Capar"*	91
25	A Gentleman Farmer at Heart	93
26	Running Away from Home	105
27	A Boy's Best Friends	111
28	A Bad Dream Comes True	115
29	Rebel with a Cause	119
30	A Philosophy of Underwear	123
31	End of Paradise	129
32	The Bully	133
33	First Holy Communion	137
34	Summers at the Beach	143
35	Yearly Audit and Crocodile Tears	147
36	Lean Years	151
37	Written in the Stars	155
38	A Night to Forget	157
39	The Refuge of Faith	165
40	The Consolation of Giving	169
41	An Interim Abode	173
42	Long Journey Into Darkness	175
43	Bicycles Are for Boys	179
44	Nena's Insistent Gay Suitor	185
45	Looking for Domestic Help	189
46	María "Picadillo"	195
47	*"¡Yo soy muy macho!"*	199
48	Teenager in Havana	205
49	The Club	209
50	Another Call	213
51	The Cursed Plantation	217
52	Sugar and Slavery	219
53	*"El Marañon Aprieta la Boca"*	223
54	"I Believe in God"	227
55	Building Up the Spirit	237

56 First Cracks of the Faith	241
57 Brother Balloon	245
58 "¿Y Tu Abuela, Dónde Está?"	247
59 "Mens Sana in Corpore Sano"	255
60 "De Eso No Se Habla"	259
61 Two Years of Terror	261
62 A Beach House at Last	265
63 Love and Prejudice	269
64 Quest for Freedom	275
65 School for Toy Soldiers	279
66 A Teacher Who Could Not Teach	285
67 "I've Got Wheels!"	289
68 Playground of the Caribbean	293
69 Chaperones	297
70 Puppy Love	301
71 Graduation and a Prom of Sorts	305
72 Starved for Culture	309
73 Recreating the Garden of Eden	311
74 From Hope to Despair	315
75 The University of Havana	321
76 *Alea Iacta Est*	323
77 The Bay of Pigs and a Police State	337
Acknowledgments	343
About the Author	345

Preface

From the very moment that I set foot in the United States, on July 18, 1961, and particularly after I moved north, to the Chicago area, I was assailed with questions about myself, my origins, my background, the circumstances surrounding my exit from Cuba and arrival in the United States, my political alliances, the composition of my family, my religion, and countless other details of my life. Americans are a curious people, and they have no qualms about asking questions that in other cultures and countries are considered indiscreet, in bad taste, or taboo. Without embarrassment, they ask about your job, your profession, and even your money. Who are you and where do you come from? From where does your family originate? Are you Cuban or Spanish? How come you look white coming from Cuba? Do you have any black ancestors? How did you get out of Cuba? Was it easy? Were you a counter-revolutionary? Did you have to leave or did you just feel you wanted to leave? Did you come alone or with your family? What did your father do in Cuba? How did Cuba change when Castro took over the government? What do you think of the Revolution? Was Castro a Communist from the very beginning? Was it the fault of the United States that he went over to the Soviet side? What was it like to live in Cuba before the Revolution? And after the Revolution? What do you think about the U.S. embargo? Was your family rich? Are you Catholic? Are Cubans generally Catholic? Are there Protestants in Cuba? Where did you live in Cuba? Did your father have a profession? Did you live in Havana? Were other members of your family able to leave Cuba? Did you take any money out when you came to the US? How many siblings do you have? Did you attend public schools? Do you or your family believe in voodoo?

    This is a small sample of the questions I have been asked by Americans throughout the years of my life in the US. Indeed, there seems to be no end to the inquiries as long as I am willing to answer and elaborate. The curiosity of Americans is insatiable and understandable, particularly because Cuba has been at the center of world and American news ever since Castro's Revolution triumphed. Also, many Americans had visited Cuba before the Revolution and many have visited Miami and seen how the presence of Cubans has changed that city since then. They are particularly curious about how the political changes in the island have affected ordinary people. They want to learn about Cuba and its people, who they are, their concerns and idiosyncrasies. More significantly perhaps these questions led me to explore questions that I had never considered.

Over the years I have tried to answer these questions, but I have frequently been dissatisfied with my answers, although I have always answered truthfully, albeit not always fully. Reality is always more complex than one can express in words at any given moment. And parts of my experiences seemed too personal to be revealed in casual conversation, making me uncomfortable from time to time. Yet, in time I have come to appreciate the curiosity of what came to be my fellow Americans. There is an openness in them, and a climate of freedom in the country, that is not just engaging, but also refreshing. Americans are a free people, free in a way no other great nation has ever been. Freedom defines us more than anything else. And we are curious both because we consider ourselves part of humanity-at-large, and, we are comfortable asking and answering questions about some of our most intimate experiences. We fit well in our skins and we are not afraid to talk about our lives and tell about who we are, our present, and our past.

There is never an end to what any of us can say about ourselves, our experiences, and our circumstances. The reservoir of lived history we individually carry with us is inexhaustible because, even though the events in our lives are limited in number, the perspectives from which they can be viewed have no boundaries. For many years I repeated myself here and there, but after a while I realized that, at some point, perhaps I should tell as much as I remembered and considered important. That is, give all those who want them, the answers to their questions, to casual acquaintances, colleagues, friends, and family who show some interest in Cuba, Cubans, and Latinos in the U.S. But how to do it? How can one tell a complicated story that involves so many others besides oneself, and tell it in a way that would be interesting and fruitful both to me and its audience?

After some thought, I came to the conclusion that one good way of doing it would be by focusing on a family, for everyone has families, everybody understands what families are about, and everyone experiences the vicissitudes that they endure, their struggles, feuds, tragedies, and successes. What better way to get to know other persons, their recent histories and culture, than to do it in the context of the families of which they are a part? The family is the primary social institution; it is where everything converges and is centered; and it is what ties together a society, an ethnos, a race, and a nation. The family is the key to a people and its history. Families have close members and extended ones. There are poor and rich members in most families. Many families count with adventurers, rogues, as well as paragons of virtue. Some of their members are handsome and some ugly. Some live long lives and some die early. Some are highly educated and some not so much. Some are smart and some stupid.

Ultimately what all of us want to know about others is something about ourselves, to know about *our* lives through *their* lives, for in them we see ourselves reflected and it is through people that everything makes some sense to us. We are not greatly interested in storms and floods unless they are related to people. We care about events, even about cataclysmic ones, only when they become calamities measured by human suffering. Humans are provincial and clannish. Yes, we are curious about science and history, but mostly because they tell us much about ourselves. Learned accounts, insulated from the human element, have a limited appeal. People are interested in people and the human dimensions of events. This interest can only be satisfied in a human context, and what context can be more appropriate and closer to us than the basic social unit, namely, the family?

The subject matter of this book, then, is a group of people related to each other as mothers, children, fathers, siblings, cousins, uncles, aunts, nephews, nieces, friends, acquaintances, and even those related through service, for they all comprise the human context in which I live and about which I know best. It is about them and the odds they encountered, their sufferings and pleasures, their idiosyncrasies and their humanity. Indirectly, then, it is about life and death, health and disease, love and hate, destiny and freedom, faith and doubt, rebellion and submission, betrayal and loyalty, honor and shame, choice and destiny.

Will this satisfy readers? It all depends on what they are searching for. But let me say that it has satisfied me in the sense that composing this narrative has allowed me to better understand myself and those who have lived close to me during an important period not only of my life, but of the lives of Cubans and even to some extent Americans. It has made me understand Cuban culture and society: the country in which I was born, my roots going back a while, and my history. And through contrasts and similarities, it has made me understand better my adopted countries, Canada and the United States. But this is not all, for insofar as this is a story of humans, I have been able to understand humans better, our similarities and differences, and many of our idiosyncrasies.

Human beings are products of ancestors, genes, the past, and circumstances. In particular, we are historical creatures, where memory plays a fundamental role in the formation of our identities. An acquaintance with our history helps us begin to see why we look the way we do and why we think and act in ways that distinguish us from others. Our past, the one that we have lived and the one that preceded us, reveals itself in our present and future. And our contemporary times provide challenges that explain our choices and actions. Understanding how it all hangs together is a journey of discovery that perhaps all of us should make at some point in our lives, for each of us is unique. We occupy places of our own, and in that sense we are special. But we are not alone, like separate islands in an ocean. We are part of humanity, integral constituents of a continent, to paraphrase the poet John Donne. Through the accounts presented here, accounts of various persons and their stories, peculiarities, virtues, and follies, I hope readers will indirectly learn about themselves and each other.

Because I am a philosopher perhaps readers will think that the following pages will be full of philosophical speculations, ruminations, and counsel. Indeed, there are some brilliant precedents for composing such an account. Think of Aristotle's *Nichomachean Ethics* and Augustine's *Confessions*. These narratives are full of theory and advice about how to lead a good life. This account, however, is nothing quite like that. It is not intended to expound a philosophy or make recommendations, moral or otherwise. Because I am a philosopher, what I write cannot avoid having what might be called a philosophical edge, a slant that perhaps other books of this sort may not have. But I tried to stay away from excessive preaching, sermonizing, teaching, or philosophizing. Whatever readers learn from reading it is up to them. I merely present the facts as I remember them and let readers draw their own inferences.

This is why, just as every account of human life, my account contains both humor and tragedy, success and failure, frustration and satisfaction. It is composed of pieces of a puzzle that sometimes make no sense but which are part of the baggage I carry with me on my journey. Events, people, and experiences, some sad, some happy, but all personally significant, even though at first some of them might appear banal. They constitute a small part of a whole, the tracks of my life in Cuba for nearly twenty of the most tumultuous years in the history of Cuba, of events I witnessed and people I knew, but also of events I never experienced and people I never knew but who were part of the lore that surrounded me.

Recounting these facts does not strictly constitute an autobiography. Autobiographies paint pictures their authors want to be seen, theories they try to defend, and accounts they aim to settle. They are full of justifications, confessions, accusations, apologies, revenge, and gossip. The memories in this book are not intended to do any of that. As snippets of my past, weathered by years that have remained in my mind, or of events recounted by others to me sometimes directly and sometimes indirectly, they lack the artificial cogency and goals of an autobiography. And yet, they make up a story that reveals much about me, my family, and Cuba, but more importantly, I hope, about humanity as a whole, for it is the particular that uncovers the universal. More than anything else, this is a story about people struggling to survive and understand themselves, about their hopes and disappointments, in moments of joy or despair.

I have not thought to tie these memories together except insofar as they are all connected in some way, closely or loosely, to me. And I have not cleaned them up according to a blueprint. Nor have I tried to fill in gaps in them, or look for sources to complete those gaps. This is a book of memories and memories are incomplete, discontinuous, vague, and to some extent unreliable, although they can also be sharp, indeed sometimes sharper than the experiences that give rise to them. Some resemble dreams and some resemble facts. They pop up in our consciousness at unexpected times, prompted by associations that are often unclear to us, and for all we know, respond to chance. And so, these memories appear in no particularly strict order, except for a rough temporal sequence mirroring my life that even at times is violated. To readers they might appear chaotic, but are not our lives so as well? Where is the pattern, the model that orders them? Do we have any control in what we are and what we become? Who among us can say that they had plans for their lives and have executed them successfully? And yet we do have goals and make plans, whether we succeed in bringing them to fruition or not.

Chapter One

Names and Identity. What's in a Name?

Everything and nothing! Proper names are of the essence; they single us out as the individual persons we are thought to be. Indeed, they do more than this, because they also suggest. Their very sound often conveys and arouses feelings, emotions, and views whether positive or negative. It is one thing to be sweet Susan and another to be imposing Gertrude! And they bring out associations that brand us. It is one thing to be called Jesus, and another thing to be called Judas. And we know it, for how many people are called Judas in the Western world?

Some names are feminine, others are masculine. A friend of mine who was rather peculiar, stuck-up in a misguided sense of history and privilege, named his son Claire. Imagine being called Claire in front of a class of school boys who are anxiously looking for ways in which they can make fun of other boys to hide their own inadequacies, insecurities, and fears! Poor Claire, the humiliations he may have suffered because of his father's insensitivity marked him for life and created a resentment that has not been erased in spite of the many decades that have passed since then. Obviously, there are feminine and masculine names, although in English the line that separates them is not as clear as it is in, say, Spanish, most names point one way or the other. To have a name that is contrary to one's gender is to ask for trouble.

Names connote meaning in subtle ways, and often miscast and humiliate us, presenting us in a light that has nothing to do with who or what we are, or opening the doors to ridicule by those searching for ways to have fun at our expense, or even to do us harm. I had to suffer endless teasing in school because of my last name, Gracia. The name means grace, and that is not something a boy would like to be or be called. We would rather be thought of as tough and macho, particularly in Cuba, where machismo is rampant. To boot, this unfortunate name was always confused with "García." "Gracia" is not as common as "García" and it is unusual in comparison with other common Spanish names such as Rodríguez, Pérez, and González.

I lost count of the times I wished my last name had been Dubié, father's mother last name, not only because it would prevent the teasing from my peers and the confusion with bureaucrats, but because a French name always carried some éclat. In Latin America in general any name that is not Spanish, unless it is non-Western, has class and French names are at the top of the social hierarchy, followed by English and German names. To have one of these names means that you come from a family that is not Indian, Black, or Spanish, all presumably undesirable ancestries. Slavery weighed heavily against anything that suggested African ancestry. Pre-Columbian descent counted against anyone because of its ties to indentured servitude. And the cruel and crude Spanish behavior in the Americas contrasted with that of other Europeans who were seen as both cultured and enlightened.

To make matters worse, we always called each other in school by our family names rather than our given names. "Jorge" was certainly all right, but "Gracia" made my life difficult because its meaning originated in a part of Spain, Aragón, that has always been considered to be inhabited by a very uncouth and stubborn people, and it sounded somewhat feminine (in Spanish, words that end in the letter "a" are feminine). Just as some names, whether given or family names, work against us, other names help us in our social intercourse. For example, "Alexander" is a manly name with great historical connotations and a pleasant sound whether in English or Spanish.

My family took names seriously. Indeed, I was taught from a very early age to trot out all the surnames that traced our ancestry, together with my given names. When I was asked for my name, I was ready: Jorge Jesús Emiliano Gracia, Otero, Dubié, Muñoz, Suárez, Recamán, Ferro and Pimienta. Whew! That mouthful was quite enough, although sometimes I went beyond it to mention Ramírez de Arellano and others. The first three names were given, but the others traced my descent. It was a genealogical tree in sounds that presumably identified how I came to be who I am, even though I hardly knew anything about my ancestors and knowing their names did not help me much getting to know them.

In the Gracia-Dubié branch of the family in particular, babies were burdened with long and often unappealing names for reasons that were never completely clear to me. Why the long list of given names? Why the double, or even triple and quadruple, family names? No one in the family was expected to have only one or two given names, for how could a baby be deprived of a substantial nomenclature to help it throughout life? Perhaps it was a way of making our identity unique, distinguishing us from everybody else, living or dead, for even to this day, I am probably the only person in the world, at least according to the Internet, that is named Jorge Jesus Emiliano Gracia Otero, et al. Indeed, as far as I know, I am the only Jorge J. E. Gracia.

A minimum of four given names was de rigueur, and five or six was even better.

Among the given names were the names of saints whose feasts were celebrated on the days in which the children had been born. Imagine someone who was born on the day of celebration for Segismundo or Gumercinda! Saint names were meant to keep the babies in good graces with influential figures in the right heavenly circles, assuming of course, that the dead behave exactly as the living. No matter that few people in the family really believed in saints—still, this was a good precaution. Obviously, the French side of the family kept up the Voltaire tradition of playing it safe.

The names of the saints were usually chosen from the calendar, which in Cuba listed the names of saints that had died on each day. This list was called *santoral*, that is, list of saints. This led some country folk to use *"Santoral"* or *"Santoral al Dorso"* as names for their children because they did not know the difference. In addition, there were the names of Jesus, the Virgin Mary in her various apparitions, such as Caridad, which was one of father's given names, and sometimes additional names of favorite saints. These should also help insofar as the saint of the day might not be powerful enough, and there is no contest when it comes to the clout of Jesus or the Virgin Mary.

Finally, the children should carry the names of several members of the family, for diverse reasons, such as tradition, respect, influence, power, and money—nothing to sneeze at. The results were rather long strings of names, so heavy that the babies were burdened with large linguistic loads from the very beginning of their lives. If they survived this, they probably would not need to be afraid of anything else. My only cousin from the Gracia-Dubié side of the family had six names because her mother was one for tradition.

Occasionally a name would be truly unfortunate. One of my paternal grandmother's babies was named Soila Pura, which added to the family name Gracia became Soila Pura Gracia. The problem with this string of words is that it sounds just like *Soy la pura gracia*, which in Spanish means "I am pure grace." Once, when I was discussing our names with my cousin, she said that it was lucky that the baby died at two, for living with that ridiculous name would have been a burden very difficult to carry. What were these people thinking? For all the sophistication and éclat they thought they had, the Gracia-Dubiés family did some very stupid things, and this was one of them. I am all for respecting traditions, but only if they are sensible. Of course, if there is a matter of ingratiating a child with a wealthy relative, then obviously a name becomes a valuable commodity.

My siblings and I were luckier than my paternal cousin because mother had some influence when it came to our names. Mother's family did not put too much stock on given names, nor was father as bound to tradition as his relatives. Father, of course, had plenty of names, and weird ones at that: Ignacio, Jesús, Loreto, de la Caridad, etc. *Loreto* for the Virgen de Loreto, and *de la Caridad* for Our Lady of Charity, patroness of Cuba. But we were generally spared. We were given only two or three given names each, chosen for family or religious reasons. I was particularly lucky because when I was born, in 1942, my brother was fourteen, and he insisted that I be given a simple, ordinary name. "Don't burden him with weird names, please." My brother had influence; he was the heir and a favorite. So, I was given the name "Jorge," but also got "Jesús" as a result of mother's promise: "if the birth and the baby are fine," she promised, "I will name it Jesús or María, depending on the gender." I also got the name of the saint on whose feast day I was born: "Emiliano" (you really do not want to antagonize the saint on whose day you were born). Not a bad show after all.

The Spanish Otero-Muñoz side of the family was not as bound by tradition as the Gracia-Dubié side. They favored shorter names which nonetheless, and contrary to the Gracia-Dubiés who always were called by one of their given names, they avoided using in everyday discourse. It was not only that they might dislike their particular names, but that they did not relate to them. Perhaps they thought they were cold, uniform, lacking the familiarity and personal touch that a name created out of love had. This was not unusual in Cuba. At the beach, we were friends with a family whose members had nicknames of the same format and somewhat similar sound. Quique (the father), Queca (the mother), Cuqui (the oldest daughter), Coca and Quiqui (the middle daughters) and Queque (the youngest son). To keep the names of members of that family straight was a feat! Imagine talking about the family: "I saw Queca today, she was still sick." "Queca? Was she sick? Or did you mean Cuqui?" "No, actually it was Quiqui." It took me a whole summer to learn their names and keep them straight.

In mother's family no one, with few exceptions, was called by his or her given name, regardless of the name, and our family adhered to this custom. Mother was Niña (girl), because she was the youngest child in her family. My sister was Nena, which is another term for "baby girl," and I was Chucho, which is the usual nickname for "Jesús." No one ever called me Jorge. The exception was my brother whose name was Ignacio, like father, and was called Ignacito. As the heir of the family name he was treated differently. The use of nicknames was so pervasive that when father died, we received condolence letters addressed to La Niña de Gracia (Gracia's girl). People who had known our family for decades did not know mother's name, Leonila. Everyone called her Niña.

The custom of nicknaming extended to everyone. For members of the family, the nicknames were not nasty, but endearing, perhaps highlighting an event or a feature, although there were exceptions. Mother called me "Mi negro" or "Mi negrito" because I was the darkest member of the family. Mother was not unique in this. This endearing use of language descriptive of blacks was usual in Cuba, a remnant of the time when slavery was common and blacks were seen as dependent on whites. Many whites had a paternalistic and patronizing feeling toward blacks who were considered less fortunate than whites, more like children, and therefore as worthy of eliciting what they thought was a kind of protective love. Loved ones, then, frequently were called *negros*: A lover would refer to his female lover as "Mi negra" or "Mi negrita," regardless of the race involved, and this was extended to children. Obviously, how people nickname each other reveals much about the mores of the society in which they live.

Not all the nicknames used among ourselves in the family were flattering. Sometimes they were meant to emphasize a defect. Nena, for example, dubbed me *Babosa* (slug) when I became a teenager, because of my bad habit of leaving a trace of disorder anywhere I went, and *Lobo feroz* (ferocious wolf), a reference to the story of the three little pigs, because during my teen years I was moody and had a nasty temper, blowing up frequently. But she did not intend these names nastily; she meant to make fun of me in order to correct my bad habits. At no time did I ever hear mother or father say to her not to do it, after all they were quite aware of my faults and were not about to leave them unnoticed.

When it came to other people, names were chosen to emphasize something funny about them, or to call attention to an anecdote that pointed to something ridiculous in the person's behavior. There was often some malice in the naming, but it was seldom nasty. The sense behind it was always to bring out humor, which Cubans have in abundance. There is practically nothing about which Cubans cannot make a joke. Of course, when the reason for the name was a physical defect, the naming could be cruel, and was never used in front of the person in question for obvious reasons.

There was *La pelilarga* (the long-haired female), a young woman in our neighborhood who wore her long hair loose in a way that mother thought was not only *déclassé*, but in fact indicated that she was too racy, a sign of loose morals. *El tuerto* had lost an eye. *El de la nariz virada* had a crooked nose. *La de la sonrisita* was a poor woman who had dared to laugh in a nervous funny way once she was visiting us. *Mira pa mis yentes* was a woman who wore a permanent, forced smile in order to prevent wrinkling her face—the name suggested the difficulty of smiling while talking. A man who seemed to have an important role in a store because he paraded around it became *El importante*; another who behaved arrogantly was dubbed *El arrogante*; one who frequently passed by grandmother's home was called *El pasador*; and still another who had a head shaped like a pumpkin became *Cabeza de calabaza*. The favorite nicknames were derived from something the person had said that struck members of the family as weird, inappropriate, or funny. One that I thought was particularly hilarious was the name made from a phrase that a young girl once used while she and her mother were visiting us. She was small, but chubby, and ate a lot. At lunch, when her mother served her plate, she said: "*Mamá, con pila*," (mother, with a heap). From then on, she was always called *Mamá con pila*. No one escaped. Indeed, my maternal uncle Jaime, who was himself one of the greatest offenders, used to say, referring to grandmother's knack for nicknaming people, "*el que escape queda loco*." The list of nicknames was very long. Mostly they were created by grandmother and Jaime; those two never called anyone by his or her given names. For years I thought this was a peculiarity of our family, but then I traveled to Spain and realized that this is a widespread custom, in Southern Spain in particular. For us the custom came through my maternal great-grandfather, *El Curro*, who was from Andalucía. I never met him, but it appears that he spent most of his life making fun of everybody else. To this day, I have difficulty remembering names that are not in some way descriptive. So, readers of this book, claim yourselves lucky if you have ordinary names, they are few, and you live in a society where people like my maternal grandmother and my uncle Jaime do not live.

Chapter Two

"Je Suis Française!"

Following our family custom of giving nicknames to people based on idiosyncrasies, my paternal grandmother, Mercedes Dubié Ferro, should have been called, and sometimes was called behind her back, "*la francesa*," because she frequently and proudly said "*¡Yo soy francesa!*" ironically in Spanish, whenever anyone started talking about ancestry and family in our home. The fact is that, although she was the daughter of a Frenchman, and therefore we all had some claim to being French, the bulk of our ancestry on father's side was Spanish. Nonetheless, the Gracia-Dubié's thought of themselves as French. Their sympathies were with the French, French literature, French cuisine, French art, French politics, French history, and anything French. They went so far as to argue that France's *La Marseillaise,* was the most beautiful and inspiring national anthem in the world! And for the most part they despised anything Spanish. Their admiration for France and French civilization was unbound. France was a symbol of culture, sophistication, and enlightenment. Anything not French was considered to be of lesser quality, inferior, insignificant, and derivative.

They had some sympathy for the British, but it paled in comparison with their attitude toward the French. Mother, whose father was Spanish, did all she could to make us appreciate the Spanish culture and music, which she loved, but she was thoroughly ignored and overwhelmed by the Francophiles. The sense of undisputed superiority with which anything French was regarded by the Gracia-Dubiés won us over for years. Of course, it did not help that some other people thought of us as French and said that we looked French, probably because of our large and convoluted noses. This happened to me even in Spain, where I was generally identified, to my delight, as French, and even in France, where I was generally deemed a native except when I opened my mouth. It was not until I came to the United States and found myself being identified by Americans with the Spanish, and I had a hard look at my ancestry, that I had to accept that I spoke Spanish and my culture was fundamentally Spanish, rather than French, whether I liked it or not. It was only then that I began to think of myself as not French, and could not help feeling that I had been cut down in size. Obviously, we can be brainwashed by our families to such a degree that we live comfortably in a world of pretense. And pretense often has a rough ending when confronted with reality.

Chapter Three

Escaping Mexican Wrath

The story of grandmother and the French side of father's family begins in Mexico, not in Cuba, Spain, or France, as one would have expected, and more pointedly in Mérida, a town in the North West coast of the Yucatán Peninsula. When I visited Mérida in the 1990s, it was still a sleepy town, mostly forgotten except for the occasional tourist. Mérida had been an important urban center at the turn of the century. The rubber industry had a good run there, and the remnants of the former prosperity were still evident in the town. Its broad avenues were lined by elegant mansions in various degrees of decay. Genteel poverty was revealed in that some of the mansions had been broken up into apartments and some had become business offices or museums. Nonetheless, there was still a gracious ambiance about the town, with well-planned plazas, numerous trees, and the air of past grandeur, like a lady who had seen better days but still kept a certain hauteur, the remains of prosperous times. The beach was bordered by a *malecón*, a broad promenade with expansive vistas of an inviting gulf. White sand, calm clean waters, and a limited population that contrasted with the oppressing humanity of Mexico City were unquestionable attractions.

The rubber industry had been dying for almost a century, but tourists were beginning to discover Mérida. It was in many ways a pity. Things would change. Large buildings and resorts would go up to accommodate the insatiable appetite of American and European tastes. The views of the ocean would become blocked by concrete walls, shielding tanned, half-naked visitors, from native inhabitants. McDonald's would open franchises, and the greasy fumes of hamburgers and Kentucky Fried Chicken would knock you down when you inadvertently passed by. Then there would be ambulant vendors attracted by the lure of easy targets. Petty thieves would multiply, scrounging around for neglected purses, forgotten shopping bags, and dropped coins.

Loud music, the one Meridians think tourists like, would clog your ears and overwhelm the rhythm of the waves as they licked the sand. Life would become different and Mérida would cease to be what it once was and become something else that could not easily be determined, although undoubtedly worse.

By the time I visited, Mérida was still the charming forgotten lady of former grander times. I traveled with my daughter, Leticia. I had received one of those promotion deals, or travel miles. Two free airline tickets to use by a certain date, which was very close. Only one destination was still available—a flight to Cancún—but Norma, my wife, could not accompany me. She had the dubious disadvantage in life of having a regular job.

I had the free tickets, my wife could not accompany me, but my daughter, Leticia, could. Her classes at Trinity College in Toronto were over, and her wedding had been scheduled for June of the following year. So, we took off. The plan was to fly to Cancún, rent a car, and then visit all the Mayan ruins in Yucatán. We did this, but we had not anticipated Mérida. We expected to be awed by Chichén Itzá and Uxmal. We had read and prepared for the spectacle that ruins from formidable pre-Columbian civilizations would offer us. And we were appropriately impressed, when we got there. Few archeological sites on Earth match the splendor of Mayan ruins and fewer still surpass them. The delicate splendor of Uxmal in particular is hard to match anywhere in the world. But Mérida? Who had ever heard of Mérida?

Well, I had, vaguely, from grandmother Dubié, daughter of Jean Dubié and Mercedes Ferro Ramírez de Arellano. I give you the full names I know—the rest have been forgotten—not to show off our pedigree, but simply because that is how people of this ilk called themselves and for the sake of satisfying your possible curiosity and interest in ancestry. I am not and have never been, although I have an interesting set of ancestors as far as I know—adventurers and rogues some of them—who made and lost fortunes repeatedly. Indeed, if there is something that characterizes our family is the uncanny ability of its members, on both the maternal and paternal sides, to make and lose fortunes.

Great-grandfather Jean was originally from Tarbes, France. In one of our many trips to France my wife and I visited Tarbes, we noticed two Dubiés listed in the phone book. Anyone else would reach out a possible relative, and Norma urged me to do so. Instead, I jotted down their telephone numbers and to this date have not contacted them. Still, we did have someone check the name in France's computerized telephone directory at the time and it turned out that Dubié is not a very common name—we could find only two persons, or families, in Tarbes and one in the Isle de France. Although there are Dubiés in Santiago, Chile, who are related to us, and in Argentina who may be related. In the forties, one of the Chilean Dubiés, an admiral in the Chilean Navy, visited Havana and met with two Dubiés of my family, my grandmother and her sister, María (known as Mina). After visiting Santiago and learning that the Dubiés own a large winery in Chile, I was tempted to contact them—maybe they would give me a case of their best wine out of kinship? But I've never done it. Who knows, they might think I wanted to ask them a favor and shun me, and if they are like some of the Dubiés I have known, they probably would!

Our family's connection with Mérida goes back to the nineteenth century. Jean, who was no doubt poorer than he thought he deserved to be, was part of the group of Frenchmen that accompanied Maximilian when he came to Mexico as emperor and, like most adventurers who came to America, he wanted to make his fortune—*hacerse la América*, as we say in Spanish—except that he was French! But we all know what happened to Maximilian and his short-lived empire. A nasty little patriot by the name of Benito Juárez did him in, in a bad way. He was executed in 1867, and Carlotta, his presumably lovely wife (that is the usual epithet when you talk about "persons of quality"), who had earlier left Mexico, went mad. And the Mexicans have not wanted to hear anything about them ever since. The feeling goes deep. A few years ago I was told that someone had bought Carlotta's set of china, with the Emperor's crest, for practically nothing and tried to dump it on a museum in Mexico, but the Mexicans would not hear of it—the hatred of Maximilian and the French runs deep. This sounds very shortsighted to me. You want to preserve every bit of history and historical artifacts you can get your hands on, even if it comes from politically incorrect sources—so much of it is lost! But I guess some Mexicans are still wrapped-up in an ideological, nationalist flag that does not allow them to see the full value of history.

After Maximilian met his doom, the remaining Frenchmen scattered about Mexico. They sought refuge primarily along the east coast, in part because this was an easy escape if further flight was necessary. Veracruz was one of the main destinations; Mérida was another. My great-grandfather went to Mérida. And there, the presumably dashing fortune hunter found it in the lovely Mercedes. Isn't a rich wife the greatest treasure a man with limited means can find? Truly, it did not take much to accomplish the feat. At the time, the population of Mérida was minuscule, and the number of *señoritas* who would qualify as wives of an ambitious Frenchman under penurious circumstances would have been infinitesimal. And from her side, who could resist a well-appointed Frenchman with a dangerous history? So, Jean married well. Indeed, I am told that the Ramírez de Arellano are still a powerful and well-known clan in Mexico.

Some ancestors of early Cubans who came from Spain and Mexico live in the federal district, rather than in sleepy Mérida. When Leticia and I visited Mérida, I checked the telephone book and I found two listed as Dubiés, but following my usual diffidence in pursuing these matters, I never called them. Again, I may have lost a real opportunity for advancement! But that is the story of my life! My advice to you, readers, is to act differently if you want to find your ancestors.

Jean and Mercedes had two daughters, one of whom was my grandmother. Unfortunately, life in Mérida was not altogether secure for a Frenchman who had been associated with Maximilian, so eventually my great-grandparents felt they needed to leave town and headed for Cuba, where my great-grandmother had a wealthy brother willing to give the family shelter. They left in a hurry as those things go, and arrived safely in Havana two weeks later. However, soon after their arrival, Jean and Mercedes died from typhus. My young grandmother and her sister, Mercedes and Mina, who each spoke French and Spanish, were left in the charge of an uncle they had just met. He was a Jesuit priest.

Chapter Four

The Jesuits Stole My Inheritance

In all honesty, I should say that sometimes I have toyed with the idea that, if I outlive my wife, I will enter a Jesuit monastery somewhere and spend the last years of my life in seclusion from a world that I find increasingly troubling. After all, another Jorge, who was also a philosopher, did it, and with some success, although he called himself George rather than Jorge. But this fancy speculation is not motivated by the vocation to save souls, religious piety, or a desire for great spiritual enlightenment; it is merely a selfish desire for untroubled peace. Who does not want to live *"la descansada vida de aquel que huye del mundanal ruido"* (the rested life of one who flees worldly noise) of which Fray Luis de León wrote so eloquently?

Still, in spite of the respect I have for the Jesuits, I have a grudge against them, for they cheated grandmother, and thus indirectly me, of a substantial inheritance, and losing money is always a sore point with the Gracias. We all understand that making money is not easy, nor is it easy to keep it once one has it, a fact illustrated repeatedly in my family's history. That aside, how did the Jesuits cheat grandmother Dubié?

When my Mexican great-grandmother and French great-grandfather died of typhus in Cuba, their daughters were left in the charge of their uncle. He was a Jesuit living in Havana, a city he loved, being originally from Cadiz, a city that is often called *"la Habana sin negritos"* (Havana without blacks). This liking dated to the time before he had joined the Jesuit Order as an adult, and only after he had already acquired very substantial parcels of land in the area where the water intake for Havana is located, around Regla and Guanabacoa. Knowing how greedy religious orders can be, and given his desire to live in Havana, before he joined the Order he made a deal: He would deed his land to the Jesuits if he was never moved away from the city. Naturally, the Order promptly agreed—no one can accuse the Jesuits of ever not taking advantage of a good deal—but my great-grand-uncle did not realize who he was dealing with. He had not yet studied casuistry and he naively believed what the Jesuits appeared to say. He did not make sure of what they meant.

Violating their presumed promise to him, the Order moved him for reasons I don't know, and consequently he changed his will, bequeathing his property to grandmother and her sister. But the Order was powerful—when people believe that you control their fate after death, they do not want to mess with you, and the Jesuits have always succeeded in persuading some people that they control the keys of the Kingdom. Only very few members of other religious Orders and the regular clergy of the Catholic Church have ever effectively challenged this claim.

In time, the lands grandmother should have inherited became very valuable. The Jesuits did what they needed to do, and the orphans had to be content with little but a dubious social position. One appeared to have married well, to grandfather Gracia, but the other married a free spirit who only thought of having a good time, a charmer and fortune hunter who must have been disappointed when he realized the heiress he thought he had married was far from being as rich as she appeared to be. Still, he was enough of a gentleman never to reveal his disappointment.

Our family's efforts continued well into the end of the Batista regime, in the 1950s, to recover the inheritance stolen by the Jesuits. Indeed, Cuban dictator Batista gave an audience to members of our family, including father and grandmother's surviving sister, to discuss the issue. We were all quite excited about the prospects. Father said the inheritance would be distributed among the living descendants, including children and grandchildren, so my sister and I were already dividing up the spoils, which would have been considerable.

Father's family had been softening up government officials through intermediaries and things looked hopeful. But in corrupt Cuba, nothing moved without proper grease. At the audience, Batista made clear that he expected a sizable sum of money up front, and a cut of the proceeds after settlement, to move the legal claim forward. No one in the family had that kind of money to spare but father, and he said he did not want to risk his own money with a man like Batista. Of course, he was right. The negotiations continued for a while, but father's death in 1957 put a stop to them, and two years later communism entered Cuba and inheritance claims did not survive. In short, the Jesuits owe me one, and I intend to press my claim, whether in heaven or hell.

Chapter Five

Poetry, Spirits, and Flair

The younger of the two sisters who had been orphaned shortly after landing in Cuba was the more glamorous of the two. To visit Mina and her daughter, Baby (pronounced *a la cubana* "*Bebee*"), was a treat for all of us. Baby was contemporary with mother and so they got along well. She had married an old Asturian, Don Aquilino López, devoted to naturalism. Asturias is one of the most traditional parts of Spain. Located in the North of the Iberian Peninsula, it was the last remnant of the Visigothic Kingdom which replaced the Roman province of Hispania, from which the country takes its name, and became one of the two earliest foci of resistance to the Moorish invasion in 711 AD. The Moors were never able to conquer and pacify it. Accordingly, it has to this day kept a certain profile of individual ruggedness and a sense of non-negotiable superiority, similar in some ways to those that characterize Scots, which is passed on to its inhabitants and which Don Aquilino exemplified well. While to be a Galician in Cuba did not provide any superior status, to be an Asturian was regarded as something worth notice. For an Asturian to be confused with a Galician was nothing less than an insult.

The family lived in an extraordinary penthouse very close to the corner of Galiano and San Rafael, a crossing at the very center of the elegant commercial district in Havana. El Encanto, Havana's most fashionable clothing store, and Fin de Siglo, the second, were just around the corner. And close-by were other stores, such as La Opera and La Epoca, and of course the proverbial *Ten-Cents* (which later became Woolworths), where one could buy ice cream, hot dogs, hamburgers, and other recently imported American fare on blue plates, after going to a show in Radio Cine América. This theater presented shows and performances by many artists of note including Josephine Baker, who my parents went to see in 1950 when she took Havana by storm. It was obvious why mother loved to visit Mina and Baby.

Don Aquilino was old but still vigorous, evident from the fact that he had fathered a child well into his eighties, Martiana, of my age, and whom I took out to dances a couple of times when I became a teenager. In line with the naming customs of the Dubiés, she had been given an odd and ugly name in honor of José Martí, father of Cuban independence, because she had been born on January 28, the day Martí had been born. But everyone called her Cucha.

Don Aquilino credited his vigor to a carefully balanced vegetarian diet. It was in this house that I first heard of the benefits of eating potato peels and raw garlic. Don Aquilino's breakfast every morning consisted of a large serving of raw garlic, eaten with olive oil and a bit of salt spread on whole wheat bread. Then, in order to counteract the overpowering smell of the garlic, he ate a generous portion of raw onions. To me, he still reeked of garlic, just like the priests in the confessional that I met when I felt the need to be absolved of my sins and to suffer some accompanying penance through their stink. The difference was that the smell of garlic was mixed with the pungent smell of onions. The last I heard of Don Aquilino, he was still going strong in his nineties.

Mina and Baby were fashionable people, and fashionable not in the silly sense of being social butterflies. These people knew everything you needed to know when it came to real fashion, that is of course French fashion, as well as art, literature, and the theater. After all, Mina, like grandmother Mercedes, thought of herself as French, and looked down on anything that did not come directly from Paris. She styled herself a poet, and could, like mother, create a poem in response to a request at a moment's notice. I still have the poem she wrote for me and Cucha during one of our visits.

Like a vain woman of fashion, she did not want anyone to know her age. Many of the Gracias and Dubiés hated to reveal their age. Among the most notorious were uncle Julio and grandmother, but the worst was Mina. Once, Mina was asked how much younger she was than her sister (my grandmother). She answered, in all seriousness, that she was twenty years younger. In reality she was merely two years younger! I guess one could excuse her by arguing that she confused two with twenty?

The penthouse where they lived was a place of enchantment and mystery. It consisted of many rooms, mostly unconnected and only united in that the spaces around and between them were covered by a pergola with a wonderful climbing bush, whose flowers beautified and perfumed the atmosphere. The vistas from the penthouse were superb. You could get to the penthouse through an elevator, but I preferred climbing up through spiral stairs that turned and turned until you became dizzy. The floors below the penthouse, where Don Aquilino conducted his business, were an uncontrollable enticement to a young and curious explorer such as myself. The place was cavernous, and you could easily get lost in endless passages, which looked to me like enormous salons, with dark, frightening corners and confusing labyrinths of a Borgian quality. Guests were offered special baths, saunas, and all the paraphernalia available at the time to those who were nature's devotees. You could get any treatment you wanted, from massages of various sorts to mud baths. Don Aquilino also ran a kind of hotel or spa, where people came and spent time being cleansed from all the impurities to which they were exposed in daily life, and reestablishing their health and natural balance. Baby was as knowledgeable about the business as Don Aquilino, and both were charming people, although as a child I was intimidated by the man, his serious demeanor, his heavy Asturian accent, and the pervasive garlic smell that he emitted.

Mina did not only style herself a poet. She also thought of herself as a spiritualist, and dabbled, like many of the Gracia-Dubiés, in the occult and Eastern religions. It was at their home that I first saw a Ouija board, when Mina offered mother a consultation in one of our visits. I suppose this was more a matter of fashion than religious belief; it seems to have been the thing to do at the time.

Mina's presence was as impressive as everything else about her. She was very thin, almost cadaverous by Cuban standards, and always dressed in the latest fashion. She had her hair styled at the hair dresser every other day, a reason for her thinning hair according to mother. Her fingers looked like skeletal paws and were covered with large, odd rings. She was the first person I saw wearing rings on many of her fingers. She also wore bracelets that looked like they belonged in the world of the One Thousand and One Nights, and brooches with large, rare stones with images of what appeared to be landscapes and planets. Occasionally she would wear a pendant with a rock—it was that big—that I would have thought fake, had it been worn by any other woman. (Probably it was fake!)

Looking at Mina was a treat, and hearing her talk about art, literature, religion, or anything whatever was mesmerizing. She had a low, raspy, and hypnotic voice. And her diction was exquisite—you may not understand the sophisticated jargon she used, peppered with French expressions and the language of literature, but you could spell every syllable uttered. The sibilants in particular were carefully articulated, adding a musical cadence to an enchanting speech. When we went to visit, Cucha wanted to play in the nursery, which was filled with every kind of toys, but I would rather sit and listen to Mina spin her stories. I was particularly entranced by her tales of the spiritual world, populated by ghosts and spirits, which were at once intoxicating and frightening.

Visiting that house was like entering a world of magic, where reality became fiction and fiction became reality. If I'd had any choice, I would have stayed there forever, exploring the mysterious labyrinth of endless salons and passages that could not help remind those in the know that the Minotaur was not far. Perhaps he was Don Aquilino, who looked the proper age.

Chapter Six

Treasure Trove for Christmas

The less glamorous of the two Dubié sisters was grandmother Mercedes. She and Mina could not be more different. Mina was glamorous, a great dresser, an enigmatic spiritualist, and a presumed poet. She inspired interest and fun. Grandmother offered a great contrast in comparison. Neither of the sisters was beautiful. Beauty was not a feature common among the Dubiés. But Mina was mysterious and arresting. Grandmother was neither, and from the photographs I have of her, it looks as if she was rather plain. I never evaluated her appearance in vivo—I loved her too much to judge her objectively. But now I can say that she looked not very different than the wicked witch of the West, with the enormous and undulating nose, unruly hair, eyes too close together, and a premature bent back. It did not help that she kept her dentures in her pocket instead of in her mouth because they bothered her. And she dressed uniquely—her small print dresses, too long and unfashionable, did nothing for her appearance. Obviously, she had no taste in clothes, and she had a very ambiguous attitude toward any kind of religion and least of all, unlike Mina, toward spiritualism. She also never thought of writing a poem, as far as I know. She did not inspire interest and fun, but she inspired love and happiness. Not that she was dull, or did not like to have fun. On the contrary, she was quite animated, and learned, and when it was time to go out and have a good time, she was the first one to get in the car. I loved her dearly. Whereas my love for my maternal grandmother was somewhat ambiguous from the time I got to know her because of how difficult and self-centered she always was—my love for grandmother Dubié was unqualified.

She visited us rarely, but when she did during Christmas she stayed with us for a month or two and came loaded with gifts. I still have yet to meet a child that is not mercenary, and I certainly was no exception to the rule. She traveled with two large trunks. In one she brought her clothes and other personal items; the other was filled with gifts. She always brought something precious for mother, and various things for the other members of the family, but most of the trunk was devoted to me. Opening that treasure trove was one of the most exciting things I remember from my childhood. She always brought the latest available in Havana in terms of toys. Contraptions that were not only entertaining, but also beautiful. I remember some of these toys and trinkets to this day. A musical box that played a Strauss waltz and had dancing figurines inside; a miniature cuckoo clock in which the bird came out at certain times to announce the hour, a pack of cards with mysterious images, glass marbles whose appearance changed with the light, story books with marvelous images, a toy train, materials and instructions to build houses, cottages, and buildings, and so many other things!

When she arrived, I was anxious to see what she had in the trunk, but mother had warned me that I was not to say anything about it. Fortunately, grandmother was as anxious to see my reaction when she opened the trunk as I was to see what it contained. But don't get the idea that I loved her only for what she brought. She also endeared herself to me in other ways. From the time that I was very small I was fascinated by stories, and she was a great story teller. In her visits, she came armed with many tales, and so I sat on her lap while she transported me to a world of wonder. Her voice was not like that of her sister; it was soft and pleasant, with a cultivated accent that made it more enchanting. And then there were the daily walks through the garden, examining the flowers, the bugs, the butterflies, the ornamental bushes and fruit trees. She was always keenly observant and noticed many things the rest of the family did not. Once she found a little pet turtle that had escaped from its cage and was thought to have been lost. It was a miracle, considering the size of the gardens, the fact that they were covered with grass and flowering bushes, and the time that had elapsed from the moment we realized the turtle was missing. But grandmother knew the turtle had to be somewhere, and every time she went walking in the garden she looked for it. She also knew the names of plants and animals, and had stories to go along with them. She was a rich source of information for me, and I particularly liked that she talked to me in a serious, interested manner. I spent my time with her asking about why this or that, and she always had something unusual to answer.

In the afternoons she said the rosary. She was not religious and, given the debacle with the Jesuits, she had very little use for Catholic clergy or religious orders. There was also a grain of Protestant in her, because she did not like saints, although she did pray to Jesus and the Virgin Mary. I asked her once why she did not pray to saints, and she answered that it was useless to do it since they did not have real power. Why would she bother with saints if Jesus was God, and it is He who controls the show? But what about the Virgin Mary, I asked? Did she not also lack power? Her answer was that she prayed to her because she was a mother and had suffered much and thus perhaps was positioned better to understand other mothers' troubles. Her reasons convinced me and, from then on, I decided to pray only to Jesus and the Virgin. To Jesus for grandmother's reasons, and to the Virgin because she was like mother, and mother was more loving to me than father was.

Father and the rest of grandmother's children and family always addressed her in the formal way, *de usted*. Only the grandchildren were familiar with her. But this did not mean that she did not get into the fray of everyday life. In many ways, she reminded me of my maternal aunt Maruca. These were people who never caused friction and always brought happiness with them. Grandmother was considerate even in dying. She lived with aunt Rosario, and one night after she had turned eighty, Rosario heard her make a noise in the middle of the night. She got up to see what was happening, and found her breathing with difficulty. She went to the bathroom to get something that would help, but when she got back, grandmother had expired. She died at the age of eighty in 1950. I felt very sad when I heard the news. I would not see her again, and truly I did not think of the trunk, although I was selfish in another way, thinking of the hole her absence would make in my life.

Chapter Seven

Promising Future Comes to Naught

In spite of grandmother's ordinary appearance, she was the Dubié sister that caught the most promising husband, grandfather: Ignacio Gracia Suárez, for short. He was the son of a well-established bureaucrat in the Spanish colonial administration. (It was ironic that great-grandfather, grandfather, father, and my brother were all called Ignacio, the name of the founder of the religious order that had swindled grandmother Dubié of her rightful inheritance.) My paternal great-grandfather had come to Cuba as part of the entourage of a newly appointed Spanish governor, with a position in the area of finance. A morally upright man, he had an impeccable reputation. Having established an excellent track record, he rose in the colonial bureaucracy and he and his family lived accordingly. His home was a fairly substantial structure, located on Carlos III and Belascoin. It was eventually demolished to make room for the Masonic Lodge in Havana. Great colonial houses and estates had been built on Carlos III, in one of which the king had stayed during his visit to Cuba. I am told that until the very end, great-grandfather kept a coterie of twelve servants and dressed impeccably, spending as much as he earned living a good life. But when he died, he left mostly debts.

After Cuba became independent in 1902, his reputation assured him a good position with the Cuban government at the Ministry of Finances, and so he kept living the life he had lived until then. He did not spare any expense when it came to his well-being and those of his children: a son and two daughters. His son was given a first-rate education and became both a physician and a pharmacist, but his sisters, Ninfa and Chichita, remained spinsters. After he married grandmother Dubié, his father sent him and his family to the Canary Islands to accompany Ninfa, who was very sick with tuberculosis—the great nineteenth century disease—and had been told that the climate of the Islands would be good for her. They traveled on a luxurious liner in grand style, and they rented a palatial home in Tenerife whose living room, I'm told, accommodated forty chairs.

I am not sure whether the climate of the Canary Islands was effective in curing grandfather's sister, but after a year they returned to Havana because their father was ailing. Grandfather ran for Congress twice and was elected both times. However, he was very distressed at the state of politics in Cuba. The dishonesty and corruption grated on him and so he decided to abandon politics and devote himself to his profession and the investigation of cancer. When his father died, leaving a limited estate, he moved the family to the town of Yaguaramas, in the province of Matanzas, established in 1560, which boasted of a church founded by Fray Bartolomé de las Casas. There he set up a medical practice and continued his research. He wanted to test some of his ideas about the treatment of cancer and this situation allowed him to do it particularly because the town had a high incidence of the disease.

Apart from the practice, he associated himself with a partner who ran a pharmacy for him. Interested in his patients and research, he neglected both the pharmacy and his own health. He died at forty-seven of throat cancer. Uncle Julio, one of his children, claimed that it was there that he contracted cancer because of his close contact with the cancer patients he treated. Whether there was any basis to this claim is indeterminable, but I tend to think that, given the recent findings that associate certain types of cancer with viruses, Julio may not have been too far off the mark.

Although the family was relatively large, they could have survived comfortably had it not been for the partner who managed to end up with everything of value. It was a sad end. At birth, grandfather's future had seemed assured. He was the son of a man who had an important position in the government and had social connections. A political career appeared promising. And he made what seemed to be a good match in grandmother. There was no reason why he should not live a long and successful life. However, reality turned out to be very different. He died relatively young and left his family in financial straits.

Although resources were limited, grandfather was buried in a bronze casket, as befit his station. But two years afterwards, when uncle Julio had the tomb opened to transfer his bones to the ossuary, the casket was missing and the bones were scattered on the floor of the vault. Following a well-known pattern in history, thieves, probably the very people who had buried the body, had stolen the casket. Robbing tombs was not just an Egyptian custom, in Cuba it was a common affair at the time of my grandfather's internment. Some Cubans left valuable mementos with the bodies they buried, such as jewelry and even money. And when there were no valuables, the thieves stole caskets or parts of caskets made out of bronze or other expensive metals. A casket, if stolen early on, can be easily reused with little modification.

After the burial, grandmother moved the family back to Havana in search for greater opportunities. There were several children of various ages. Rosario was the oldest and nineteen when grandfather died. Father was the second and fifteen. Julio was thirteen. Mercedita was six and Carlos was three. Two other siblings had died earlier, Luis Felipe from tuberculosis and Soila Pura from the measles. Grandfather's sisters reached old age. Although I met them, I only remember Chichita because of a rather unpleasant experience. She was living in an old-folks home near Bellamar, the place of the well-known caves. When I was five, the family went to see the caves and took the opportunity to stop to visit Chichita. She was at the time very old. I remember the occasion because I had a panic attack in the caves and cried inconsolably until we exited.

Chapter Eight

Una Señora Muy Aseñorada

After grandfather's death, the family was held together by grandmother and two of her children, Rosario and father. When I think of Rosario, I always recall a Spanish riddle that goes like this: *Una señora muy aseñorada, con veinte remiendos y ni una puntada* (a very ladylike lady, with many patches and not one stitch). The answer to the riddle is a hen, because hens, especially when they have chicks, are very proud and self-important but their plumage looks like a stitched patchwork. They are small, but they walk around puffed up as if they were something very special, even though they seem to be dressed in mended garments. Not that Rosario had any patches! But she was the epitome of a lady, a formidable one, indeed. When I was small, I was terrified of her. She was always so composed, so formal, so authoritative. Her diction was perfect. And her manner was that of an aristocrat whose word was to be taken as the law. In keeping with the Dubié family looks, she was not a beautiful woman, but she exuded character. Her expression was one of *gravitas*. There was nothing light about her. She was not tall or big, but she had some bulk. And her jaw projected in such a way that made her chin look firm without being protuberant. It said clearly: "You better not mess with me!" She used to wear her hair braided and secured in a kind of arrangement similar to that of Frida Kahlo's in one of her most famous portraits. In later years she wore it short, in a business-like fashion. Her skin, like that of all the Gracia-Dubiés was very fair, so much so that it was covered with freckles which she tried to disguise with powders and creams. Her lips were very thin, like those of most Gracia-Dubiés, and her eyes not large, but piercing. Very few people could resist her gaze.

Rosario was the repository of much of the Gracia-Dubié family lore, and I learned many interesting things from her. She was very proud of her lineage—she came from "people of substance" as she put it, with lands in Jerez de la Frontera, in Spain, going all the way back, through a detour in Galicia, to the roots of the family in Aragón. Whether this was true or not, I could never establish. She was well educated, an accountant by profession who had worked outside the home at a time when women were both uneducated and stayed at home to take care of domestic chores. At a mature age, however, she married a well-to-do widowed physician, much older than herself, and from then on, her life revolved around managing her home, which she did as an army general. She did not have a large crew of servants to help her, only a cook, a maid and, while her husband lived, a chauffeur. But she kept busy making sure everything was in perfect order.

The center of her life was her daughter, Marta, a last gasp of middle age for herself and of old age for her husband. This child became her main obsession, and Rosario did everything possible to make sure that Marta had everything she needed or wanted. No expense or care was spared. She was dressed like a princess and every whim she had was satisfied. Her father spoiled Marta, although she never became a spoiled brat. I loved to talk to her. Her father would go out every day to take care of professional and business matters and when he came back, he always brought with him a gift. Over the years, the number of gifts—trinkets of various sorts such as delicate glass figurines, little silk dolls, miniature tea sets, imaginative music boxes, rag clowns, jewelry, and the like—grew and grew, to the point that in time they were gathered in glass cabinets all over the home. I was fascinated with them when I was a child and visited my aunt's house, but I was never allowed to handle anything. They were considered too precious to be touched by anybody but Marta; no one but her had the right to break them. That grated on me and my sister a great deal.

The keys to the coffers and wardrobes that contained the family treasures—precious heirlooms, jewels, diamonds, broaches, chains, watches, fabrics brought all the way from France, lace from Belgium, porcelain from Germany and France, painted miniatures, rare Murano vases, Sevre and Meissen porcelains and exquisite china—were securely kept by Rosario on a chain she carried with her at all times. No servant was ever given the keys to any of the chests, cabinets, and armoires where the treasures were stored. The house resembled a museum, because, apart from the trinkets given to my cousin, it was full not just of the things that had resulted from the alliance with the physician, but also objects Rosario had inherited from her parents, grandparents, and great-grandparents. She, as the only surviving sister, took everything, accumulating bibelots through many decades. Most important were the jewels, particularly diamonds going back generations. I particularly remember a set of diamond earrings that apparently had belonged to Rosario's great-grandmother and were very heavy. She wore them only when she wanted to impress someone.

A bone of contention between mother and father's family was a diamond ring. Father was the favorite nephew of his aunt Ninfa, who owned a ring with a very large diamond solitaire. At her death, she had stipulated that she wanted the ring to go to father who was her favorite nephew. But grandmother, who lived with aunt Rosario, kept the ring, because father had no one to give it to at the time. Later, when father became engaged to mother, aunt Rosario saw the danger of the ring going to mother, so she asked grandmother to give it to her. Grandmother liked mother, but she lived with aunt Rosario, so it was hard for her to oppose Rosario's wishes. Likewise, it was hard for father to resist Rosario when in fact he had not yet married mother and Rosario took care of grandmother.

This is how the ring ended up with Rosario, and eventually with cousin Marta. My mother felt that was unfair and always resented it. Not that mother was interested in jewelry. She was not. The only rings she ever wore were her wedding band, an emerald in an oval shape, and a diamond ring that I took with me when I escaped Cuba and came to the United States. But it was the principle of the thing. Mother thought the ring should have gone to her, to be passed on in time to her own daughter. But the Gracia-Dubiés were very possessive when it came to property of any kind and particularly precious heirlooms. They were hoarders and keepers, and Rosario could not let this treasure slip away.

Eventually the Revolution swallowed everything up. But Rosario and her daughter's family were able to live much better under the shortages the Revolution caused thanks to the hoard they had accumulated. Some of it was bartered or sold, and materials were used to make clothing for the family. Who knows where the diamond ring that caused such a sting is now!

When I was small, I felt lost and overwhelmed when we visited aunt Rosario. I vaguely remember meeting the old doctor, but I only became familiar with Rosario after he had died. There was also a daughter from the doctor's previous marriage who occupied one of the bedrooms in the house and had a full-time caretaker looking after her needs. She was mad and I saw her only occasionally. Her shadowy existence, and the fact that I only heard whispers about her, created an atmosphere of mystery and even fear around the home. At some point, she attacked Rosario with a pair of scissors, but Rosario was able to resist her and was not wounded. After that she was placed in a sanitarium.

After her husband's death, Rosario, my cousin, and my grandmother came every year to spend Christmas with us, staying for a month at the orchard in Ceballos. The first time they came I remember they were in deep mourning, all in black with hats and veils, and traveled by train. From then on, I saw them more frequently. Cousin Marta would come and spend some weeks during the summer with us, to keep my sister company and enjoy the amenities that the country provided—horses, a carriage, hunting, excursions around the area, a jeep, and swimming in the nearby creek.

It was not until we moved to Havana and close to where they lived that I began to see them more frequently. I came to love the visits. I talked for hours with Rosario about books and places to visit. She was extremely well read, like all the Gracia-Dubiés, and liked to discuss ideas. These conversations made me appreciate literature and culture. She could talk knowledgeably about anything—opera, ballet, classical music, zarzuelas, history, architecture, and great cities of the world, even though she had never traveled outside Cuba—and she loved to have me for an audience. We would sit in her large living room, near the piano, on top of which she kept the untouchable Sevre porcelains—these were so untouchable that I worried even looking at them—and talk until I decided it was time to go home. Father also visited her regularly and I wondered what they talked about. Probably about the same things that we talked about, because father also loved ideas and books. Like father, Rosario seemed to have read everything, and she had a substantial collection of books, primarily by French authors as one would have expected, from which I borrowed frequently.

At first, I was intimidated by aunt Rosario. Going to her house was like visiting a forbidden place where you had to be very quiet and careful not to break anything. There were so many rules and so many fragile trinkets! The place had an air of elegant clutter which captivated my imagination. How I longed to have a house like that, full of bibelots! I inherited the tendency to collect clutter from the Gracia-Dubiés, but this was fortunately balanced with my mother's tendency to minimalism. As a result, I have always been torn between Baroque excess on one hand and Japanese sparsity on the other. I have spent a great deal of my life trying to balance these two tendencies, finding a middle ground, a compromise, which has eluded me most of the time.

Aunt Rosario's husband left the family well off, but nonetheless she took extreme care with financial matters. To say that all the Gracia-Dubiés, except uncle Carlos, were frugal was an elegant understatement. In some ways they were just stingy, although they would have been appalled at anyone saying so. It is true that they did not have any problem dropping good sums of money on things they thought important, such as fashionable clothing and precious objects, but other expenses were carefully managed.

When my cousin became a young lady, the hunt for a proper husband was on. For years she had a handsome Air Force pilot as beau, but eventually that did not bear fruit. Time passed and she remained unmarried, so the fear of her never marrying was evident. Eventually, Marta married but this was only years after Castro's Revolution had triumphed. This posed difficulties finding proper accommodations for the newlyweds which they solved quite creatively. The house in which they lived had very high ceilings, so they divided the house into two by adding a floor between the original floor and the original ceiling. It was an ingenious solution to a vexing problem. Unfortunately, the marriage did not last. Two children came and were looked after with extreme care, but there were difficulties, and the father unexpectedly committed suicide.

Aunt Rosario died shortly after this tragedy, at eighty-five. Everything she had worked so hard to build was at the verge of destruction. Her treasures had to be traded for food and the bare necessities of life, in response to the increasing scarcity in Cuba, and her family was in disarray. I wonder whether she ever thought of similarities between the Cuban and French Revolutions. Perhaps the Cuban Revolution was not as bad as the French, since although she lost all her treasures, her head did not end up on a pole.

Chapter Nine

Unexpected Success

Father was the second oldest of his siblings, after Rosario. He was born in the Canary Islands on December 10, 1897, while the family were residing there. The family waited for the return to Havana in order to register father's birth on December 31, so as to show that he had been born in Cuba.

Father was fifteen when his father died, and the financial struggles that followed his death shaped his goals and ideas about money. The family kept up a good front, although few of their social relations and friends extended a helping hand, and they soon realized that they had to rely on themselves. They thought that the key to a prosperous future was education, and so everyone was stirred toward a profession. Aunt Rosario became an accountant, following on the footsteps of her grandfather. Uncle Julio chose law, and father intended to become a physician, like his father. Uncle Carlos was a baby at the time, so his future would have to be determined at a later date.

To help with expenses, those who could work did. Aunt Rosario in accounting, uncle Julio doing legal errands, and father joining the army when he became eligible so he could get an education and contribute to the family's support. Before then, he attended a well-known prep school in Havana, the Colegio Mimó. Life in Havana was not easy, but the family managed to survive and do so without compromising their principles and social aspirations. This hard experience molded father's opinions. Two of his siblings died young of diseases that perhaps could have been prevented, and he could not but think that under different circumstances perhaps they would not have. The need to live an organized and hard-working life created habits that were going to shape the rest of his days. The military academy in particular, with its emphasis on discipline, helped him develop an iron will when it came to work and saving.

Although his dream had been to become a physician like his father, he understood how difficult this would be under the family's present circumstances and decided to become a pharmacist instead. His qualifications, and no doubt some social pull, secured him a position at the most prominent pharmaceutical establishment in Havana, Droguería Sarrá (founded in 1853). I visited it with him. It was a grand establishment, with exquisite mahogany cabinets where all the jars with medications were kept. It looked more like a museum than a regular pharmacy, but still at that time there were many clerks and pharmacists taking care of the clientele.

The job at Sarrá made possible for father to work and study at the same time, which he did until he graduated with a straight A record (*sobresaliente*) at the University of Havana with a Doctorate in Chemistry and Pharmacological Sciences. The easiest path for him after graduation would have been to continue at Sarrá. He had already distinguished himself there and had a secure position. Eventually he would have to climb the business ladder, but this future was too ordinary for him. He would always be an employee, or at best he could have become a partner, but only after many years. The financial prospects were secure, but not brilliant. Was there a better alternative available?

Yes, but it was a gamble and required sacrifices: going to the country and opening a pharmacy in a town where there was limited competition. Imagine for a moment what this meant for a young man raised in a bourgeois family and, although recently under financial stress, used to a pleasant life style in the capital, surrounded by educated people and having the benefits of culture and refinement. But he did it. He borrowed three thousand pesos from grandmother and left Havana to make his fortune. The gamble paid off handsomely. He set up shop in Chambas, a town of five thousand inhabitants in the northwest of Camagüey province, near Morón, where there was only one other pharmacy. The other pharmacist was not happy about father's intrusion into his turf and tried his best to undermine father and bankrupt him, but father's competence, persistence, and savvy, made his pharmacy the favorite in the town.

One of father's great advantages was that he gave medical advice freely, and the advice was effective. After all, his own father had been a physician and he had picked up much information from him and Sarrá. And he read widely. He owned all sorts of books about medicine he had inherited from grandfather. In addition, he developed various concoctions that proved to be effective for treating certain ailments.

More important perhaps was that he transformed the pharmacy into a place of social gatherings for the leading men of the town. He set up a chess board on the pharmacy counter and there was always a game going. He would play with anyone and challenged anyone who walked through the door. He was good, and so the town's men came in to meet the challenge. Father was considered a superb chess player, and the town's men tried vainly to defeat him. I was never able to do it myself, although perhaps that was because he died when I was fourteen, and I was hardly seasoned enough to carry out the task. Keep in mind that these were the times when the legendary Capablanca (he died the year of my birth) had made chess a very popular game in Cuba — everyone was trying to duplicate his feats.

In less than twenty years, father made a not insignificant fortune. He owned a cattle farm, a citrus orchard, a sugarcane plantation, a pharmacy, our home, the home where my maternal grandmother and aunt Maruca lived, and some rental properties whose income supported his in-laws. He had accumulated a substantial amount of cash in the bank and had paid back grandmother's loan. His success had been due to his business savvy and hard work, but also to his personal charm. One of my greatest sorrows was that father died when I was so young.

The pharmacy had never been father's real interest, instead agriculture became his true vocation. He discovered it when he bought his first farm. He immediately realized that he loved the challenge of turning around a poorly run piece of land into a productive garden. He enjoyed the life of the gentleman farmer, and hosted big parties for friends from all over who came and spent time on his land.

Father had several obsessions. Food, dress, intellectual excellence, and books were all very important in his life. Above all these, he was obsessed with the idea of financial security. He never became a millionaire but by the standards of the time he managed to become what most Cubans would consider to be rich and I would call comfortable. During this time millionaires were very rare, as rare probably as billionaires are today, but when he died father left a very substantial estate, which, thanks to the Cuban Revolution, dwindled to nothing very quickly. Father frequently repeated the saying that "a widow's money lasts only seven years," and this prediction came true of our family, although not for the reasons he thought and on which the saying was based. It was not that mother squandered our money, but simply that private property ceased to be allowed in communist Cuba.

Although father liked having money, he was not interested in living the profligate life associated with the wealthy. He did not have any use for fancy cars, jewels, travels, parties, or any of the paraphernalia so common among "the beautiful people." He was interested in good food, clothing, and books, and these were not expensive. His financial interests had to do with security. He had been born into a prominent, well-to-do family that had lost its financial base, and for his entire life he struggled to prevent the repetition of what happened to his father's family to his own family. The result was that, in spite of his success, we always lived well below our means, something everyone in the family, except him, resented. In short, father was, in current language, "the millionaire next door," comfortable but frugal. Warren Buffet would have approved.

Chapter Ten

The Storyteller

Most families count a storyteller among its members, and some are lucky to have more than one. Our most successful example of this was uncle Julio. Unlike father and uncle Carlos, uncle Julio was short, a bit overweight, and a perennial loafer. A chronic student of law who never graduated, he earned a living doing paperwork for other people, *gestionando* as this kind of activity was called in Cuba. People like him are useful in societies burdened with exhausting bureaucratic rigamaroles that only the initiated can sidestep because of their familiarity with them, the right acquaintances among the bureaucracy, and particularly their charm, the last of which Julio had in abundance. There was nothing we liked more in my immediate family than to have Julio visit. And when we moved to Havana, to a neighborhood close to where he lived, he came to see us almost every day. Of course, there were also excuses for his visits. After father bought an apartment house, he gave Julio its management. Julio never did a very good job on this or anything else, and after father died, mother threatened to take the job away from him, but who could do that to Julio? It was impossible. His charm shielded him from any retribution or harm.

The charm worked well with women, of course. And he had an endless line of girlfriends and mistresses of various sorts, although he kept them to himself. None of them were ever introduced to any member of our family. Eventually he married a spinster who lived next door to aunt Rosario and whom he got to know in his almost daily visits with his sister. They were both middle aged, in their fifties, well past the age of romance, but they behaved as if they were teenagers. In our somewhat puritanical family, in which open expressions of passion were considered to be in bad taste, their kissing and embracing in public, and their touching and petting, were considered scandalous. But the new, although old, lovers could not care less. They behaved as if they were the only people in the universe. Fortunately for my straight-laced parents, they seldom visited us together, and separately they were the epitome of propriety.

Having Julio around was a feast, because he had always something new to tell us, including stories of his travels and adventures. One of his trips was to the United States. He loved everything he found there, from the coffee to the system of government. "Imagine," he would point out, "the superb idea of making weak coffee and then pouring thick cream on it to taste!" How could Cuban *café con leche* compare with this? And the way in which the cream came, in little plastic containers with individual portions, was so clever! Everything else was also superb! How smart those Americans are!" he would say full of admiration for the country to the North. Indeed, he postulated, to go for independence had been a serious mistake among the fathers of our country. Cubans should have gone for annexation. (Annexationists formed a group of Cuban patriots who favored annexing Cuba to the United States rather than independence.) He then would recite the list of distressing results of having failed to make Cuba part of the United States: corruption, disorder, and destructive politics, to name a few. Of course, he was in favor of independence from Spain. After all, the Spaniards were stupid brutes! Remember, he was a Dubié. But the only alternative that would have made sense for him was to join the United States, since France, which had the superior culture and an enlightened ideology, had become unavailable.

Julio had a large repertoire of stories to tell about ghosts and spirits in particular. I remember loving his narratives, at the same time that I was terrified by them and spent many sleepless nights, frightened at the evil things that lurked under the bed, in the closet, in the next room, or in the dark. Many of the stories were autobiographical, which makes me wonder whether he was simply a storyteller that did not believe what he told or believed in them but was crazy. I remember one in particular that for some unexplained reason chilled my bones.

He was out very late one night, walking home on a deserted street after having had a few drinks at a well-known bar. All of a sudden, he felt a compulsion to look back, an unusual attraction, a pull, almost physical, and when he did, he saw his friend looking directly at him very intently from far away. He did not understand how this was possible, since he had been with his friend earlier that very evening at his home. He wanted to call out, but something stopped him. It was as if his mouth could not open, while he simultaneously felt the hairs on his head stand up. He walked some more and then, anxiously, looked back again. His friend was still there, looking fixedly at him, his eyes larger than usual, as if they had grown in the few seconds that had passed. He appeared to want to say something, and his neck was unexplainably long and straining to see Julio. Uncle realized this was not natural, so his legs started trembling and he hurried on his way. But he could not prevent himself from looking back again and again, and each time he saw his friend, the eyes growing larger, and the neck extending farther, becoming so long that it looked as if it were made of rubber, straining like a tentacle of a gigantic octopus in order to follow him. Eventually Julio overcame the weakness of his legs and broke into a run which did not stop until he got home. The next morning, he learned that his friend had died just at the time he had first seen him on the street.

Julio never had a proper family; he married late; he never had children; he never became financially stable; and he made no contributions to the family or society. But he was a wonderful storyteller, which made him welcome anywhere he went, and particularly in our home.

Chapter Eleven

Bedroom Suite for a Pompadour

The youngest of my father's siblings was Carlos. He grew up at a time, after grandfather's death, when the Gracia-Dubié family was in financial straits. As a consequence, he could not attend the university, having to go to work instead. When father settled in Chambas, he brought Carlos to work for him and be trained in the business. In a few years, father set him up in the pharmacy of a sugar mill, Central Falla. The beauty of this was that each of these large mills had a community of people living around it that was isolated from larger towns where they would have access to various sources of healthcare and medications. It was a captive audience and so pharmacists could charge for medications—at the time pharmacists prepared most of these—whatever they wanted, within reason. Father used to give the example of one that all pharmacies sold: rose water. This was merely a compound of tap water and rose essence. The ingredients costed less than a penny and the small bottle sold for one peso (100 pennies). Pharmacists who went to such towns could do very well financially because there was no competition. It was always the case that there was only one pharmacy in the town, because the sugar mill owned the land and had to approve its establishment.

Although uncle Carlos did not have a university degree in pharmacy, as a result of the family situation at the time, and so could not legally be at the head of the family business, he hired someone who, for a fee, would be the front man. But Carlos coveted my father's title: Doctor in Chemistry, and his standing first in his class. The plan worked. In five years not only had uncle repaid father, but he had saved fifty-thousand pesos. This was a considerable sum of money at the time and could, with proper management, be the beginning of a fortune. However, Carlos was a city boy from Havana and he felt that he could not stand the countryside any longer. In spite of father's objections, he sold the pharmacy and moved back to the capital, where he started studying toward a university degree and could enjoy what a grand playground for those with money could offer.

The desire to obtain a degree was not the main motivation for Carlos' decision; he wanted the good life he could have in Havana. Among the things he coveted were women. In the country he had been isolated and few women were available to a young bachelor. He was not particularly handsome, but he was six feet tall, with sandy hair, light eyes, and the distinguished countenance of the Gracia men. The contrast with the general male population was strong and in his favor, and he had plenty of money, which he did not mind spending. It took no time at all for him to fall in love with a woman in Havana. She was attractive and presentable, the kind of woman that would make him look and feel good. He could be the envy of other men. Still, she was not the sort of woman the family would consider appropriate, so instead of marrying her, he set her up in grand style as his mistress, in a lavishly furnished apartment in a nice building in El Vedado, a fashionable neighborhood of Havana. Carlos' extravagance can be epitomized by the price of the bedroom suite he bought for his mistress, one thousand pesos, which at the time was half a year's salary of a bank manager.

As it often happens, the relationship soured with time and the two lovers separated. She kept everything he had given her, including the grand bedroom suite, which no doubt she shared with other men, including (if we are to believe mother) on occasion with father for a brief period years later. In five years, my uncle had spent all his money. The only thing he had at the end was a degree, and he had to go back to father to borrow money. Father dutifully set him up again in business, although this time in Havana. This meant that the set-up cost more than the first time and the profitability of the business was not nearly what it had been in the country. Moreover, father kept a large interest in the pharmacy, just to make sure that he had the last word if need be. What else could father do? Carlos was his kid brother and Ignacito's godfather. And he was an articulate and charming fellow we all liked. Besides, father always felt a duty to help and provide for his family as well as for mother's family. In the end, all of it worked out for father because our pharmacy was to be the first in a chain of pharmacies father envisioned, starting with the one shared with Carlos in Cuatro Caminos, a busy part of Havana. Unfortunately, this plan did not materialize for a variety of reasons I will mention later.

Carlos learned his lesson and from then on became very discriminating about the women he dated. Eventually he ended up getting married to another pharmacist, a woman in middle age like him, who seems to have made him happy.

In the mid-seventies Carlos visited Miami with his wife, and I went to see him with my wife and our two daughters. He looked fine and fit. He ran every day and ate a healthy diet. And he meditated as he had learned to do from his readings of Hindu sages. Although he did not agree with Castro's government, he had been put in charge of the overall distribution of pharmaceutical drugs in Havana because of his competence and strict ethics. The government knew that he would neither double-cross them nor steal from them. He seemed happy, and he loved to see me again after so many years and to talk about our family. Indeed, some of the information about the Gracia-Dubiés included here derives from our conversations.

As was to be expected, our talk during his visit drifted to father and life as it had been in Cuba. He told me that when he was young, he was obsessed with winning the lottery and frequently bought tickets, selecting the numbers on the basis of dreams and spiritual revelations he might have had. This was typical of Cubans, even among educated people like himself. No one seems to have been aware of the contradictions it implied. Uncle Carlos added that whenever he discussed this with father, he would ask Carlos why he wasted time with such nonsense. What he needed, if he wanted to be rich, father urged, was to set himself up in a business and work hard at it. In short, father's advice was to follow the formula he had proven works. This confirmed one of my beliefs about father. He never thought there was such a thing as a free lunch, at least not for our family. And I can vouch for it. Whatever I have achieved has been the product of hard work and ingenuity, although I have had my share of luck. But I have never won the lottery, a fact I've always resented. Of course, how could I, since I never buy lottery tickets?

Chapter Twelve

"¡España Es Nuestra Madre Patria!"

"Spain is our motherland and Cuba is its faithful daughter." Many Cubans thought and still think in this way about Spain and its relationship with Cuba. They consider themselves to be close to Spain, and yet Cuba is as African as it is Spanish, and in the eyes of some more so.

In most of Latin America this feeling for Spain is generally absent, particularly in countries where the majority of the population is of Amerindian origin. Not only do they not consider themselves Spanish in any way, but they resent being considered so by others because of the abuses that imperial Spain committed in the almost four hundred years in which it was a colonial power in Latin America. This is evident even in the United States in the way some persons with Latin American ancestry object to being called Hispanics because of that term's association with Spain. Although some Cubans also have resented Spain and tried hard to separate themselves from it, most of them appreciate Spanish culture and the Spanish roots of the population while objecting to Spanish politics.

Mother's family had one advantage over father's French branch: they were who they thought they were, and did not have any pretense or illusions about themselves. They did not worry much about their identity. They felt comfortable in their culture of origin and could care less about what others thought. Considering themselves Spaniards or descendants of Spaniards, they loved the motherland, Spain, although they regarded Cuba as their fatherland. My grandfather fought along Spaniards and against Cuban patriots in the War of Independence. Even father, who belonged to the French branch of the family, acted often as if he were Spanish in his criticism of Spain.

Spanish culture is superbly rich, but Spaniards are generally thought to be uncouth, a byproduct of the long subjugation under the Moors, and the need to live in a country at war for the seven hundred years that it took for it to achieve liberation. Until well into the twentieth century, most Spaniards were farmers or soldiers and many still behave as such to this day. Indeed, many Cubans regard Spaniards as uncouth, unsophisticated folks. A fact that contributes to this judgment is that the Spaniards who came to the island in large numbers before Cuban independence were for the most part uneducated country folk from Extremadura and Andalucía, traditionally rural and poor areas of Spain or, after independence, from Galicia, a province that was also rural and poor and its population spoke Galician, rather than Castilian, as the mother tongue. But there were other reasons as well. In general, Spanish social manners are unpolished if compared with, say, French or English manners. Yet, who can resist the appeal of an Aragónese *jota,* or fail to admire the Catalan Romanesque?

There is something very authentic in typical Spaniards, regardless of which part of Spain they come from. Most of them have in abundance what they metaphorically call *salero.* A *salero* is a salt shaker. Salt defines the taste of food, by making everything taste as it should. Like the English wit, but different from it, it is an attractive manner of talking and behaving *con gracia,* that draws others to those who have it. Nonchalance shamelessness mixed with a bit of cockiness and smartness makes Spaniards, particularly from the south of the peninsula, *simpáticos.* So, it is not surprising that many of us feel strongly about our Spanish roots in spite of the crimes Spaniards committed in Latin America during colonial times.

Chapter Thirteen

Better Marry Than Burn

Carmen Recamán, the mother of my maternal grandfather, José María Otero Recamán, came from an important family in La Coruña, the large city in Galicia, the Spanish province where the Celts settled when they overran Iberia. Her brother was a bishop, which at the time in Spain was as good as being a general or a member of the landed aristocracy. But she married for love and to a man belonging to the bourgeoisie, a physician. To be a physician in nineteenth-century Spain did not have much éclat, and certainly did not involve a great deal of money.

In spite of her marriage into a lower social class, my great-grandmother was not disowned by her family and she continued to maintain good relations with them and especially with her brother. Grandfather was born in 1857, and when he came of age and had to decide what to do in life, the family assumed that he would go into the Church. With a bishop for an uncle he could be assured a good position and perhaps, in time, would open the possibility of succeeding him. Everything would be set up for advancement and wealth. Ecclesiastical nepotism was not alien in nineteenth-century Spain.

Unfortunately, grandfather liked women too much, and he disliked the idea of sleeping with women on the sly, as many members of the clergy did. Still, rejecting the profession planned by his family for him was not possible as long as he remained in Spain, so he decided to flee the country, and at the time the best destination for that was Cuba. The rest of Spanish America had become independent, and Puerto Rico and Santo Domingo were backwaters and offered limited prospects. Cuba was the Pearl of the Antilles.

After a few months at the seminary, grandfather escaped with the help of his mother, who as she had proven with her own marriage, believed in love. She sold some of her jewels and gave him enough money for the ship's passage to Cuba and a little extra to set up some business there. She also gave him what to me was a treasure box, containing precious objects, as both mementos from her and insurance in case he found himself in financial difficulties. The objects were beautiful, embroidered in gold, with semi-precious stones, and delicate filigrees. I used to covet looking at, and holding them in my hands when I was small and visited grandmother. They made me dream of enchanted places in long forgotten principalities and kingdoms, and of knights and princesses. Grandmother kept them with her until her death in the 1960s. After that, they were bartered by mother for things she needed in the scarcity that ensued in the aftermath of Castro's Revolution.

Grandfather's departure from Spain was unexpected to everyone except his mother. His father knew nothing of it, and he kept secret the exact date of it even from his mother. When the day came, he left for the port very early in the morning, quietly rushing to make sure he awoke no one. He had been spending a few days at home on vacation, away from the seminary, and one morning his mother noticed he had failed to come to breakfast early, as was his custom, to drink a sweet, hot cup of thick chocolate *a la española*. Fearing he was not feeling well, and not anticipating his departure, she went to his room. There she found a farewell note. In a letter she subsequently wrote to him, she recalled how she came into the room and saw the unmade bed, with the indentation in the feather pillow from his having slept on it. The wrinkles on the sheets made her heart ache, and the emptiness of the room pierced her heart. Would she ever see José María again? She concluded rightly that she would not. She picked up his note and read it, sitting on the bed and caressing the place where he had spent his last night. Then she went downstairs and gave the letter to his father, and they wept together.

Chapter Fourteen

The Marquis' Mistress

Grandfather was born in Spain, but grandmother was born in Cuba. Her mother, my great-mother, was Epifania Pimienta. She had become widowed early on, and had been left with three children: Casimiro, Susana, and Dolores (a.k.a. Lola). Her first husband had been a wealthy landowner by the name of Pozo, whose family had a high profile in Cuba and one of whose members eventually included Justo Luis Pozo del Puerto, mayor of Havana in the fifties, under the regime of the dictator Fulgencio Batista. Lola's father was assassinated, for reasons that were never made clear, on his return from Havana on one of his business trips. He had gone to the capital to retrieve a large sum of money and was returning on horseback when he was shot. He managed to ride his horse home, but collapsed when he arrived and died shortly after from the loss of blood, unable to explain what had happened. One story that circulated at the time was that he had been shot by an administrator of one of his farms he had fired because of the cruelty he used with the large number of slaves he kept. Another was that he had been shot by a band of *cimarrón* slaves who had escaped one of his farms and had formed a band of outlaws. The money he had brought with him from Havana, a bag full of gold coins, was intact when he arrived home, but in the commotion that his appearance caused, no one paid attention to it, and when things settled down it was missing.

Great-grandmother did not wait long to remarry. She took as husband a charming, profligate rogue without money, Diego Muñoz, who helped her go through what remained of her fortune quite quickly. They lived with the three children from the previous marriage and had five additional ones: Angela (a.k.a. Angelita), Miguel (a.k.a. Miguelito), Edelmira, Leonila (after whom mother was named), and grandmother María.

Chapter 14

Perhaps the most interesting member of grandmother's family, other than grandmother, was Lola. She was grandmother's half-sister and an independently minded woman. She was also regarded as a beauty in spite of a major flaw. Her light blue eyes had been a wonder celebrated all around Vuelta Abajo, the area of Pinar del Río where she lived with grandmother's family. Unfortunately, when she was very young, she was helping the cook to roast coffee beans in the kitchen and a bean exploded in the hot oil, flew out, and hit her right eye. She lost her sight in it immediately and eventually had to have the eyeball replaced with a prosthesis. After this event everyone thought that she would not find any male to become interested in her, but to everyone's surprise her glass eye did not deter her from wreaking havoc with men's hearts and being quite discriminating with those who courted her. She was an intriguing woman and the queen of the household, who, because of her misfortune, was allowed to do as she pleased.

A neighbor and frequent visitor to the house was Ramón Argüelles y Alonso, first Marquis of Argüelles, an enormously wealthy landowner and railroad magnate, perhaps the wealthiest man in the Spanish empire at the time. His title had been granted to honor him for his services to the Spanish Crown. Apart from his fortune, he served as Colonel of Volunteers in the army that Spain used to fight against Cubans in the war of independence. Unlike so many other Cubans who had purchased aristocratic titles from Spanish nobles in financial distress, he was the real thing.

In the nineteenth century, and particularly in the early twentieth century, a great many Spanish aristocrats lost their money and were in serious economic straits, so they began to sell their titles to the Cuban nouveau riche. As a result, there were plenty of counts and marquises in Cuba. And there were even some princes. Next to our farm in Ceballos lived the Príncipe Ruspoli, for example, who had a train stop next to his property named after him, but he was an Italian prince, rather than a Spanish one. He visited us a number of times and I recall hearing that he had been impressed by my mother's garden and flowers. Frankly, he did not impress me at the time. He appeared to be as ordinary as anybody else, and perhaps even more ordinary. One of father's close friends in Chambas of all places, was Count (or Marquis) de Peñaranda. Indeed, he suggested to father that he buy himself a title, but father scoffed at the idea; he considered himself a progressive free thinker and the last thing he would want was to be associated with a bankrupt aristocracy through the purchase of a title.

But, as I was saying, the Marquis of Argüelles was the real thing. He was already married when he visited great-grandmother's home, although his wife lived in Spain. In time it became evident that he was attracted to Lola and Lola to him. Great-grandmother was alarmed, but what could she do? You can't easily forbid a wealthy marquis to visit your home and she had never been able to control Lola. One day, when Argüelles was visiting, Lola went into her bedroom to make her bed—she had decided to sleep with the Marquis that night (in her mother's home of all places!), and leave with him following morning. Great-grandmother pleaded with her to abandon this idea. Had she thought about what she was about to do? What were the consequences for her and the family? But Lola had made up her mind and brushed aside her mother's concerns, responding like the willful, spoiled child she was: "*Sí, ya lo pensé, lo pensé, lo pensé.*" Her step father was called to help, but he could do little. Since he was not Lola's father and the money that supported the family was matrilineal, he knew better than to antagonize Lola or the Marquis! So, the Marquis stayed the night and next morning left with Lola, who had become his mistress.

Their union produced an issue, Elicio Argüelles y Pozo, whom the Marquis recognized as his son. He did all he could to advance Elicio in society, except allow him to inherit the title—that, and whatever went with it, was reserved for the daughter he had fathered with his lawful wife, who lived in Spain. Cuban high society has always had a penchant for titles and money and, in spite of the usual gossip, no one of consequence denied Elicio entrance in their homes. It is certainly better to be a marquis' bastard than a legitimate *don nadie*. Indeed, Elicio married one of the Menocal women, María Luisa Menocal y Cueto, and thus became part of a very select Cuban elite, since Mario García Menocal had been president of Cuba and belonged to one of the most important families in the island. Eventually Elicio entered politics and became a senator. Indeed, the influence of Elicio reached all the way to my grandfather who was twice a member of Congress, until he was disgusted by Cuban politics and resigned.

Lola, the Marquis' mistress, lived well for the rest of her life. First, with her lover the Marquis of Argüelles, and later with their son Elicio. He saw to it that she had every comfort, although she kept a low profile. Elicio was a loving and dutiful son who, in spite of his social position and duties, visited Lola every week until the end of her long life. For many years, she was the head of a sprawling crèche for abandoned children in a swank area of Havana where, in addition to the caring for the children, she kept a menagerie of birds and domestic animals as was fashionable at the time. I particularly remember a flock of peacocks parading elegantly through the gardens.

Chapter Fifteen

Ruined by a Hurricane and Resentment Against Spaniards

With the small capital his mother gave my grandfather, José María, when he left Spain for Cuba, he settled in the region of the province of Pinar del Río, where grandmother's family lived. The area, known as Vuelta Abajo, was reported to grow the best tobacco in the world. Having an enterprising nature, he saw the advantage of getting into the business and began growing the crop, first by leasing some land and later buying it. Things went well for a few years. He increased his land holdings and was able to marry grandmother. He was thirty-three and she was seventeen when they married in 1890. They had seven children, one of which was stillborn. The surviving children were José María, Carmen, Jaime, Epifania (a.k.a. Juanita), María (a.k.a. Maruca), and Leonila (a.k.a. Niña, my mother). José María was born three years after the marriage. As a good Spaniard, grandfather joined the Spanish Company of volunteers fighting against Cuban patriots in which the Marquis de Argüelles also served, and became a captain. This, together with perhaps too much ambition and bad luck, was going to cause his eventual downfall.

After Cuba became independent from Spain, grandfather saw the opportunity to increase his fortune. Commerce was growing now that Spain's tight commercial monopoly on the island had been broken, and new opportunities for exports of tobacco were opening up. In order to take advantage of the new situation he needed to increase his crop, and this in turn required more land. Following an ambitious plan, grandfather negotiated a large mortgage under conditions that, unfortunately, were to prove disastrous. Grandmother told me that he expected to have no difficulty in paying the mortgage with the rent he would get from farmers to whom he would lease the land to grow tobacco. Initially things progressed as he had envisioned and he made good money.

However, in 1910 a major hurricane hit Cuba and devastated the province of Pinar del Río. Known as *El Huracán de los Cinco Días* (the Five-Day Hurricane). It lasted for more than five days. Heavy rain, together with violent winds, savaged Vuelta Abajo, where grandfather's *vegas* (tobacco farms) were located. The entire tobacco crop was lost, farm animals were drowned, and most structures were heavily damaged or entirely destroyed. Even the family's home and the country store grandfather kept suffered irreparable damage. Nothing of this magnitude had hit the area before, according to the collective memory. The farmers to whom grandfather had leased land lost their crops and some lost their homes as well (as did my grandfather). Unable to pay father, and having nothing more to lose, they abandoned the area leaving father with large mortgage payments and debts that he could not discharge. His creditors saw a unique opportunity to recover the land they had sold after having initially received a considerable amount for it.

Some ill will among Cuban creditors against grandfather lingered because he had sided with Spain in the War of Independence. Nationalistic feelings were very strong and trumped common sense, justice, and compassion. In the very family there were serious divisions between Cuban patriots and supporters of Spain. Casimiro, grandmother's half-brother, went so far as not eating scrambled eggs with tomato because the colors of the dish were the same as those of the Spanish flag. Of course, the Marquis de Argüelles did not have to suffer such treatment; his money and position were enough to keep him safe, but not even he could save grandfather from bankruptcy. The creditors called their loans and he had no way to pay them. Finding no alternative, grandfather declared bankruptcy and relinquished the land.

Broken, embarrassed, and in disgrace, grandfather moved the family to Zaza del Medio, a town located in the province of Las Villas, in the center of the island. The town had two virtues: It was far away from Pinar del Río and therefore it was a place where no one knew him or his disgrace; and, it was near Taguasco, the town where his eldest daughter, Carmen, resided. She was married to a prosperous merchant. Grandfather earned a living there working as a bookkeeper for his son-in-law, and other businessmen and farmers in the community. The job was painful to him because he considered it beneath his social station. His rapid rise and success in Cuba had come to end. But tragedy was not done with him.

Ten years later, Carmen was left widowed and in financial straits so that grandfather's main means of support collapsed, except for the wages the two sons brought home from working on farms. The naturalist treatments for the asthma he suffered, which improved his health in Vuelta Abajo, were now unaffordable. He continued to adhere to a vegetarian diet, but gone were the therapeutic baths, special treatments, and massages. The ruins of the glass sun-bathing facility that he had built and enjoyed in Vuelta Abajo was the thing that remained of his establishment. His health deteriorated markedly and rapidly. Severe asthma attacks became increasingly frequent and the medications he used to control them finally damaged his heart irreparably. He died in 1906, the year mother turned fifteen, a broken man, leaving his family in very difficult circumstances. The one grace of his early death was that it occurred three months before his eldest son, José María, was killed. He did not have to suffer that final crushing blow.

Chapter Sixteen

Tears from a "Bileless Dove"

Mother's mother, *"Abuelita Belé"* in my childhood lexicon, thought of herself as an innocent victim of her husband, her children, her in-laws or in-laws to be, the circumstances in which she lived, and life in general, *"una paloma sin hiel"* as she put it. She always recounted her unmarried years with nostalgia, the only memories that caused sweet, rather than bitter tears. She seemed to have enjoyed her sisters and the life in Vuelta Abajo, whereas marriage brought obligations, children, the distress caused by a womanizing husband, and eventually their move away from the country. From that time on she spent her life shedding bitter tears. There were tears for every occasion. Everything was high tragedy for her, deserving a good cry. She cried when she remembered any of the misfortunes that, real or imagined, had happened to her. She cried when she thought that someone was abusing her in some way. She cried when she did not feel well, which was most of the time, for she was a relentless hypochondriac. She even cried when people were kind to her and she felt grateful, although in such occasions the tears were not bitter.

I remember how she cried every time mother gave her some money, which was constantly because she lived mainly from mother's handouts. She cried whenever anyone was going away, even for very short periods of time, and when anyone arrived. Saying goodbye immediately caused her eyes to water. She would pull out one of the many embroidered handkerchiefs she always carried in case of emergencies and try to dry her eyes, but the tears kept flowing. One needed a handkerchief the size of a bedsheet to control the flood. When I was going to school in Ciego de Ávila, staying with her and aunt Maruca, my parents would come to get me on Fridays to take me back to the orchard in Ceballos for the weekend, and bring me back on Sunday evening. Well, grandmother cried when my parents came to get me and when they left, and she cried when they brought me back and left. There was never an occasion when a good cry was not in order for *Abuelita Belé*.

Living with a person who was constantly in tears had serious consequences for mother and her siblings. They all had acquired a tendency to cry which was passed on to my sister and even to me. We also cried. One of the great advantages of mother's religious conversion to Evangelical Christianity many years later was that she decided that it was wrong to cry so much. Crying when you had no serious reason to do it was, thanks to some use of tortured logic, morally inappropriate. Indeed, mother went further, because she believed that God's grace and mercy were so abundant, given the serious nature of our sins, she came to think that nothing, no matter how dreadful, merited crying. We should instead rejoice in what we have, a la Candide, no matter how dreadful the circumstances are. And since mother was the leader of her family, the family followed the golden rule: she who has the gold rules. What mother said was law. So, slowly, crying was reduced and eventually eliminated, even by grandmother. But it was not easy to reform the whole family, and to this day I am prone to shed a tear when others are not, which is quite embarrassing, being a male and all that the title entails if you are Hispanic or Latino. But, of course, it must have been, or was, particularly difficult for grandmother. A life of crying was difficult to stop.

Part of the reason for so much crying was that grandmother was self-centered and felt sorry for herself. She considered herself a martyr. This showed in many ways: in the power she exercised over her daughter Maruca, in her constant complaints about her own discomfort and ailments, and in her difficulties living in peace with anyone. For years she had a kind of neck ache of which she complained constantly. She could not find a comfortable position and went everywhere with special pillows for her neck. Then there was the problem with her hair bun and scalp itching. It was her custom to comb her hair in a long braid which she, as was usual with old Cuban and Spanish ladies, rolled over into a bun at the back of her head, down toward her neck. This caused itching on that spot, which in turn caused her to constantly complain about it, yet she wouldn't change her hair style. No one could figure out another way of solving the problem, so she continued to complain.

Mosquitos were a particularly vexing problem for grandmother. In tropical Cuba, mosquitoes are ubiquitous. Even in houses that have screens on windows and doors, mosquitoes often sneak inside. In houses without screens people used mosquito nets. At one time or another, grandmother lived in houses of both types, but anywhere that she was you could be sure that, if there was one mosquito in the neighborhood, it would find its way to her and prevent her from sleeping. Once the mosquito made its unwelcome presence known, there would be no peace in the household. Everyone had to get up in pursuit of the bug, which of course smartly eluded its executioners most of the time. But grandmother made sure that no one else in the house slept until the mosquito met its demise. Finally, someone would kill it, although by then it was too late and grandmother had lost her sleep. Tea would have to be brewed, *un cocimiento de manzanilla* or *tilo*. Perhaps the tea helped to soothe conversation so eventually, if we were lucky, produced some peace and sleep. Then grandmother would fall into a relaxing slumber until well into the day, while the rest of the household had to get up and go to school or work.

Insomnia was another problem. Grandmother never acknowledged that she had slept well. At night I frequently heard her snoring away in perfect sleep, but in the morning when she got up and the first order of business was to ask her how she had slept, the answer always was that she had not slept a wink. Aunt Maruca and I would knowingly look at each other, but neither one of us would ever dare to say to grandmother, "I heard you snoring, so you must have slept some!"

Then there was the fact that she suffered from motion sickness. This meant that she never went anywhere by automobile or bus if it could at all be helped. Whenever she had to travel, a horse carriage had to be contracted for the journey. Imagine the difficulties this created! Fortunately, in most Cuban towns there were always some horse carriages around the main plazas for the sake of tourists. So, someone had to go there to contract for the trip since telephones were generally unavailable. This was a great nuisance. On the rare occasion when no horse carriage could be secured and she was forced to travel by car, grandmother carried with her one of her embroidered hankies, soaked in alcohol, and smelled it constantly. The reason, she said, was that it was not just the motion of the car that made her sick, but the smell of gasoline. Of course, I loved to ride with her in the horse carriages! This was one of her habits that was a source of enjoyment for me. So she and I rode in the carriage, with the sound of the horse's hooves striking the road, talking pleasantly to each other, and enjoying the light and the sun. She always carried a *sombrilla* (umbrella) so that the sun would not burn her fine skin. I ran from seat to seat observing the world around us.

Perhaps more remarkable than grandmother's motion sickness was the fact that I never heard anyone complain about all the inconveniences that her complaints created for the rest of the family, even when she was not present. The only comments ever voiced were directed to making her as comfortable as we could all do. But I should tell you that I inherited her propensity to motion sickness, and ended up vomiting a number of times on the side of a road or in an amusement park. Oh well, it is in my genes! But I have the redeeming quality that I sleep like a log and I have never claimed to be a dove without bile!

Grandmother's feelings toward herself were revealed in the way she managed her hands, which she rubbed against each other, twiddling her thumbs in a nervous gesture that indicated her impatience and frustration. She thought all the commotion she caused with her sleep and health complaints was the most natural thing in the world. Her comfort should be the primary goal of everyone around her. And what about the discomfort that she caused others? I don't think it ever crossed her mind that she ever caused any! For as long as she lived grandmother managed to be a constant center of attention without thinking that she was.

One point of frequent contention surrounding her was the place where she would live after aunt Maruca got married and grandmother's household was dismantled. This meant that she had to live with one of her daughters, and of course Maruca was the obvious choice since grandmother had lived with her while Maruca was unmarried. But that turned out to be difficult, because after a few weeks of living with her, grandmother wanted to move somewhere else. And then after another few weeks, still somewhere else. One of the factors common to her daughters that irritated grandmother was the husbands, whom she did not suffer well—as the saying goes, *los masticaba pero no los tragaba* (chewed them but did not swallow them). The way it worked was that she would be content for a while, but eventually she began to idealize her daughters, and finally quarreled with the husband of the one with whom she was staying. This would make it imperative that she move, and this in time was repeated at the new place, and so on.

Father, who was a respectful and orderly man, wrote grandmother a letter after one of these disorderly moves that created much havoc and anguish among her daughters. He explained to Doña María, as she was called by everyone except her children and grandchildren, that it made sense for her to live at least two months in each of her daughters' homes in rotation, for various reasons which he enumerated carefully. Unfortunately, grandmother took the letter as an insult. She never forgave father for it, even though he supported her from the time he married mother until he died. No final arrangement concerning where she would live was successful until father died and she could move into a home where no in-law resided. The main obstacle to her contentment in our home had been removed.

Don't get the idea that I did not love *Abuelita Belé*. True, I did not like her as well as I did *abuelita* Mercedes, whom I preferred to any of the other women who played a role in my early life, with the exception of mother, my sister, and Aunt Maruca. But I did love her, although my love was always tempered by the sense that she created too much trouble for others that I also loved and some that I loved more than I loved her. Later in life, when she had adapted to life in our home, I spent many interesting hours listening to the stories from years gone by that she liked to tell. Indeed, many of the anecdotes in this narrative come from her recollections. She told her tales with passion, as if they had just happened. A strong indication of her hold on her daughters was that mother did not seek to leave Cuba until grandmother died, even though grandmother could have stayed with Maruca.

Grandmother thought that her misery had started with her marriage. She married for love, but grandfather had an eye for women and is reputed to have engaged in infidelities that grandmother found intolerable. Children came regularly, and that also was a source of preoccupation and work, although she had servants that helped her, and for whom she cared well. I remember the story of one of her cooks, who was Chinese, and who worked for her until his death. He had no family and was considered part of the greater household. When he was taken ill with the disease that killed him, grandmother saw to it that he was cared for and kept comfortable until the end.

Grandmother's life took a particularly bad turn when grandfather lost his land and they had to leave Vuelta Abajo, the place in which she had lived all her life and where her family resided. In a few years grandfather died, and shortly after came the death of her eldest son José María. This last event destroyed her chances of any further happiness, although she still had another son, Jaime, who replaced the eldest in her affections. And there was Maruca. Sometimes I think that Maruca in fact was more important to her than anyone else, although grandmother never explicitly recognized it. The way Maruca treated her, always with so much love and affection, even when she was irritating and wounding, was quite inexplicable to me. Maruca had been a sickly child and later in life was also prone to serious asthma attacks. Grandmother was lost without her, and when she married, grandmother felt betrayed.

Abuelita Belé lived a long life, but from the time I first remember and she was in her seventies, whenever anyone mentioned buying her clothes or shoes, she would put a face of compunction and say, whimpering, "for the few days of life that I have left, what I have is more than sufficient." She was a very fastidious and prudish lady, who until three months before her death would not allow anyone to wash her undergarments—they were too private to be exposed to someone else's eyes. Then she felt sick and very quickly became comatose. She lasted three months that way, and died a peaceful death at the age of ninety-three, in 1966.

Grandmother's wake was held at the Caballeros Funeral Home, which had also been the place for my Aunt Carmen's wake. She was buried in the Cementerio Colón, like other members of my family who had died in Havana. Mother wrote to me that everything had been done properly in spite of the shortages common in Cuba, and that she had bought a shroud of white carnations to cover the casket. Being able to do this was a great consolation to mother. It was a proper farewell to her mother.

Chapter Seventeen

Murdered by the Guardia Civil

The main source of grandmother's suffering had been the death of her first-born son, José María. I never met him, or his wife Leonarda, who was supposed to be both sexy and to have had a roaming eye for males. The allusions to José María in my family were always veiled in mystery, although his son, named after him, but called Pepe by everyone, frequently stayed with us and even worked for father occasionally. The name "Leonarda" was anathema, and the mere mention of it, after what she is supposed to have done, was unthinkable.

I knew early on that José María had died young, but the circumstances of his death were never discussed. One day, however, when I was about fifteen, grandmother told me the story of his tragic demise, although the narrative was incomplete. The missing parts I had to surmise and put together from occasional comments by other members of the family.

My uncle's death happened ten years after grandfather had lost his tobacco fortune in the Five-Day Hurricane and the family had found refuge in Zaza del Medio. Before the family moved to the town, Elicio, the illegitimate son of the Marquis de Argüelles and grandmother's half-sister Lola, offered to take José María under his wing to study in Havana. But José María was young and because he was very attached to his family, he did not accept the offer. This close family attachment was to be his undoing, just as to some extent it also was of my brother years later. Instead of taking the opportunity to forge a future for himself under the patronage of a willing and powerful sponsor, he forsook an education and buried himself in the country, where his prospects of ever becoming somebody vanished.

Familial attachment can be a cruel master. I have often thought of how life would have been if he had accepted Elicio's offer. He would have grown up in Havana, surrounded by people of means who belonged to the highest levels of Cuban society. Perhaps he would have married well, for he is reputed to have been both handsome and charming. Surely Elicio would have seen to it that he had position and power, for Elicio was a loyal member of the family who took good care of his mother and her siblings. By contrast, José María's decision opened a road that led to death and destruction, one made on the basis of compassion and filial love perhaps, but more likely fear and a false sense of duty, maybe even tinged with honor and pride. Pride also can be a source of great mischief as the story in Genesis illustrates. For José María and the family, the consequences of his decision were devastating, although for me they were fortuitous insofar as if he had gone to live with Elicio, most likely mother would not have met and married father and I would not be writing this today. As Borges conveyed in one of his stories, life is a garden of forking paths, where a decision opens up an infinite number of choices whose ultimate outcome remains a mystery.

In a few years, José María married and became the bailiff of a large farm owned by a wealthy absentee landowner who resided in Havana, so he was doing relatively well. Sadly, his wife liked flirting with other men even after she got pregnant. José María suspected that she was having an affair with a handsome *guardia civil*, someone he knew, and was eager to have the opportunity to confront and challenge him. He did not have long to wait. One day when the suspected lover and his partner were making their rounds in the countryside, uncle came to meet them. No one knows what actually happened, since the story was told by the two *guardias* responsible for my uncle's death and what they told did not make much sense. According to them, harsh words were exchanged and José María, who was hot tempered and had been mulling the situation for weeks, pulled out his machete, the only weapon he had with him at the time, to attack the rival who was attacking his honor. The reaction of the *guardia* that accompanied Leonarda's presumptive lover was to take out his gun and shoot him dead. He was thirty-one years old. Of course, no one believed this story, for José María, even partially blinded by anger, would not have behaved so stupidly, attacking his rival, who was accompanied by another *guardia* and well-armed, with a mere *machete*.

The two soldiers then explained that they loaded uncle's limp and bleeding body across the saddle on his horse and proceeded to the *cuartel*, from which they sent someone to notify his wife and grandmother of what had happened—grandfather had died three months earlier. José María was young and the apple of grandmothers' eyes. How did she react? She was almost incoherent when she told me the story, still unable to describe with equanimity the events that transpired next, even though several decades had elapsed since then. Imagine then what the reality had been!

Someone had come to the door of the house; she could not remember who. Mother, who was fifteen, answered the door and talked to the visitor.

"Who is it?" grandmother asked from her bedroom. Then she heard mother crying. 'What is it Niña?" But what could mother answer? Choking back tears she answered: "Mamá, mamá, it is José María!"

And then, grandmother answered in a trembling voice "José María? What happened? What's wrong?"

"He has been shot!" From then on, events took a life of their own, as in a movie reel fast-forwarding the pictures out of control. Nothing was clear in grandmother's narrative, but I was able to piece together some of the events. Mother's sisters, Maruca and Juanita, hearing the commotion, came out of the kitchen where they were preparing the evening meal, and joined mother and grandmother. The women confronted their tragedy together. Jaime, the remaining brother, was away working and it fell on the women, a group of women as was the case with Christ, to fetch the body. Legally, José María's wife should have done it, but she was brushed aside in anger when the story of who had killed uncle came out.

It had rained and the streets were muddy. Grandmother kept telling me that she did not want to have her shoes dirty, that she could not meet her son like that, as if she were reliving the moment. But she could not find proper shoes to wear. The group of women walked to the *cuartel* and there, laid on a dirty table, they found the body. The wound on José María's chest still fresh and oozing. His face surprised, as if death had caught him off guard, as if it had been unexpected. Perhaps trying to tell his mother something, to assuage her pain, to say the last farewell. A cart was fetched from the stable, the body placed on it, and the women went back with it, now with their sorry load, to their home. Then my uncle Jaime arrived.

The story was all over town now. The sisters began to prepare the body for the wake and burial. It was getting dark. Candles were lit. The mother could do nothing but caress uncle's face. The sisters washed the body. A doctor came to declare José María dead. After the body was washed and dressed, it was first laid on the dining room table which had been covered with the tablecloth used at grandmother's wedding. The body was eventually placed inside a modest coffin.

Friends and acquaintances began to congregate. Everyone knew about the feud, for both José María and his enemy had talked publicly about their grievances. People crowded the house, whispering. They brought flowers, tears, cries, wailing, and voiced threats. Every one that came prompted a new burst of sorrow in those who had arrived earlier. José María's friends. His associates. And his wife, where is she? Where is "the whore, the bitch that is the cause of everything?" Grandmother could not bring herself to name her, but she also did not call her the names that were coming up to her mouth. She wanted to cry out *"Puta, maldita hija de puta!"* but she was too much of a lady to do it—bourgeois women in Cuba did not use that kind of language even in extreme circumstances.

Grandmother was reliving the experience while she talked to me. The scene was harrowing, but nothing new. It repeats itself frequently, even if it is never easy to take in. This version was hers to suffer. The mother, *La Dolorosa,* grieving with a pierced heart.

That night, José María's killer disappeared. A rumor went about that he had fled because he was afraid for his life. He was right to fear. A couple of days later his fate was known. The body was found in a nearby field, with the penis cut and placed inside his mouth. He had bled to death. No one ever found out who killed him. The *guardias* were not popular in the town, and my uncle had been, so no inquiries were undertaken. The authorities were afraid of further repercussions. Still, the way grandmother told the story, and the nervous gesture with which she signaled how the penis had been stuck in the man's mouth, were chilling. Justice had been done. Blood was paid with blood. A life for a life! Justice demanded it! But where was the consolation, the relief?

From that moment on, grandmother dressed in black, and only in her very old age, at the insistence of her daughters, did she consent to wear printed dresses of black on white, and rarely with a dash of blue or gray. Her mourning for her eldest son, whose life had been terminated at the peak of his manhood, never found closure while she lived. From the moment of his demise onwards she had a virulent aversion to anyone who wore a uniform. She always referred to them as *"el dos de espada, la última carta de la baraja."* They were trash.

What became of the family after the tragedy? And what became of the widow? Leonarda gave birth to a child, cousin Pepe. Her situation was dire and she could hardly support herself and the child. And Carmen, who had no children, adopted Pepe and raised him as her son, but she did a bad job of it, spoiling him rotten. Pepe never amounted to anything and until his mature years he had difficulty holding on to a job or behaving appropriately. Father tried to help him repeatedly, but he always failed to satisfy basic standards of behavior. Mother said that he took any loose money he ran into and stole anything of value he thought he could sell or barter. Yet, years later, in Miami, his widow told my sister that he had been a loving and unimpeachable husband. It was hard to believe, but perhaps it was true.

Chapter Eighteen

La Dolorosa's Miracle

After José María was killed, grandmother gave up on life. Sons are favored in Cuban families and being the oldest of the siblings made uncle doubly important. For mothers, family life revolves around them. The premature and unexpected death of my uncle was an irreparable blow to grandmother. Her deep mourning never ended. There was nothing to live for. Not her remaining children and not the few grandchildren she eventually had. A disagreeable hypochondria trapped, enslaving her to real or imagined disorders—rheumatism, sleepless nights, and all the paraphernalia typical of a melancholic temperament and a depressed mind.

Only one thing seemed to help grandmother, a statue of the Virgin Mary as *La Dolorosa* (Our Lady of Sorrows) that she kept in her bedroom. Her bleeding heart, pierced by seven daggers symbolizing the seven sorrows that she suffered as Christ's mother, seemed to have a calming effect on grandmother. She prayed to it morning and night, and whenever a further crisis occupied her mind. Her shrine, located in a corner of grandmother's bedroom, was a refuge, a place of peace where grandmother could shed tears without being disturbed. She kneeled in front of the Virgin Mary statue and prayed.

The statute was about four feet tall, carved in wood with glass eyes and gilded details on the carefully decorated clothing. Her face was compassionate, one hand signaling her heart and the other in a becoming gesture that showed empathy for other sufferers. She had also suffered. She had also lost a grown son. Who else could better understand grandmother's plight? Who else could be her companion and share her grief?

The story of the statue was miraculous. Miracles are not regarded as odd happenings in Cuba, a world whose roots go back to the Mediterranean and Africa. The tale told that the image had been famous for her effective powers among the people in the area of Vuelta Abajo. She had the place of honor on the altar of a small chapel in the countryside and pilgrims came from far away to pray to it, to leave her *votos*, and to fulfill *promesas*. The walls that surrounded her were filled with gifts left by those who came to visit: messages of love, devotion, and gratitude; small reproductions of healed limbs; and photographs of the sick or the dead, waiting for healing or everlasting life. The small chapel was built of wood. It caught fire, apparently due to candles lit-up by pilgrims. The chapel burned to the ground. Everything was destroyed except for the statue of the Virgin Mary. Although the holy statue was covered in soot, and had a few charred spots on the veil, it was completely spared. What could this be but a miracle?

Grandmother asked for the statue as soon as she learned about the accident. She had it restored and found a place of honor for the holy statue in her home. It became the source of grandmother's consolation, her defense against the vagaries of destiny, her strength and companion, and a comfort in times of trial.

The Virgin Mary statue comforted grandmother for years. It responded as desired. It became grandmother's crutch at times of need. It witnessed the financial ruin of her family. It helped her carry on in spite of the death of her husband and first son. It stood by at the death of her eldest daughter, Carmen. And about a year later, grandmother witnessed her second daughter Maruca being severely burned. And then, she helped Maruca endure a very long recovery. Yet, grandmother could not survive the ideological shift of the family after the accidental death of my brother, and mother's conversion to Evangelical Christianity. Once converted, mother could not rest until the Virgin Mary statue was destroyed. Her new faith could not tolerate what she considered to be idolatry, and so the Virgin Mary statue, which had faithfully comforted grandmother for years, was not just dethroned with the shrine sanitized of heresy, but it was broken up and burned. Mother's fanatic iconoclasm triumphed over grandmother's decades of devotion—the miracle was undone!

Grandmother never complained. Perhaps mother convinced her of the evil symbolized by the statue of the *La Dolorosa,* so she was content with how things turned out. But I missed the statue, standing on its shrine in the corner of grandmother's bedroom. There was an emptiness there, and I could not help but look for the statue's kind face every time I entered *Abuelita Belé's* sanctuary.

Chapter Nineteen

Promising Beginning and Sad End

Aunt Carmen was mother's oldest sister. She was second in age to José María. As I remember her, she was an elegant lady, with a good figure and impeccable manners. She took pride in them and was so intent on giving the right impression that she adopted a fine Castilian accent in her speech. Spanish accents in Cuba were not particularly favored, or considered chic, but Carmen was smart enough to adopt one that separated her from Galicians and Andalucians, who were generally considered rough and uneducated, and emulated Castilians and Asturians, who were at the top of the Spanish social hierarchy. This even though her own father was from Galicia and one of her grandfathers was from Andalucía. She could have spoken like other educated Cubans, but she sought to inspire a higher level of sophistication. Not that she appeared phony. I never heard anyone in my family, or outside of it, say anything against this particular idiosyncrasy, perhaps because she was not only thoughtful and urbane, but also pretty. Indeed, when she was fifteen she had been dubbed *"la perlita"* (the little pearl), because she was so beautiful.

Carmen's strategy, added to her appearance, seems to have worked to her advantage for she married a man of some means, owner of a general store and some land in Taguasco, the small but prosperous town where she lived with her family. This was far from Pinar del Río, where my grandparents lived and she had been raised. But the separation did not seem to bother her. Although she did not have any children, the marriage appeared to have become particularly fortunate even for the rest of the family after grandfather lost everything and had to seek refuge from the financial debacle the Five-Day Hurricane had caused. Carmen's husband gave grandfather a job and the family was able to get by without further humiliation.

Unfortunately, still quite young, Carmen's husband became ill and weakened markedly and rapidly. His business needed careful attention and his inability to give it caused it to falter. After trying various local treatments that failed, Carmen decided to take him to Havana to see a specialist. She shut down their business and gathered all the money they had in cash, most of which she packed carefully in a bundle, and left for the capital. In Havana they stayed at the home of one of grandmother's sisters, Angelita, who had married and not yet gone to live with Lola.

Worried about the substantial amount of money she had carried with her, Carmen told Angelita and her husband what she had brought, thinking that perhaps they would need to stay long in Havana for treatment. Ostensibly to unburden her from a needless preoccupation, Angelita's husband, who was a very charming man, suggested that she leave the bundle of money with him for safekeeping. Trusting him, Carmen gave him the bulk of it after taking out what she thought she would need during her stay, and devoted herself to restoring her husband's health. After many months and a progressively deteriorating condition, he died. Carmen buried him in Havana, got her bundle of money from the uncle in law, and went back to Taguasco. There she had a nasty surprise waiting. When she arrived and opened the bundle where the money was supposed to be, she found only pieces of newspapers. The rascal had carefully cut pieces of newspaper in the exact dimensions of the pesos in the package and substituted them for the pesos, which he pocketed.

The pesos he stole constituted a good portion of Carmen's savings and the blow devastated her finances. The business that her husband had ran so successfully had been declining rapidly during his illness, and the closure during the months Carmen and her husband spent in Havana had given it the coup de grace. Now, without her husband, alone, and having lost a considerable amount of her savings, the only course of action Carmen had was to sell what she could. With the proceeds she was able to set up a small business making slippers which she ran with sufficient success to support herself but not sufficiently to help her father, mother, and sisters. Grandfather's family had to rely on the wages that José María and Jaime brought home, but the death of grandfather and shortly after of José María made their situation much worse.

Carmen was a strong and enterprising woman, and eventually re-married, this time to an older man, a retired Coronel of the Cuban army. They lived together well for a few years. He was a jolly man I remember distinctly because, when they visited us for Christmas, he organized games, dressed up in various costumes, and put on shows. Destiny was not yet ready to give Carmen a break, however. In time she developed cirrhosis of the liver as a consequence of a bout of hepatitis she had when she was young. Aunt Carmen died five months after the diagnosis, and her death was neither fast nor painless.

Mother visited her often at the clinic in Havana where she was and I accompanied her some times. I remember how the disease had ravaged her.

Her skin appeared sallow, and the loss of weight was alarming. She looked like a skin covered skeleton, but with a large belly, swollen with liquid that had to be extracted with long and foreboding needles. She declined fairly rapidly, and suffered considerably, but she was always cheerful and optimistic when we visited. I don't know whether she suspected, let alone knew, that her death was inevitable and imminent. She appeared to be not so much resigned as at peace. Nor did she take a strong turn toward religion for comfort. I recall the room where she was, with a crucifix hanging above the headboard of her bed, reminding us of Christ's own suffering and death. In all this affair, Carmen behaved as she always had, like a lady. She never told her aunt of her husband's betrayal. And everyone else respected her silence.

Chapter Twenty

Is Having to Work Punishment for Sin?

Contrary to what many believe, the Bible makes quite clear that work is a bad thing. We were intended to have a good, relaxing time in Paradise and the idea of toiling did not enter into it. However, according to the biblical story, our first ancestors made a mistake and we are stuck with work as punishment for their mistake. Several members of my maternal family could not agree more.

By the way, it is hard to believe that a nice guy like God would hold all of Adam and Eve's progeny to blame for their foolishness and transgression. Imagine that any of you, readers, were to be punished because of some crime that your great-grandmother and great-grandfather committed! Would you regard that as just? And would you think fair that your great-grandchildren should suffer the consequences of your mistakes? But that is exactly what some tell us God does. So, we are stuck. Our job is either to cooperate, or not to cooperate, with the punishment. Some believe we should cooperate. Perhaps they do not quite accept the word of God in spite of protestations to the contrary, as they do not also accept St. Paul's recommendation about drinking wine. Indeed, they are no better than others they frequently criticize who think they know better than God what He means. Still, it is possible that they just feel they need to cooperate with God, and we should not resist in any way the punishment we deserve because of Adam and Eve's transgression.

Cubans generally are more faithful to the biblical message. They like to relax and enjoy life; let others do the work so we can have the fun. Of course, not every Cuban shares this attitude. Many are hard-working, but even those who work in order to live, do not live in order to work.

On the maternal side of my family there is a strong current that believes that God is right, and work is something bad. We infer from this that we should resist work as much as possible, rather than embrace it cheerfully.

This view may come from one of my great-grandfathers, the father of my maternal grandmother. He originated from the south of Spain, the Moorish side, where a penchant for good living was the foundation of the Islamic kingdoms in Iberia in the late Middle Ages. Like some "cool" men from that part of Spain, he was called *El Curro*. He did not like to work and was lucky enough to marry a woman whose previous husband had left her a good living. His aversion to work was not inherited by grandmother, but it was passed on with a vengeance to some of her children—uncle Jaime, mother, and her sister Juanita—in addition to Uncle José María's son.

Jaime seldom did an honest day's work in his life. Well, maybe I am exaggerating. Perhaps he did work hard more often than I thought. But he never had steady work, let alone a profession, and studying was no part of the chart for his existence. Mostly he drifted from job to job, and lived as much as possible on borrowed money. His negative attitude toward work was so strong that he refused to eat fish because of the trouble it takes to separate the meat from the bones! He lived with grandmother whenever he was not living with one of the women that paid attention to him, of which there were not few, and this helped him get by.

Father tried to help him in various ways. First, he set him up in the business of selling cloth, but Jaime failed. Then, when father invested in his first plantation, El Anoncillo, he put Jaime in charge of it and built him a house, but he proved to be a disaster as administrator. Father had to fire Jaime, although he kept him on the payroll doing odd chores. Even that did not last. Jaime broke a rib and the doctor informed him that the rib was not important, but that he had a serious condition: his aorta had become stretched and any physical effort could make it rupture and kill him. That was good news for someone who did not like to make an effort. Now he had a good excuse. The cause of the condition was that, early in his life, Jaime had caught syphilis and it had not been treated properly. The condition was in fact very serious. Indeed, Jaime died in his fifties when his aorta burst suddenly when he was startled by lightning.

Grandmother was never told of the true cause of Jaime's illness. She lived under the illusion that his condition was the result of a bad case of typhus when he was young. No one ever tried to disabuse her of this wrong notion so as to spare her pain and embarrassment. Besides, her story sounded much more appropriate for polite company. I learned the truth when I was a teenager, from my grand-uncle Miguelito, who was a rogue of sorts and delighted in taking family skeletons out of the closet. So perhaps we should not blame Jaime for his aversion to work. Perhaps he had not felt well all along and that is why he disliked work so much.

Aunt Juanita was also very lazy and had no excuse of a serious condition. She married a guy who was even more lazy than she was. They lived like hippies before hippies were invented, and worked only as a last resort. The name of her husband was Lara Miyares. He had a very profitable trade that could have made him a wealthy man. He knew how to make all sorts of brushes and had invented models for every purpose you could think of—washing bottles, cleaning pots, brushing nails, dusting engines, scratching your back, cleaning your ears, untangling hair, and so on ad infinitum. If you had to clean something that was very difficult to reach and you asked him whether there was some contraption to make the task easier, he either already had invented it or he did on the spot.

Father was so impressed by his talent and designs that he offered to go into business with him. Lara would put-in his expertise and father would invest the capital. But, of course, the enterprise had to be run like a business, steadily and consistently, and Lara would have nothing to do with that; he was not interested in anything steady. Here is his *modus operandi:* when he ran out of money, he would go into his shop and make brushes of all kinds, which he then sold to businesses. Once he got enough money, he stopped and waited until he would run out of money again, when the cycle would be repeated.

Father was not the last person to be impressed with Lara's skills. After the Castro government abolished private property, it confiscated Lara's workshop, and made an offer to him to continue as manager in charge of production. In Cuba, at the time, this was a great opportunity for him. It would ensure him a good salary by Cuban standards and keep him in the good graces of the Revolution. However, Lara would not have anything to do with it, not because of resentment for the confiscation of his property, or because he was against the government, but because he did not fancy the idea of having someone dictate to him what he had to do, or for him to be the boss of other people. He was a free spirit that merely wanted to have what was absolutely indispensable to live and be free to do as he pleased, to get up at whatever time in the morning felt like, to go to bed at whatever time in the evening struck his fancy, and to not have any responsibilities. After he rejected the government's offer, he and Juanita lived with small amounts of money they could scrounge around. It was not an entirely pleasant life, but it was a free one, and that presumably made him happy.

Before Lara married aunt Juanita, he had adopted a child, Oscar, which became a thorn on Juanita's side. Juanita regarded him as a bad seed, completely unredeemable. He would get onto everything that was considered bad. He smoked, he stole, and he lied. One thing I remember, from the time I was a little kid, is that, whenever we visited aunt Juanita, Oscar would try to play sexual games with me. That seemed to be his only interest. I mentioned that to Juanita, and after that Juanita kept a careful watch whenever Oscar was around.

Juanita kept a tolerably clean house, but the idea of doing anything other than the bare minimum was as foreign to her as steady work was to Lara.

One of the many things she abhorred was cooking, and since they could not afford a full time cook, Lara had to do it. I did not like to eat the food he cooked, though. He had lost several of his front teeth, and when he spoke he often sprayed people, which made me think that the same thing happened while he was cooking, and I was not thrilled about eating his spit. Fortunately, being lazy, Juanita and Lara preferred to eat out as frequently as possible, and when we visited them it was rare that they cooked for us. Usually we would go out, and guess who ended up paying?

The case with mother was different from that of Juanita and Lara, because she always had plenty of people who did her work for her. She never had to do anything, as her fine hands and manicured nails demonstrated until the very end of her life. Mother never knew what a callus or dry skin were. She took meticulous care of herself—I guess she thought it was her duty to maintain her good looks. After all, she figured father married her for her looks, since she had no money or skills, and so she had to maintain her image. When she came out of Cuba, my wife and I had two girls, and both of us worked. We thought we could rely on mother to keep an eye on the girls when they came from school in the afternoon, until one of us got home. But the idea of doing this was enough to make mother pack her bags and leave for my sister's, where she had someone who would take care of her. She abhorred work and used to say that God had punished humanity by making it necessary for us to eat, because if we did not have to eat, who would ever do anything? Once in a while I feel that maybe there was some wisdom in what she said.

Mother's idea of a good day was one devoted to conversation. She was a great conversationalist until she converted to Evangelical Christianity and became obsessed with religion. Even then, she was occasionally funny and sharp. Unfortunately, she also enjoyed keeping a running commentary on her many ailments, as many Cuban women of her generation and station tended to do. She particularly complained about her weak heart. This was a complete fabrication. Mother's heart was strong as that of an ox. Endless tests were made throughout her life to see if the symptoms of which she complained were related to a heart condition, as she believed. Many trips were made to Havana when we lived in the country for consultations with specialists. But nothing was ever found. Still, she never walked more than half a block, and never did any strenuous exercise. Mother was very talented and creative. She loved to sew and write poetry. But she had an aversion to physical work. It was so severe that sometimes she did not pick up things that fell to the floor. She considered the effort was too much for her heart . She died at ninety-three of old age and other complications that had nothing to do with her heart.

Chapter Twenty-One

Broken Promise

Aunt Juanita was the second oldest of mother's sisters. Mother was blonde and had very fair skin, Maruca had jet-black hair and fair skin, and Carmen, when I met her, had streaks of gray highlighting her auburn hair. Juanita, however, was swarthy, like my maternal grandfather, a dark Galician Celt, and her hair turned gray in her early twenties. The contrast with her Mediterranean olive skin was most striking. She was baptized Epifania, after her maternal grandmother, and was at first called "Fanny" for short. When she grew up, she realized that "Fanny" had a connotation she did not like, so she changed her name to Juana, and became known as Juanita.

Juanita was supposed to have been an attractive woman, with the dark eyes characteristic of mother's family and a fun-loving nature, a kind of saucy wench. But when I knew her, she had lost her looks and had developed a bitter countenance. Very few signs remained of her former self. She seldom smiled, but when she did her face lighted up, the sour countenance disappeared, and a twinkle appeared on her eye that made her look like someone different from the person we all knew. Although it took a long time before I learned her story, and, when I did, I understood why she had become what she was.

The tale goes back to her youth, when she was engaged to a debonair and fashionable young man by the name of Manolo. Apparently, he was extraordinarily handsome in a rugged, masculine way. From what people said, they made an outstanding couple, and they loved each other with a passion that was unusual. Both were high spirited, full of life, and had strong, intense, even dramatic, personalities. It seemed impossible for them to be apart from each other, but it was also difficult for them to be together. He was a womanizer. How couldn't he be, when women threw themselves at him everywhere he went? That was the excuse used to justify his behavior. His looks and personality attracted women and he could not resist. Women did not leave him alone, and his presumably hot Cuban blood could not fail to respond appropriately. So went the common talk.

A stream of gossip about his affairs, some well-intentioned and others meant to make Juanita suffer, reached her constantly. This talk disgusted her, even when she knew that some was ill intended. The romance between her and Manolo was stormy, because he could not stop philandering and Juanita could not stop complaining. Quarrels, recriminations, fights, embarrassments, humiliations, together with reconciliations, promises, and love characterized their relationship. Eventually, the negative side of the relationship predominated. Juanita was so unhappy that she lost weight and became almost mentally distraught. Whenever she met him after news of one of his bouts of unfaithful behavior had reached her, she confronted him and there was a scene, sometimes in front of others. He always claimed that Juanita was the woman he truly loved and these others she had heard about were of no consequence; they did not mean anything to him. These words sounded to Juanita like boiler plate, although, unlike many unfaithful lovers, he was a fair man and he did not lie to her. He never denied having affairs with other women, albeit he claimed that they did not signify even though he could not stay away from them.

This was not sufficient for Juanita. She brooded constantly and could not take her mind off the affront of his infidelity. Things went on like this for a while. Often the lovers would quarrel, but she could never bring herself to end their engagement. Still, her jealousy began to eat into her mind and appearance. She became consumed by her suffering, and the moments they were together became painful to both. Eventually, he told her that this could not continue; he could not live in this permanent state of confrontation. This time, unlike many others, she agreed and so they permanently broke off their pledge. But he could not let things be. In a tragic impulse at the breaking moment, he promised her that he would never marry anyone else until after she had married.

For Juanita, life without him was painful, particularly at the beginning, but time heals the worst wounds and she slowly recovered her poise and peace of mind, although she did not accept the attentions of other men. She could not love anyone else while she knew that he was alive and unattached, and she continued to suffer when she heard of his exploits.

Two years passed. Rumors circulated about Manolo, a new engagement, a wealthy heiress, love. Then, Juanita heard that he had become engaged, and later that he was to be married. The agony this produced was excruciating, and the peace of mind she had achieved disappeared, but at least there was an end in sight, the moment he would marry she would begin to forget him.

Manolo's marriage was to take place in a town not far from where Juanita lived. She knew perfectly well the fateful day, but neither she nor anyone else in the family mentioned it. Juanita did not want to hear about the details, but on that day the radio brought rather startling news. In the early evening, after dinner, the family was gathered in the living room and were listening to the local radio broadcast, when it was interrupted for a piece of flash news. The broadcaster said that Manolo had killed himself shortly after the marriage ceremony had concluded. The details of the story eventually reached the family. The wedding had taken place, but during the reception that followed, Manolo excused himself, went to an adjacent room and shot himself.

I heard the story thirty years afterwards from *Abuelita Belé*. Grandmother was still moved when she told it to me and got to this point of the narrative. She said that the moment Juanita heard the news she became unresponsive. They took her to a bedroom and called a doctor. For days afterwards she was in a state of delirium. She couldn't swallow any food and her conversation was inarticulate. They feared for her life, and the family kept a vigil. The morning after the event, her hair, which had been black, began to turn gray. This was hard for me to believe, but I did not question it since grandmother sounded certain. It took Juanita months to become a functioning person again. No one ever mentioned Manolo in her presence, but further details of what had happened filtered in slowly.

Everything had seemed quite normal at the wedding, although the groom appeared to be unusually preoccupied. After the ceremony, when the couple were about to sit down for the wedding banquet, Manolo had asked his bride to excuse him. Then a shot was heard. People ran to the room from which it had come, broke down the locked door and found him on the floor on a pool of blood. They found a piece of paper with a single line. It was addressed to no one in particular. "Forgive me, this is the price for not keeping my promise."

Grandmother knew of his promise to Juanita, but she never learned whether Juanita found out about Manolo's note. She thought it best not to mention it, and, should Juanita learn about it, better she hears it from someone else.

Juanita nearly lost her mind. It took months before a semblance of normality returned. In time she married Lara who was poor and lazy, but who seemed to love her in a peculiar sort of way. She was never a happy woman, but she survived. Her face lined with suffering. One cannot help but think about how often she thought of Manolo. Did she hold herself responsible for his death? Did she regret her jealousy? In a quirky turn of events, both she and Lara became Jehovah's Witnesses. One would have expected this would yield a certain relief, but it did not. Instead of peace, the new faith generated a painful dogmatism and proselytism that alienated everyone that came near them. Their lives were transformed into a struggle against unbelievers, including members of our family. The great advantage of the new faith was that it gave both of them a reason to live, the spread of an idea, that may have kept Juanita from thinking about what her life could have been with the man she had loved so much. She died at the age of eighty-six, two years after her husband.

Chapter Twenty-Two

A Twenty-Five Year Engagement

Aunt Maruca was not just my favorite aunt, but one of the people I loved the most when I was growing up. In fact, her place in my affections was not too far below that held mother, and sometimes I felt warmer toward her than toward mother. Mother was mother, of course, and her place was secured beyond question in my affections because of it. Maruca was one of those very few persons who make herself welcomed and loved in every place she is. She spent long periods of time with our immediate family, and her presence was always like a breath of fresh air. She was a favorite of everyone. I thought of the time she spent with us as a holiday. I loved the way she treated me, the way she helped me with my homework when I was going to school and staying with her and grandmother, and the stories she would make up to entertain me. Most of all, I liked that she treated me like an adult, not like a child. She did not patronize me, and when I did something nutty, she was completely matter of fact, explaining why it was unacceptable. Mind you, she never preached or nagged! And she very rarely lost her temper, and never with me. With grandmother, who was difficult and demanding, she was always gentle and loving! She called her "*Mi viejita*" (my little old woman), a term of endearment, even though grandmother was a terror.

Maruca was no pushover, however. She was the only member of our family that stood up to father when it came to table games. She defeated him frequently and would not tolerate any of the shenanigans that occasionally he tried to pull. I tried to follow her example once and ended up with one of the two spankings that father ever gave me. Father was quite formidable, but Maruca was not intimidated by him. Of course, she was in no danger of being punished! Father thought of her as an equal, and that did not happen often with him. In fact, she was father's favorite among mother's relatives.

I remember Maruca as a middle-age woman, still good looking. She had been a beauty of sorts in her youth. She did not have a perfect face, and the Otero nose, with its parrot-like curve, detracted from her appearance. But she had enormous, dark eyes, her hair was jet black, and her skin very fair. Her eyes looked at you with an intensity softened only by her pleasant and kind manner; it was as if they penetrated into your soul. The combination of these features must have been stunning when she was young, and surely captured the hearts of many an eligible young man. One in particular, named Gabriel, seems to have been the love of her life. Yet, at some point he decided to leave for the United States and abandoned her. Maruca took his desertion stoically, but I am told that some time passed before she paid attention to any other suitor. By the time she did, everyone thought that she was a spinster and she could not aspire to marry anyone that was any good, or even to marry at all, although she was not yet thirty.

Nonetheless she did find a beau, Fernando. Her courtship with him became quite predictable. He lived in the small town of Majagua, where he worked for the sugar mill. Maruca lived with grandmother in a nearby town, so Fernando would travel to visit her at least one night a week, but whenever possible two nights per week, on Tuesdays and Thursdays. I remember his visits because I stayed with Maruca and grandmother for two years when I first went to school.

In his visits, Fernando always brought a box of pastries, as fine as you could get in a place like Ciego de Ávila. The box was quickly passed on to me and then he and Maruca sat in the living room, speaking in low tones that I could not decipher. This went on until about ten o'clock, at which time he left. At some point during the visit Maruca would offer him coffee, which he accepted, but he never ate anything and he was never invited to dinner. Nor was he ever invited to a meal at my parents' home. Grandmother and I would stay out of the living room for the duration of Fernando's visits.

This routine seemed to suit everybody directly concerned. Maruca had her beau, Fernando had a fiancée who comforted him, and grandmother had Maruca to keep her company and manage her home. Maruca had the misfortune to be grandmother's favorite daughter, part of the reason for which was that Maruca had delicate health when she was a child. She suffered from asthma and as a small girl had required special attention. Mother was the youngest child in the family, and because of it enjoyed a special status, but Maruca was the favorite. Of course, as was generally the case in Cuba, none of the girls occupied the favored position of the males.

As mentioned earlier, in Latin cultures, one of the female children is supposed to remain unmarried so she can take care of the mother in her old age, devoting all her efforts to her comfort. This is considered a small sacrifice to make for a child who owes her life to the mother and was raised and cared for by her. The task of a 'mother-caretaker' usually falls on the favorite daughter. So Maruca had been implicitly anointed with that responsibility. Of course, not everyone in our family approved of Maruca's lot, and they kept asking, when is Fernando going to set the date? Is he serious about getting married? Why shouldn't some pressure be exerted on him? The main mover behind these questions was mother, who understood quite well the sacrifice Maruca was making and her increasing frustration. Her only prospect for liberation from grandmother's tyranny was Fernando, but he showed no inclination to change the status quo, so things continued as they were.

Then something happened that changed everything. I was living at grandmother's house at the time. Maruca was preparing some concoction for grandmother's real or imagined rheumatism, which had some alcohol in it. She was heating it on the stove on a metal container and, thinking that it had not yet become very hot, grabbed the container with a bare hand. *"¡Ay!"* The jar was too hot to hold and she dropped it. The container hit the counter and then the floor, splashing the burning liquid on her. The alcohol ignited and set Maruca on fire, instantly turning her into a living torch.

It was late in the afternoon. I had already come back from school and was sitting in the living room doing homework, when I heard Maruca cry out in the kitchen. I looked up and saw her enveloped in flames running from the kitchen to the bedroom through the dining room. I was eight years old then, but I did not waste any time. I ran to the kitchen, filled up a pot of water as fast as I could and ran after her to put out the fire. Maruca had smartly thrown herself on the bed and by doing it had extinguished the fire on her face, neck, and partly on her arms. But flames were still burning her arms and torso. I threw water on the flames and after they had been extinguished, ran out of the house shouting at the top of my lungs. *Auxilio, socorro!* While I was busy doing all this, grandmother was kneeling and praying in front of the Virgin Mary statue, *La Dolorosa*. The neighbors came, Maruca was taken to a hospital, and mother and father were notified.

Later that night we went to visit her at a private clinic, Clínica Olazábal, where she had been taken after having received emergency treatment at the public hospital. She was completely covered with cotton and looked like an Egyptian mummy. The only parts of her body that were visible were her eyes, nostrils, and mouth. The frightening sight indelibly carved itself in my consciousness. I can still see her on the bed, immobile, only her dark eyes moving when anyone spoke to her. Her voice was just a raspy whisper coming out of a slit in the cotton on the place where her mouth was supposed to be. I was frightened and worried about her. I approached the bed and she moved her hand covered with cotton. She asked me whether I had been frightened by the accident. I could hardly understand her. I let her touch me, but I was afraid because I could not see anything that I recognized as aunt Maruca.

For days that seemed an eternity to all of us, it was not clear she would survive the shock—her bladder was not functioning, and the other organs in her body appeared to be shutting down. But she did survive, although she spent months recovering. There was no end to the procedures and surgeries she had to undergo. She squeaked through but was marked for life. In spite of multiple skin grafts at various times after the accident that extended for months and even years, she was never able to completely lift her head because the skin and muscles of her neck had been so damaged. Her arms continued to show the scars of the ordeal. The skin on these badly affected areas was very thin, like mucous membranes, through which veins and muscle were visible. It was not pretty, but she covered the most obvious places with special make up and always wore long sleeve blouses with high collars even in the hot summer months. Fortunately, her face was not disfigured.

During this entire process, Fernando was very attentive. He spent hours with her whenever his job allowed it; he brought gifts, many of which I consumed; and he seemed truly moved by the experience. Everybody was wondering whether now that the goods had been seriously damaged he would scamp away. He didn't. When Maruca came back home, the long routine in which they had been locked for years resumed: Tuesday and Thursday visits, with boxes of pastries to which I did proper justice.

But this was too much for mother to tolerate; she had had enough. Maruca was a middle-age woman and Fernando was her older contemporary. Her engagement had lasted more than two dozen years. Mother was not one to sit back and let things take their course; she often believed in forcing an issue by giving ultimatums. Sometimes this strategy backfired, but most of the time it worked and she thought it was time to take the risk. She worked hard to convince Maruca that the situation was unsustainable and suggested that, on a particular Thursday, without any warning, Maruca prepare a suitcase with some of her most indispensable things, and when Fernando showed up, that she tell him: "Either I leave with you now, or our engagement is over." The discussions about this that followed were frequent and heated. Eventually, Maruca came around, in spite of the objections of grandmother who was opposed for reasons we knew had nothing to do with the reasons she voiced. Grandmother realized that if Maruca left with Fernando, her reign was over and she was going to lose her daughter-servant. She probably thought that the whole family had ganged-up on her, but she never let out that she did. Her pride would not permit it.

I was present the day when Maruca confronted her beau, and so was mother, who had made a point of being there to lend Maruca moral support and make sure she went through with it. Poor Fernando, he had no clue when he arrived for his routine visit what that Thursday had in store for him! He was the lamb brought to the slaughter house. But when confronted with the situation, he did the right thing, to everyone's relief. He called a taxi and took

Maruca to his mother's home in Majagua, until they could get married, which happened a couple of weeks later. Fernando's mother was surprised but welcomed Maruca as a daughter; she had always loved her and had wanted for a long time that Fernando marry her. The twenty-five-year engagement had ended, and both Fernando and Maruca seem to have enjoyed its ending. Fernando lived well into his early eighties, and Maruca died later still, at eighty-eight. No one else from our family was in Cuba at the time of her death, but she died surrounded by friends who loved her. For mother, her death was a great sorrow, because she had nurtured the illusion of having Maruca come to the United States to live with her.

Chapter Twenty-Three

Romance on a Scale

When I look back at the members of mother's family, I see plenty of romance but very little in the way of happiness. Perhaps the only success story is that of mother's, although at first it did not look as if it was going to turn out that way. Mother was very young when her father lost his fortune and they moved to Zaza del Medio. There she found first love. She was only fifteen when she became attracted to a young man who loved her. He appeared to be *un buen partido,* as the saying goes; he had a business and had already established himself. Indeed, in a few years he would become a very wealthy man, wealthier than father ever became. Mother was so much in love that she took the initiative to talk to her father, explaining that they loved each other and that, if he was predisposed to accept him, her suitor would come to ask for her hand in marriage.

However, grandfather said "No." The reason he gave was that she was too young, which of course was not a good reason at all, since grandmother had married him when she was seventeen.

True, mother was merely fifteen, but the young man was in his twenties, and these were different times. Indeed, grandmother had married at seventeen, which means that her courtship had started well before then.

The true reason behind grandfather's rejection was that the young man was darker-skinned than was acceptable to him. In short, he appeared to have some black blood, and that was certainly something that grandfather was not willing to allow in his family. Given the future of the young man, it is obvious that this act of discrimination cost the family quite a bit.

Mother suffered much, but abided by grandfather's decision and eventually put this unfortunate experience behind her. The young man was frustrated, as young men are, but he also accepted the decision and left for Havana to distance himself from mother. Shortly after, grandfather died and uncle José

María was killed. The family, devastated by these events, chose to move to Chambas, a little town in Camagüey Province, where uncle Jaime had secured a job. This was the same town where father had set up business as a pharmacist, and where he and mother met.

Father was immediately smitten by mother. She was blonde, had an engaging personality, and was a bit of a coquette. Father claimed that she would come every day to the pharmacy with one of her sisters or a friend to weigh herself on the scale. Father could not resist and in time they talked and their romance began. Father was a serious, formal man, so he asked grandmother for mother's hand and so they were engaged. Mother was sixteen and he was twenty-five. The engagement lasted five years, giving father time to build a house, which costs him a little over 5,000 pesos. Following father's enlightened ideas about religion and mother's indifferent faith, a judge, rather than a priest, married them, which I assume makes me a bastard in the eyes of some members of the Catholic Church.

My brother, Ignacito, was born exactly a year after my parents were married, and Nena two years later. I showed up when mother was thirty-six and father was forty-five, clearly the result of an accident, at a time he had already decided that he was soon going to retire and leave Chambas.

The marriage was based on love, and father was deeply enamored of mother. He complained about her profligate ways, but in reality, she could do no wrong. He was in love with her until he died. And she also loved him, although not perhaps with the same intensity. For many years I wondered whether she regretted not having married her first love, until an incident after father's death convinced me that she truly had loved father.

It was in the first anniversary of his death. We were in Havana and he had been buried in Ciego de Ávila. Mother had been nervous and agitated all week. She felt that she should be at his tomb, by his side, sharing this anniversary with him. But there were complications. My school, Nena was pregnant, among the many things that are part of a life. Still, she could not put out of her mind the thought that he expected her to remember him by going to his resting place with flowers, recalling the years they had shared. I had seldom seen her so distraught. But she could not make up her mind. Finally, on the anniversary day she sat down and did something she often did when her emotions overcame her. She wrote a poem. It was a tribute, and a confession to him about their love. She finished it quickly, but it changed her. The tears and anxiety turned into consolation and peace. She read the poem to Nena and me. It was clear that her words had come from the heart, expressing both her loneliness and desolation at his absence and her gratitude for their years together. She wanted him to understand that she cared, that she loved him even in death.

Years later, when I gathered some of mother's poems into a little book, she insisted on changing the original version. She included in it something about her belief in Jesus. I tried to convince her of the value of the original, but her almost fanatical religious faith won out. The poem was no longer about her and father, but rather about some doctrinaire religious feelings quite foreign to the original experience and thought.

For mother's family, the marriage to my father was the break they had hoped for. Father's financial situation was steadily improving and, after years of genteel poverty, the family could look forward to years of financial security. Father did not disappoint them. He was a generous man who from the moment he married mother, became the support for the entire family.

Chapter Twenty-Four

"Te Voy a Capar"

Although none of us remembers the moment of our birth, all of us have a few recollections of early events. Perhaps that reveals something about what we care about, our context, and what has made us who we are. In my case, these memories are of terrifying events. Unlike some people who shun terror, a few of us are fascinated by it. I have seen all the classic Dracula movies and even wrote an article on them. There is nothing I like better than to be terrorized in a movie theater or by a book. And yet, psychologists claim that a self-preservation mechanism we have developed through the evolutionary process makes us forget the terrors of our childhood, whereas we generally remember happy times. My experience contradicts this view to this extent: My earliest memory involves terror. It dates from before the time that I was three years old and I can recall clearly very little else from this period of my life.

At the time we lived in Chambas, the small town in which father had cast his lot. Father was one of the most important persons in the town, along with a couple of physicians, the judge, the mayor, and the head of the local army unit, among others. In keeping with father's social station, he had built our house across the street from the town square—not that the town square was much of anything, still it was the town square. Nor was the house a very impressive structure, but by the standards of the town and the times it was pretty good, particularly considering that father had been a relatively young man and at the beginning of his professional life when he had it built.

After I learned to walk and before we moved out of Chambas when I was three, it became part of my daily routine to take a stroll by myself, as naked as I was born, pulling a toy truck with a string behind me, around the town square. People would smile at me and say hello, and I felt like the king of the world. One day, an old friend of the family, a rather sour and imposing man, came after me, with a machete in hand, yelling that he was going to cut off my balls. *"Ven aquí, que te voy a capar!"* I was terrified and ran as fast as I could, holding onto my little truck, into aunt Maruca's arms. She had seen what was happening from across the street and hurried to rescue me from a dreadful fate! The vision of my little bundle of goods being mercilessly severed and laying somewhere on the sidewalk, was terrifying to me and I have never forgotten it.

Mother was furious with the old man, but she kept quiet. He was a good friend of father's, and he was so rich that he had bought himself a title in Spain. I do not remember what happened after Maruca rescued me, or know how deeply the experience impacted my psyche, although I am sure Freudians would love to trace some of my neuroses to that event. My own reading of it is that this experience may explain, at least in part, my fascination with terror as a need for catharsis.

Other humans, nature, and animals are perhaps the three most important sources of human fear. But of the three, humans are by far the most terrifying. The first experience of fear I remember was certainly the most terrifying to me, not only because the source was another human, but because I was alone. It was the first time I had to face danger by myself, without anyone to defend me. But does its memory challenge psychological theory? There is something captivating in danger, fear, and horror. There is excitement. There is beauty. There is risk. Perhaps psychologists are not completely wrong in their views because the reason I remember these memories is precisely that they were not entirely agonizing insofar as they also involved a rush, a peril that, like an abyss, both hypnotically repels and attracts.

Chapter Twenty-Five

A Gentleman Farmer at Heart

Although father was never really happy as a pharmacist, he had some fun in Chambas, and so did the family. The well-known, and often substantiated, saying, "*pueblo chico infierno grande*" (small town, large hell), is without a doubt true, but small towns in Cuba at the time often became communities where tight circles of friends lived good lives. The countryside was beautiful and there were frequent parties, excursions, and BBQs. The neighbors gathered at different farms for special events because farms were not just sources of income for most of these peoples, they also had a recreational dimension.

Father discovered his love of farming in Chambas. In time, his success rendered the pharmacy routine annoying. The pharmacy was the main source of the capital he had accumulated, but enough was enough. Father was itching to do something else, so he sold everything he owned—the pharmacy, the farm, the cattle ranch, our home, the house he had bought for grandmother and Maruca, and the rental properties that supported his in-laws. Still in his forties, he felt ready for something more interesting. He had accumulated considerable capital and felt confident about the future. Father was dynamic and loved getting involved in difficult projects and bringing them to fruition. He frequently mocked people who complained about having problems, saying that he loved problems, so he could solve them. This bravado was a symptom of what he enjoyed doing.

I had just turned three when father decided to retire. After he sold everything he owned, while he looked for new investment opportunities, we moved to Camagüey. It was one of the five oldest cities in Cuba, founded at the beginning of the sixteenth century and the capital of the province with the same name. At the same time, my grandmother, aunt Maruca, and uncle Jaime also moved to Camagüey.

Camagüey was a hiatus, a place to deliberate about the future course of action for father and the family. We knew we would not stay long, but we did not know where we would go. So, we never settled in it. Father did not buy a house. Instead, he rented one in the good neighborhood of La Zambrana. I can still picture it. The house had a garden at the front, the usual porch with Greek columns with Corinthians capitals topped by a balustrade, a large living room and *saleta* or family room, an interior patio on three sides of which were the *saleta,* six bedrooms, the dining room, and the kitchen. The kitchen was enormous, with a large bell chimney where bats occasionally nested and had to be expelled by pushing burning torches up the flue. At such times, the little newborn bats, looking pink and naked in their helplessness, would fall on the coal burning stove burners and were quickly picked and thrown out by the cook. Behind the kitchen and the dining room was a large porch followed by the back yard, subdivided into two parts, the first had a cement floor and the second a dirt floor. The ceilings of the house were particularly high and the rooms were cool and dark during the summer months.

The street car stopped at the corner of our block and Nena and I would take it directly to grandmother's house, on Calle Martí. She lived in a very old house, with those double doors, with doors within them, typical of colonial times and particularly favored in Camagüey. The town had been founded around 1515 and kept most of its colonial flavor. The backyard had a very large *tinajón,* a symbol of the town, in which it fitted well.

Father used the time in Camagüey to decide what he would do. His pockets were well padded, he was educated, he had a profession, his family had roots in Havana, and our family could travel. There were so many things he could do! What attracted him the most, however, was the land, growing things. The reason was probably that agriculture offers the chance to be creative, to improve things, to see them grow. And is there anything more beautiful than an orange grove? Father had planted oranges in El Anoncillo, another citrus grove in Chambas, but the trees had not prospered because of the poor soil. Still, the seeds of doing something like it had been firmly planted in him. Something about the land had gotten into his blood. Years later, when I read *Gone with the Wind,* I felt that I understood father and his desire for land and agriculture. Land means roots and we all desire to grow them surrounded by things that also grow roots. It took nearly a year for father to decide what he would do and to find the right place where to invest some of the money he had made in Chambas. For a while we thought we were going to stay in Camaguey. He was exploring the possibility of buying a bank and joining the university faculty, but unfortunately the call of the land was too strong. And I am sorry he did not buy the bank. Perhaps, if father had made a different investment, our lives may have avoided the tragedy that was to follow.

After a few months, he bought a citrus orchard in Ceballos. The orchard grew sweet oranges primarily, although it also grew large grapefruits, tangerines, and sour oranges. I can only think that he made this decision on an aesthetic basis. Orange trees are beautiful. When the fruit is ripe, the orange color contrasts with the dark, green leaves on the tree. And when orange trees are in bloom, they are as beautiful as, and of course more fragrant than, the famous cherry trees of Japan and Washington, DC. The orchard he bought was somewhat neglected, a good challenge for someone with the funds to improve the investment. That's why we moved to Ceballos, where we arrived on August 4, 1946. I had recently turned four.

The orchard belonged to an American couple who had owned it for many years and had reached an age in which they wanted to move back to the United States. The gardens that surrounded the main house constituted a veritable paradise. The owners had no children and had traveled throughout the world, bringing back with them seeds and saplings of plants that would grow in Cuba. Trees and bushes bloomed throughout the year; there was never a time where we were not surrounded by flowers. Flamboyan trees were ablaze with colors part of the year. Frangipani blossoms, with their delicate colors, turned your thoughts in a different meditative state. Blue *embelezos* contrasted with tulips and carnations. The purity of white, delicate *mariposas* beautified their surroundings. And lilies grew profusely in unexpected places. The owners had a full-time gardener who took meticulous care of the garden.

The house itself was at first sight quite ordinary and small, resembling in some ways the clapboard bungalows so common in the South of the United States. In fact, it had been planned well, and modeled after a Japanese tea house. The former owners had traveled in Japan, one of their favorite places, and they had tried to emulate Japanese traditional architecture and gardens.

The house was a two-level structure, with three bedrooms and the living room on the higher level and a large family room, dining room, and kitchen on the lower level. The two levels were necessary because of occasional flooding from the nearby creek. The higher level had wood floors that were waxed regularly and shined like glass, again following the Japanese model. The lower level was tiled, and sitting on the porch was like entering into nature, a place where one could be in harmony with the spirit of Zen, while admiring the wonders of the garden. Outside of the kitchen there was a small screened porch where BBQs were made.

Following the East Asian custom, apart from the main house, there were other structures on the grounds. A guest house, with two large bedrooms, served to accommodate visiting friends. Servant quarters permanently housed the gardener, the stable hand, and occasionally the cook and maid when they stayed overnight. Garages, a carriage house, and a stable for fine horses completed the structures. Farther away, and out of sight from the main house, was the bailiff's house, and further still the livestock barn, larger stables for draft horses, and other garages to accommodate trucks, tractors, grain, fertilizer, ladders, and implements related to farming.

To reach our house one had to cross a rather rudimentary but sturdy bridge over the creek. Then turn left, onto a road within the property. The road bordered a copse of trees that at first occluded vision, but just a bit ahead, opened onto a road that turned right. This was completely covered by trees whose branches arched over it, forming a tunnel of vegetation, with mango trees on the right, and mandarin and grapefruit trees on the left. After fifty feet, the house and grounds appeared. The first thing one saw was the main building, over which the branches from two enormous trees, a carob and a bay tree, met. Flowering bushes of various sorts were planted all around, and small *arecas* were located strategically so as to create areas where one could sit on benches and enjoy different views of the garden. These areas were connected by meandering paths.

The road that led to the house continued on the left toward a generous esplanade that ended at the garage and led to the servants' quarters, the place for the family car and the jeep, as well as a carriage and the stable for the family horses. The esplanade was covered with flamboyan trees that, in season, became a feast of red and orange colors. Over the garage and the servant quarters towered the carob tree, extending its branches over the main house and almost meeting the branches of the bay tree at the opposite end. Its roots spread away from the trunk like gigantic tentacles of a sea monster and were so large that we used to sit on them to enjoy the refreshing shade during the hot summer. A climbing bush, with white and blue-lilac flowers, had found its way from the garage onto the carob tree, reaching all the way to its top, creating a wall of greenery interrupted by splashes of delicate color. Behind the garage and the stables for the horses for members of the family and visitors grew six magnificent Indian pines, with their trunks covered by reddish bark thick with age, which seemed to reach the sky. They were majestic and so large that at Christmas we cut one of its branches to use as our Christmas tree. On the right of the road that led to the house was a row of twelve royal palm trees marking the border between the copse and the garden. If one went around the house, toward the bay tree, one would continue walking on carefully groomed grass among various flowering trees and bushes.

Farther to the right was a large orchard devoted to tropical fruit-bearing trees of various kinds—avocados, mangos, lemons, limes, plums, cashews, tamarinds, anoncillos, guanábanas, anones, chirimoyas, guayabas, among others. At the back of the house was the rose garden, with more than one-hundred rose bushes of different species. Walking further around the house, one reached the vegetable garden, located close to the guest and servant quarters. Beyond them was another crop of trees that served to isolate the dairy cow pasture and pig-pen from the living quarters. Beyond that was the banana patch where all kinds of bananas were grown: *plátanos machos, plátanos hembra, plátanos seda, platanos burros, plátanos manzanos,* and *plátanos Johnson.* All around the compound one could see orange trees. When these were flowering, the fragrance of orange blossoms was inebriating.

It took all the efforts of the full-time gardener to keep the garden in shape. Mother took a particular interest in it and spent many hours developing new strains of rose bushes and other plants. The previous owners also had a number of orchids growing in various trees and one of mother's greatest challenges became preserving the orchids and developing new varieties. Mother dreamed of adding an artificial pond with water lilies, strategically placed gazebos, and a fountain.

Life at the orchard had a rhythm of its own, and a routine for each of us. My brother got up early and joined the workers. He toiled right along them, doing heavy and demanding manual labor. In a short time, the muscles of his arms and back had grown thick and strong. He was an excellent worker, never slacking, and ready to do the heaviest work. His example inspired other laborers, who appreciated that the patron's son worked right along with them.

The bailiff was in charge of the day-to-day operation of the orchard but father checked on the work twice a day, in the morning just before lunch and before quitting time for the workers. The work in a citrus fruit plantation ebbs with the seasons and the crops. There is a long time needed for irrigating—which became automatic after father installed the latest available irrigation system—fertilizing, de-weeding, and spraying to control pests. The number of workers required for these tasks was low, but after the fruit had ripened, and was ready to be picked, came the busy time of harvest. Ladders would go up each orange tree that pickers would climb to quickly, but deftly, gather the ripe fruit.

Skill is required to do this, both to do it fast and to make sure neither the fruit nor the plants are damaged. Each orange, mandarin, or grapefruit had to be firmly grabbed and turned so that it would come off easily. Then it was deposited in a sack that hung from the picker's shoulders and to the side, before the next fruit was picked. A good worker does this in a continuous motion that saves time and is graciously efficient, almost like the movement of a ballet dancer who elegantly performs effortlessly what in reality requires intense effort. Once the sack is full, the picker climbs down a ladder and pours the fruit into wooden crates that have spaces between the side boards for ventilation. Alternatively, he throws the sack to another picker who transfers the fruit to the crates while the picker fills another sack. Sometimes the workers sing songs, and at other times they talk while they work. More often the only sound heard is that imagined by the observer who watches how perspiration falls in drops down from the workers' foreheads, until it reaches their bare chests and backs. The crates are then loaded in trucks and sent to a place in town where the fruit is washed and packed to be sent to distribution centers and later to markets.

First thing in the morning for us, after getting up, was a breakfast of *café con leche* and buttered toasts cut in narrow strips so we could dunk them in the *café con leche.* The milk came from the single cow kept for that purpose, a purebred Holstein that spent her life eating and resting. What a life she had! Sometimes I would visit her and wondered whether she ever stopped chewing. Her life seemed to be consumed with two continuous tasks, chewing and producing enormous amounts of milk, interrupted by farting and defecating. Her udders, when full, were phenomenal. When we went to breakfast she had already been milked by the stable hand. The milk, warm and thick with cream, had been taken to the kitchen where it was boiled so it could be used to make *café con leche* or *chocolate*. Left over milk was allowed to rest until the cream rose to the surface, then skimmed and beaten to make sweet butter.

Each morning, after checking on the workers, father came home and looked through the mail and his papers. His desk was placed on a corner of the family room and its top was crowded with papers, colorful pens made by prisoners, *secantes,* bronze paperweights in the shape of lions, and smoking paraphernalia—cigars, a pipe, and a silver cigarette case. Hanging above the desk was a photograph of Franklin Delano Roosevelt, which made clear father's political alliances and progressive credentials.

At lunch time, the family converged in the dining room for the mid-day meal around two. *La merienda*, a mid-afternoon snack, also consisted of *café con leche* and buttered toasts or a sandwich filled with *dulce de guayaba* and cream cheese, which we called *timba*. Dinner was around seven o'clock in the family room, a porch that wrapped around the front and one side of the house.

My sister was away at school during weekdays, but returned home on the weekends. Before I began school, I stayed at home and occupied myself as best I could, playing with my toys, exploring the grounds with Duque, my dog, Often I would follow Henry, the gardener, while he did chores. During the right season, the frangipani leaves were a favorite food for large worms that turned into gigantic moths. The worms were colorful, with bright green bodies and red heads. I put some of them in jars where I would keep them well fed with frangipani leaves. In time, they spun cocoons and eventually came out as moths. Observing this miracle was always exciting. Another favorite pastime was to walk to the creek to find snails and their discarded, colorful shells, of which I kept a collection. I also kept some living snails in jars, although I left them out periodically.

Although sometimes farm workers brought with them their children of my own age as playmates for me, and I did take advantage of these opportunities to socialize with my peers, for the most part I had to entertain myself.

The farm was good for that. It presented endless occasions for exploring the flora and fauna that surrounded us. My parents had their occupations, chores, or other adult guests that visited us, so generally I was left to my own devices. This allowed me to discover inner resources that still today are useful. I learned to appreciate solitude, to be alone, to listen to myself, and to find things to do independently of what other humans offered. These years taught me the company of solitude. Not that I was lonely. I could always find the company of mother, Henry (the gardener), Pedrito (the stable hand), Magdalena (the cook), and other adults that lived on the farm. Nonetheless, I learned not to depend on other people to prevent me from being lonely. Solitude and loneliness are two different things. The first presents an opportunity for delving into ourselves; the second is a melancholic state that leads to sadness and depression. Ever since then, I have felt the need to be alone. Human company is fun and I enjoy it, but I have also a need for solitude, a time to think, reflect, and be with myself, to find my bearings, to be comfortable with myself, in silence. Yes, silence is also a basic need. Noise, even wonderful music, imposes limits on our imagination and thought. We find ourselves more easily when we are away from the *"mundanal ruido"* of which Fray Luis de León eloquently spoke.

My placid and somewhat introspective life at the farm was regularly interrupted by trips to Havana. Mother loved to visit the capital and the family and friends who lived there. The city offered the opportunity to go to the theater and other activities that we could not enjoy in the country. These trips were particularly special for me. We traveled by train, which I loved. The trip began at the train station in Ciego de Ávila, where we waited patiently for the usually late train. The long wait was painful, but once the train got into the station everything changed. The porters, who were always black and dressed in blue and white uniforms, would bring out small step ladders that passengers used to get into the cars where they were going to travel.

First, you had to check with the porters to find out to which car you were assigned, and whether it was a sleeping car or a regular car. We always traveled in sleeping cars because the trip to Havana took many hours. Those traveling were generally mother, father, Nena, and I. Ignacito seldom came with us. That meant that we took two cabins. Usually one at the end of the car and the one next to it. The corner cabins were fairly large with comfortable chairs to sit on, sleeping berths, a bathroom, and other usual comforts. Father and mother slept there, and it was in it that we got together to talk or gather before meals, which we took in the dining car. My sister, Nena, and I occupied the other cabin. She slept on the top berth and I on the lower one, because for many years I would sometimes fall off my bed during the night. I did climb up the top berth just to explore.

Once we found our cabins, the porter would bring our luggage and we would settle down. Shortly after, the conductor would pass by asking for our tickets, which he examined and punched before leaving. The cabins were paneled with darker wood inlaid with various kinds of lighter wood, and the fixtures in the bathroom were made of brass and shined like gold. The train left the station in late afternoon. It began to move slowly, the locomotive burdened with too much weight to carry. Puffs of steam were released, whistles were heard and slowly the convoy of cars started moving, increasing speed as it went. I sat by the window, to watch the towns as we passed them, and countryside fields with crops of various kinds. The train stopped in some stations and vendors would come to our windows selling sweets—*coquitos acaramelados, boniatillo,* and *pasteles de guayaba.* Mother warned that if I ate the sweets, I would not have any appetite for dinner. But these trips were special occasions and I was allowed to fill myself with sweets. Mother and sister engaged in conversation, while father read the newspapers and I stayed silent, thinking about what was before my eyes and wondering whether it was the train that was moving or it was the land that did. These thoughts were the first encounters I had with the question of the reality of the world as given to us through the senses. Little did I know that philosophers had pondered this issue for millennia.

Not long after we were underway, we went to the dining car for dinner. Eating while the train was moving was an experience. The rails were not always even and cars swayed from side to side, making it difficult to keep glasses from tilting. I was a picky eater, and after having filled myself with sweets, it was difficult for me to eat much, but I did reasonably well because I liked the novelty of eating in the dining car. Everything tasted good. This was life, a life of adventure, travel, and surprises for a child of my age. After dinner I walked around the train, with my sister, exploring other cars, eventually finding our way back to our cabins. The porter had already prepared the berths for sleeping. The excitement conspired to keep me awake, but the sound of the train wheels on the rails—thump-thump, thump-thump—would overcome the worst case of insomnia, so I could not resist Orpheus and was sound sleep in no time.

Next morning, we awoke early and already close to Havana. We got up quickly and went for breakfast in the dining car. Here was a wonderful spread, but my favorite was *chocolate con leche y tostadas con mantequilla.* The train accelerated, eager to reach its destination, while passing fields of sugarcane and country hamlets. Close to Havana, it slowed down, giving us the opportunity to see what the city looked like behind the walls that hid the rails and trains. I always felt sad leaving the train, although Havana brought the prospect of exciting experiences, staying at a fancy hotel and visiting grand-aunt Mina and aunt Rosario.

More frequent interruptions to farm life than visits to Havana by train were the frequent visits to the orchard by my grandmothers and maternal aunts, who would come and stay with us for months at a time. Sister often brought home classmates from school, and friends from as far away as Havana would visit. Country life is quite routine and can be boring, and mother was eager to have visitors so that the family would be entertained. With enough horses for everyone, pleasant surroundings, good food, lively company, and hunting grounds full of pigeons, quail, partridges, and wild turkeys, it was easy to find family and friends who would join us for days and weeks at a time. Excursions to Ceballos, the little town closest to us and other places of interest in the area were frequently organized.

The family, and guests when we had them, gathered at lunch and dinner at our large dining table, except for me. I was not allowed to sit at the grown-up table until I turned seven because father would not abide bad manners and it was considered that children cannot eat properly until they reach "the age of reason."

At night we often went out to see the firmament, full of stars. It was so dark that in clear nights you could identify all the constellations. The stars shined with an intensity never seen even in small towns. The perfume of the flowers was intoxicating. We listened to the radio. Programs such as Tamacún, political commentary by favorites like Chivás, and never-ending soap operas such as *El derecho de nacer* (The Right to Be Born) were available. But while we listened, we played games of various sorts: Dominoes, Monopoly, Parcheesi, Indian checkers, chess, brisca, tute, and so on. In hot summer nights the house lights attracted insects and beetles of all kinds, colors, and sizes that stuck to the screens encasing the family room. We called them *chicharrones* because when crushed they made a similar sound to that made when one bit into a piece of fried pork rind. I would go out with empty jars and fill them up with the insects as play. When hens hatched eggs, we would bring some of the colorful little chicks into the house and keep them there as pets in boxes, until they grew up.

Special celebrations, such as Christmas and birthdays were common. On such occasions, family and friends came from all over. It was not easy to accommodate all these people in a house that was quite small. But the guest house helped, and even the servant's quarters were used if needed. In some cases, guests were put up in Ceballos for the fortnight they spent with us. Mother and sister planned ahead for such occasions. Standard items, such as a roasted pig, and stuffed turkeys and chickens, were accompanied by *tamales* (known in Camagüey as *tayuyos)*, *carne con papas, fricase de pollo, arroz con pollo, ropa vieja, vaca frita, bistec con papas fritas, pescado asado, filete de pargo con salsa portuguesa, papas rellenas, picadillo,* and *macarrones con salsa y queso*. Chicken was a favorite, and when my brother had taken our guests hunting we would have partridges and wild pigeons.

Special desserts always followed dinner, such as cakes, *budín de pan*, *buñuelos en almíbar*, *dulce de tomate*, *cascos de naranja*, *natilla*, *arroz con leche*, *crema catalana*, *dulce de tomate*, *mermelada de guayaba*, *dulce de mangos*, *coquitos acaramelados*, *dulce de coco*, *dulce de leche*, *flan de calabaza*, *panetela borracha*, *platanos flambé*, *torrejas de pan en almíbar*, *cascos de guayaba* accompanied by a famous cheese from the little town of Jicotea, and *flan*. Mother enjoyed planning these affairs and working with the cook to have a proper feast. For some occasions extra help was hired, so that mother and our cook could manage. Under mother's direction, everything was prepared and cooked at home except for the pigs that, after being slaughtered and seasoned, were taken to a bakery in Ceballos for roasting in the baker's oven. *Lechón asado* is a favorite dish of Cubans, usually accompanied with black beans, white rice, *yuca con mojo*, and *plátanos maduros fritos*.

Killing and preparing the pig was an especially fun activity for me. Father brought a butcher from town who knew how to kill and prepare the pig. Apart from getting the animal ready for the oven, additional pork meat was used to make *longanizas, chorizos, and butisarras*. The blood of the pig, mixed with onions and seasonings, was used to make *morcillas*. The internal organs were also saved and cooked in various ways (all of which I detested), and *chicharrones* were made with pig skin. Ah! *Chicharrones*! Is there anything that is as tempting as *chicharrones* to a small child, when they are crispy and break easily to the touch and the bite? The preparation of everything else was in mother's hand, who directed the cook and helper and was not afraid to get her hands into whatever required it, although her specialties were desserts. Of course, some of the family visitors helped with the food preparation, but most of them spent their time in games, hunting, and touring the orchard and its surroundings.

I was the only child at these events, and thus got a lot of attention, one reason I enjoyed them. Apart from the games, I liked to get my hands into the pork fat, stuff chickens, knead dough, or just do some mischief. It was party time.

The flooding of the creek was another occasion for exploration and new experiences. It would flood at least once a year. When the water level started to rise, father would place sticks as far as they could reach, every hour, to measure how high the waters were rising. In the meantime, everything that could be damaged in the house would be moved to the high floors. Rubber boots would be taken out of closets and everyone went to watch the rising water. The boots reached high in adults, but for me they reached even higher, to my groin. The floods lasted for a day or two, and then the waters would recede, leaving a coat of red mud everywhere they had been. The place looked as if it had been painted in red clay, every leaf, every branch and every flower up to a certain level. Inside the house the kitchen, one bathroom, and the family room were all covered with the red clay mud, which took a lot of work to clean. Most of it had to be hosed down, which was in itself exciting.

Chapter Twenty-Six

Running Away from Home

I did not think that everything on the farm was fun for me. I often felt grieved by what members of my family did. Indeed, my grievances against them when I was a child began early and ran deep. After all, they often did not do what I wanted them to do, and this was intolerable to a four or five-year-old! I tried to get even with them in various ways when they did something I considered an affront. One of my favorite ways of seeking revenge was by taking the items on tables, vanities, or inside cabinet drawers, and putting them on top of a bed. I would do this carefully so as not to break anything. The idea was not to cause harm, but to make sure the person against whom I had a grievance understood that I was mad and that reparations were required. Some pain also was exacted because all the things I had moved had to be put back, and certainly they would not be put back by me—well, sometimes.

Occasionally, I took more serious measures to bring attention to my grievances or punish those insensitive members of the family who had hurt me. For example, sister had on her vanity a collection of fancy art deco perfume bottles of various sizes, shapes, and colors. Once, when I was particularly annoyed with her, I poured all the perfumes into the bathroom sink and then proceeded to fill the bottles up with my pee. Naturally, I replaced the tops, so no one found out about my revenge until a critical moment when Nena was ready to put some perfume on. I was present at the time, for I had been keeping a watch on her, making sure I would witness the occasion when she first discovered my deed. The moment was delicious. Nena was sitting at the vanity, powdering her nose, putting on lipstick, and as a last stroke, opening one of the precious bottles, wetting a hanky with its contents, and applying it to her neck, just below the ears, as she often liked to do.

The expression on her face when the fragrance she expected sounded a note of dissonance was unforgettable. Her nose twitched, her face wrinkled, and suspiciously she proceeded to sniff the contents of the bottle. She could not quite understand the situation. Had the perfume spoiled? What was this? It smelled like . . . what? All of a sudden she realized it was pee! Then she opened another bottle and took another whiff. And, ugh! It was as bad. Then she turned and looked at me and the truth dawned on her. "*¡Chucho! ¡Mamá!*" She cried hysterically. I anticipated the commotion and had quickly vacated the premises and taken refuge with my brother, who of course shielded me from any punishment. When Ignacito found out what I had done he could not stop laughing and hugging and tickling me as if I had done the greatest deed in the world! Of course, he also had his gripes against his dear sister and played nasty tricks on her! He generally poked fun at her and two of her best friends whom he called, when my parents were not present "*las tres Marías: mierda, mojón y porquería.*"

In spite of the debt I owed Ignacito for regularly shielding me from Nena's wrath and frequently helping me avoid the consequences of my nutty actions against other members of the family, I did not spare him. Ignacito was quite a looker and he liked to dress in the latest fashion. In the forties, the rage was two-tone Wingtip Oxford shoes, and he had bought himself a pair that were the envy of everyone who knew anything about male fashion. They were black and white with alternating areas in the two colors, little circles of white on the rims of the black areas and vice versa. It took considerable care to keep the shoes looking as they were supposed to do, and the stable hand spent many an hour making sure these shoes appeared as they should when brother was getting ready for a night on the town.

Well, the temptation was too much for me to resist. This time it was not that I had a gripe against my brother, as I had with sister. I seldom did, since he made every effort to make me have fun. But I could not ignore those shoes. One day, after the shoes had been polished to perfection by Pedrito, and Ignacito was taking a shower to get ready for a party, I sneaked into his bedroom with a bottle of black shoe polish and proceeded to paint all the white parts of the shoes black. Imagine his face when he went to put the shoes on and saw them! Of course, he knew I had done it! Who else? But he was my big brother. Instead of cursing and yelling, he came out of his bedroom laughing, with the shoes in his hands, bragging to mother and father of my deed. He dropped the shoes and ran after me yelling that I was going to pay dearly with my life for this, but when he finally grabbed me, the punishment was to kiss and tickle me until I was screaming with pleasure! Is there anything better than to have an older brother? Yes, perhaps having an older sister, and I was lucky to have both.

I did not spare other people, including myself, from my mischief. I was fascinated with the way everybody had haircuts. And of course, so did I, except that my blond curls were first cut when I was three. The first cut was immortalized by my sister, who saved one of the curls until she left Cuba. At some point after the first cut I decided that I wanted to experiment with cutting it myself. Since members of the family wouldn't let me experiment with their hair, I got a pair of scissors and cut mine. The result was not pretty, although I should say that it didn't look very different from the cut that many teenagers get these days. However, my parents did not appreciate my precocious ideas about hair styling and proceeded to have my head shaved. A photo that was taken while my hair was still very short became grandmother Mercedes' favorite. And I never could figure out whether it was because, ironically, of how serious and saintly I looked, or because of how nutty I had been. Grandmother Dubié was also in my corner.

More drastic instances of vengeance against my family than these were my several resolves to leave home. This occurred at least three times. The first time it happened I was five years old. I can't remember the particular grievance I had, but it must have been very serious in my mind, for I thought the only way out was to leave home permanently. After brooding a great deal and feeling quite sorry for myself for the way I had been mistreated, I packed a few things in a piece of cloth tied to a stick, as I had seen done by bums and other drifters in comic books and, without telling anyone, left home. At the time, we were living in the orchard in Ceballos, so there was really nothing for miles around.

I didn't have a particular plan or place where to go. I merely wanted to leave. Of course, what I really wanted was for the guilty members of my family—mother and sister primarily—to apologize for the crimes they had committed against me, so I could gracefully forgive them and we could continue to live happily together with me ruling the roost. I wanted to send them a message—if they did not do what I deserved, they would lose me forever. Or perhaps I did not quite know what I wanted. But I did set out going away from home regardless. At the time I did not have a horse. So, after a while I became tired and sat down. And waited, mulling on my grievances. Then I walked a bit more, and sat down on a stone and waited. And I waited again. And nothing happened. Minutes looked like hours, but there was nothing to do but wait, hoping for a sign of concern.

The situation was becoming worrisome, because no one had come to find me. Had they not noticed my absence? That certainly would add insult to injury! Was there some way of signaling my absence without breaking my resolve or losing face? I couldn't think of one! I should have left a note, but I did not know how to write. That taught me the value of writing, but realizing it didn't help, I made a resolve to learn as soon as possible. I would have to fix that for the future.

Of course, I couldn't go back. That would be too embarrassing. My pride would not allow me to do it. So, I waited some more. I became hungry. I ate a couple of *galletas* I had brought with me, but they were not enough. Oh, what misery! Nonetheless, I hung on. My family deserved this and more! I bet they were aware of my absence and were just being mean to me. Did I deserve this? I hated them! Finally, Pedrito found me. He said that everybody was worried about me.

What a surprise! Or no, really, I knew it. Ah, sweet delight! They had noticed my absence and sent Pedrito to get me! And they were worried. They had suffered. This was vindication, a triumph. Now I could go back. But I didn't agree to do it right away. I let Pedrito work hard to convince me, to tell me that mother and sister were sorry, and so on. After all, mother and sister had not come themselves, as they should have. What kind of love did they have for me if they were not willing to try to find me themselves, and sent Pedrito instead? I was dubious on whether I should go back with Pedrito, but eventually I allowed Pedrito take me home, because I was hungry, bored, and tired.

And oh, the return was sweet, because there was no punishment at all, since I was not guilty of anything. I was sure they understood that they were the guilty ones for treating me in ways I did not deserve! They certainly had learned their lesson. If they again mistreated me, I would leave and never come back, although, when mother and sister were on their death beds I would return and magnanimously forgive them. I imagined the scene. They dying, and I, returning, also very sad, but at the same time vindicated and happy to return. I almost felt like crying, after all I was the grandson of *Abuelita Belé*.

The second time I decided to leave home I was eight years old, and we were staying at the beach. The quarrel this time was with father, although again I cannot remember what the source of it was. He probably had told me that I had to do something and I, in my usual willful way, had said no. He had insisted, and so I left home. My leaving this time was different. I did not take precautions or prepare provisions, and father was less soft than mother. I hung around the house, but did not come in. At the end of the day I was starving and Nena worked out a deal with father: I would come back, but father would spank me as punishment. I agreed because I was too hungry, but I did not give father the satisfaction of crying when he spanked me. I never cried when I was punished regardless of the punishment. My pride wouldn't allow it.

Father spanked me only twice during the whole of my childhood, and of course, he never spanked Nena since she was a girl—that was one of the few privileges that girls enjoyed and boys did not. The first time was at the beach when I ran away from home. The second was when I was eleven and we were living in Ciego de Ávila. This happened when I accused father of cheating while he and I were playing at cards. He denied it and I insisted. Father accused me of being disrespectful, and asked me to take my accusation back or he would have to spank me. But I didn't take it back. Then he led me to my bedroom and asked me to pull down my pants and lay down on the bed. He took out his belt and gave me four swats on my bum. It really did not hurt. It was clear that the procedure was not meant to hurt me in any way. Father was not angry and he certainly would rather die that hurt me in any way. I was truly the apple of his eyes, as the cliché goes. But he could not allow me to undermine his authority, and the best way he knew how to do it was to engage in a simulacrum of the infliction of punishment and pain. I had gone too far and father wanted me to recognize I had.

For me, what hurt was the insult, the humiliation. For that I felt like crying, but I didn't shed a tear. I felt I was right and he was wrong and crying would have indicated a weakness, an acknowledgment that father was right, and that I could not tolerate because I knew he was wrong and I was right. Being used to a frequency of tears thanks to *Abuelita Belé's* predisposition to cry, I did not have difficulty shedding tears when something appealed to my sentiments, but in matters of honor I could be very hard. I understood what father wanted of me, but I could not give-in, because for me there was something higher than parental authority, namely justice.

But something happened that saved me from further discomfort. *Abuelita Belé* was in the next room and had heard what had happened. She resented father, as she did all her in-laws, although if she had been told she did, she would have been shocked, denying it vehemently. She was not vindictive; she was a victim, a bileless dove, in her own estimation. But this was a perfect opportunity to do something for me and against father. She decided to have a screaming attack, although I think this was more an instinctive hysterical reaction than a deliberately planned action. I had never heard her do this, although later I found out that this sort of thing had been part of her modus operandi for years.

The display was impressive. She started screaming at the top of her voice and would not shut up. Imagine the position father was in! He didn't know what to do. Poor man! What a predicament. His first inclination was to ask mother to do something. What would the neighbors say? But grandmother would only stop for a bit and then begin again. I am sure she was having a great time, enjoying the discomfort she was causing father, and exercising the power which it was obvious she had. That certainly taught him a lesson, and I learned a lot about family dynamics! Clearly there were more important things than I, but I could become a tool to settle some old scores.

Chapter Twenty-Seven

A Boy's Best Friends

A great palliative for the occasional egregious behavior of members of my family was the company of Henry and Duque, they understood me better than anyone else. They formed a closely knit and exclusive society that I was allowed to join at the age of four when we moved to the orchards in Ceballos. Henry took care of the grounds that surrounded the house. He was originally from Jamaica and spoke with a heavy accent. He was old and black and you never had to tell him to do anything; he knew his routine by heart and kept our grounds looking beautiful all year around. He had been the gardener to the American couple who had sold the orchard to father and came, as it were, with the farm. My parents were happy to have him, because he was highly recommended by the previous owners. He also took care of a dog that came with the property, and when we got a puppy, he was very happy to take care of it as well. But his favorite was Duque, the older dog. Duque was also my favorite, although I loved the smaller, younger dog, Ali; white, playful, and sister's pet.

Duque was a boxer, and ever since then I have had a weakness for these animals, of which unfortunately I have never had another. He was big, with the striped, brindle coat typical of the breed. But he had never had his ears or tail cut. The ears hung big and heavy on the sides of its kind face, that is, kind when he looked at Henry or me. It was an expression that said "I love you, and I'm willing to die for you if necessary. You are my boss, my pal, my partner." The hanging jowls added to his patient and accepting expression. I would follow Henry around the property, and Duque would follow me around even when I was not following Henry. The three of us became great pals. I spent hours watching Henry do his chores and Duque chasing birds. Henry would talk to me when I was watching him, in his deep melodious accent, explaining what he was doing to the plants, making plant grafts, trimming bushes, watering, planting vegetables in the orchard, and picking ripe fruits and vegetables for the cook. The orchard was large because it had all the vegetables we consumed: carrots, lettuce of various types, radishes, cabbages, cucumbers, beans of various sorts, tomatoes and squash of various kinds, water melons, cantaloupes, egg plants, *chayotes,* peppers from the very small and hot to the sweet large red kind that I loved roasted, garlic, onions, cauliflowers, corn, and so on. There was even some *cristalina* sugarcane, the kind that is very sweet and good to chew.

Henry also helped with the large rose garden, although mother loved to work on it as well; she did most of the experiments with rose plant grafts, mixing different varieties. These experiments generated considerable expectations in all of us, curious to see the results. Henry mowed the lawn, which was no small proposition since the grounds were large and electric or gas lawn mowers were not available, and he picked the debris that fell from the many trees that grew in the place, keeping the gardens tidy. He fed the pigs which we fattened every year to be killed and roasted at Christmas time or when we had a big party, and took care of the chickens. Mother kept a collection of fancy chickens of special breeds, some of which needed special foods. Their colorful plumage was something to see. I often was allowed to keep little chicks as pets; they were beautiful and loved to be handled because our hands were warm and this made them feel like they were close to the mother hen. Henry took care of them lovingly. When a hen's eggs began to hatch, he would come around to tell me, so I could watch the process of the chicks coming out of the shells, and see the various colors and coat designs they had.

Henry and Pedrito lived in the servants' cottage. Food was prepared for our family and them in the main house, but they took their meals in the cottage. Duque was fed special meals that Henry prepared. He cooked them in a large, shallow pan used only for that purpose. Duque was never fed raw meat or anything other than cooked meat and corn meal. Each of the batches of food Henry cooked for him lasted three days. He was always fed at the same time and I tried never to miss it.

Duque slept in his own dog house, which was quite spacious and cozy—I can tell because I went into it occasionally to play with Duque. When I did the house became very cramped, but Duque liked the intimacy, and so did I. Once I fell to sleep in it with Duque, and mother was worried because she did not know where I had gone and feared that I had taken off as I had done once before. In the evening, Duque was chained to his house so he would not wander away. Henry groomed him every day and gave him a bath with the hose and some soap once a week.

Duque was very gentle with everyone in the family, but particularly with Henry and me. I did everything that came into my mind to him. I was a small child and he was a large dog, so I often rode him as if he were a horse. I would push him, lay on top of him, pull his ears and tail, pull his loose skin, dress him with human clothes, and do whatever occurred to me. He never complained. The only thing he would do when my actions crossed the line, was to look at me with those big sad eyes, as if saying, "Why are you torturing me? I love you so!" But I think he liked the attention, because in addition to all the pulling and rough handling, I constantly petted and kissed him and in return he would lick my face. Sometimes I would get tired of playing and laid on the lawn and then he would come and lay next to me, putting his head on top of my belly, so I would pet it. Those were incomparable moments in which I felt completely happy. Duque gave me all his love without asking anything in return, and although I was small, I understood it well. For me, he was a person and a very important one.

Although Duque was the gentlest of dogs with his human family, he was fierce when it came to defending his territory from intruders. It was as if he were two dogs, the canine counterparts of Dr. Jekyll and Mr. Hyde. No one could approach our grounds without him making a raucous and pursuing the intruder. Once a visitor made the mistake of bringing a dog with him, when we were not prepared for the visit, and Duque was loose. Poor animal! That dog did not have a prayer. Duque ran to him and grabbed one of its ears, which immediately began to bleed profusely. The commotion was enormous, everyone ordering and begging Duque to let go. Henry poured water on him and tried to pry him loose, but he would not let the intruder off. Finally, I do not know why or how, Duque opened his mouth and the victim took the opportunity to escape and run like a light out of the inferno where he had been caught, whimpering loudly. Fortunately, Henry took the opportunity to get hold of Duque's collar so that he could not pursue his victim.

Father was embarrassed with what had happened because of the visitor, and he grumbled something about punishing Duque. But of course, Duque was defending us, and he deserved a reward rather than punishment. I would have been devastated had he been punished. In the end nothing was done, and Duque continued being the gentle soul he was with Henry and me, and with the other members of the household to a certain extent, and being a fierce defender of his territory against anyone else.

When I was in school in Ciego de Ávila, I heard that Duque had been sick, so I asked to be taken back to the orchard to see him. He was in a bad way. His belly was swollen and father said there was nothing we could do for him. In a few days he was dead. I cried bitterly. Shortly after, father had a heart attack and sold the orchard. Henry eventually moved away because he could not abide working for the new owner, whose first act as an owner was to cut down the carob and bay trees that met over the house. Father set Henry up with a source of money so he would not have to be deprived in his old age. Less than a year later, he died. I don't know how old he was. He looked ageless to me. His face creased with wrinkles, his movements slow, but sure.

If we had not sold the orchard and he had stayed with us, I bet he would have lived many more years, although Duque's absence might have made a difference. My presence would have made up for it.

Chapter Twenty-Eight

A Bad Dream Comes True

For Ignacito, I was not only the kid brother he loved, but someone on whom he could lavish attention and with whom he could play. It was almost like having a son and seeing that he turned out OK. When my brother came into the house, the first thing he would do is to come where I was, pick me up, throw me in the air, and play with me until I was screaming for help. Then he would hug me tight and kiss and bite me all over, ending with a session of tickles that disarmed me completely. I always complained to mother about my brother's rough playing, but I loved it.

By the time I was five-years old, Ignacito worked in father's orchard and had money of his own, so he was always thinking about what to give me that I would enjoy. On my fourth birthday he gave me a pair of roller skates, which I did not quite master because I lacked the proper surface where to practice. The only smooth, flat surfaces in the orchard in Ceballos were the living room and the family room in our house, and neither of these was appropriate. The first because it would damage the beautiful wood floors, and the second because the place was full of furniture. On my fifth birthday Ignacito gave me a bicycle, which I enjoyed thoroughly for years, but again was not easy to use while at the orchard, where all the roads were gravel or dirt. It was not until I went to school when I was seven and was staying at *Abuelita Belé's* house that I took full advantage of the bicycle. On my sixth birthday Ignacito went all out, giving me something of which I could take full advantage. He gave me a horse, with saddle, spurs, and all the paraphernalia proper for a cowboy. This was the best gift I ever had as a child. Having a horse of my own was a dream come true.

Ignacito had thought and worked hard to find the right kind of horse. It was a small, dark bay mare, with beautiful white marks. Everything had been done in secret. On the day of my birthday, he asked me to come outside with him to show me his gift. I was intrigued. What could it be that it had to be outside? He had already given me roller skates and a bicycle, so what else could it be? It never crossed my mind that it would be a horse. When I saw it, I did not know what to think. At first, I thought it was just the saddle that I was getting, since we had many horses on the farm, but then I understood. I had an epiphany! A horse is what every kid in the world dreams to have when he is six years old, and here it was. I had it!

I approached the horse in a state of excitement that I had never experienced before. Pedrito was holding its bridle so that I would be able to come close and pet it. I caressed her soft, shiny coat and touched her mane. It felt like silk. She was expecting a treat and my coaches were prepared to make sure she associated me with pleasure. I offered her the treat they had on hand and felt her velvet muzzle. She made friendly noises and I was able to pat her cheeks. Pedrito had been training her, so I was able to mount right away. We walked around a bit, and then I took a ride accompanied by my brother. It was heaven on earth for me, and I am sure that Ignacito enjoyed it as much as I did. From then on, I lived on the mare. The first thing I did when I got up in the morning was to mount-up and ride around the orchard and neighboring farms. It was difficult for mother to get me to eat anything for breakfast because I was so anxious to take off. If mother did not force me to eat something before mounting the mare, I would be gone and not come back until lunchtime, when I could no longer stand the hunger pains. Finally, she realized the solution was to prepare a little bag with food and give it to me before I mounted the horse and let me go—I would eat it when I needed it.

My daily excursions took me to places where farm workers were harvesting fruit, loading crates onto trucks, cutting sugarcane, etc. I talked to them for a while and then continued on my equine explorations. The mare was gentle and we got along as well as expected. I loved to gallop the horse. After all, I was Ignacito's brother! He loved to see me learning many of the tricks he had mastered. Not that I could perform any significant fraction of the countless tricks he knew, but I tried my best to follow his example. My parents warned me to be careful, but how careful can a seven-year-old riding a horse be?

I did fall off the mare, but only once, and I did not mention it to anyone. I landed flat on my back and could have killed myself. In fact, I did injure myself. I lost consciousness entirely and woke up with her muzzle on my face. Maybe that was a kiss? Her muzzle was soft and she rubbed it on my skin. After a while I managed to get up, still dizzy and re-mounted. When I returned home, I never said a word to anyone about the fall. I hoped the bump on my head would not show, although it felt big to the touch and it hurt a lot. In case it was noticed and someone asked about it, I prepared a story, of course. I knew better than to say anything about falling off the horse. Who knows what my parents and my brother would have done if I had said anything? Surely, they would have blamed me and I could not risk being separated from my horse. She was my life (although my dog, Duque, still occupied a larger portion of my heart). No one noticed the bump on my head, so no one asked me about it. However, some problems I have had later in life may be related to a possible concussion as a result of the fall. Shortly after it happened, I developed a speech impediment, namely, I began to stammer. My family associated the problem with other issues. While the stammering eventually disappeared after a year, it seemed to resurface in various ways over the years. Recently, I have experienced similar problems with speech. One doctor indicated that the problem may be connected to the moment I fell off my horse as a child.

Living in the orchard taught me to love animals of all sorts, even worms, lizards, and frogs, let alone dogs, cats, chickens, and horses. From that time on, it always hurts me deeply to see an animal suffer poor treatment at the hands of some humans. Indeed, I learned to resent hunting and imposing unwanted domestication on animals. Unfortunately, at seven years of age, I was sent away to school and could not return home every weekend. This created a problem in that my horse slowly began to regard me as a stranger, and she would often misbehave when we were out for a ride.

In the summer of my eighth birthday, we went to the beach as usual. Father sold the citrus orchard, and invested in a sugarcane plantation which had no place for our family or my horse. That ended one of the happiest periods of my life, one which gave way to the saddest. My brother, Ignacito, would be dead in a few months, and our lives would be subjected to a series of tragedies that became nearly unbearable.

Chapter Twenty-Nine

Rebel with a Cause

Ignacito was the first fruit of my parents' marriage, born just a year after they consummated their union. Mother was twenty-two and father thirty-one. Father had firmly established himself in Chambas. For the next seventeen years they lived there. Father's pharmacy and other businesses thrived. One would think their lives were idyllic. My sister was born two years after my brother was born, and I was born twelve years later than she. We grew up in an atmosphere of abundance and freedom. As children of a prominent member of a very small, but significant, rural community, we had a privileged existence. Ignacito and Nena spent much of their time riding, swimming in the river, and enjoying the delights that the country offered.

Father had high hopes for Ignacito. As an ambitious man with a strict code of behavior by which he measured himself and others, father had a penchant for intellectual achievements. As a loving father, he wanted his first-born son to have the values he did and to succeed in the things he had succeeded. Above everything else for him was academic performance. Father had always excelled in his studies, having graduated with the highest grades in high school, the military academy, and the university, and now he had also proven that he could succeed in business. He expected Ignacito to be at least as good as he was and he spared no expense or effort to make sure that he had as good an education as it was possible in Cuba.

Unfortunately, my brother was not interested in books or learning. Ignacito had inherited the love of fun that came to us from El Curro, my maternal great-grandfather. He could work very hard, but he hated books and scholarly work, and he liked fancy clothes, drinking, dancing, women, cars, and horses. This was very sad for father, who loved intellectual work and, in spite of a few flings, was a steady guy. With the method of the Gracia-Dubiés, father would never have more than one alcoholic drink at a party. My brother, on the other hand, loved to drink, and often on the weekends came home with some level of inebriation. It did not help that alcohol did not agree with him; even minor amounts made him sick. I can put away five drinks of hard liquor, or a full bottle of wine, and still be ok—the only effect being that I feel happy and perhaps a little sentimental. But Ignacito had a couple of beers and his head was gone, and eventually he would be sick. This was unfortunate because in truth he did not drink that much; his drinking was a party affair, and only on weekends. He was not a drunk by any stretch of the imagination. He just liked to have a good time, and he needed to assuage a permanent sadness resulting from the disappointment he had caused father for not measuring up to his expectations. What could be worse than this for an eldest son, the heir to the name?

Ignacito needed to forget the feeling that gnawed at his existence, and a couple of beers was the only effective vehicle he found to do it. Studying was a terrible chore for him. He regularly neglected his studies, never picking up a book to read for pleasure. Nena told me that when he was supposed to be studying, he would sit with an open book in his hands, presumably reading, but he never turned its pages. His mind was elsewhere, swimming in the creek that ran through one of father's plantations, riding horses with our sister or his friends, exploring the countryside, playing table games, and in time running after girls of his age, and eventually also pursuing older women.

Ignacito's friends were young men of whom father did not approve, often uninterested in acquiring a professional education or in learning anything worthwhile. In many cases they were just manual workers among whom Ignacito felt comfortable since he had given up on an education and did not feel the pressure he felt in the company of anyone who had succeeded in school or led a professional life. For the young men Ignacito's company was special in that they seldom had an opportunity to rub shoulders with members of a bourgeois family. This gave them an opportunity to learn about a world they did not know but coveted. Aware of how little mother and father liked those friends, I used to call them derogatorily *"sus amigotes."* To boot, when my brother got together with them, he drank more than he could manage.

Ignacito's drinking began one of those times when people from the town took refuge in our home during tornados. Father was not at home, and two older guys smuggled liquor into the house and got my brother drunk. Many men look for storms, tornados, hurricanes, and similar natural disasters as excuses for partying and drinking. Mother, inexperienced in these matters and having to deal with a house full of people, did not notice what was happening until it was too late. After the danger from the tornado had passed and people began to leave the house, one of father's workers told mother that Ignacito was drunk. The poor boy did not know what to do; he had vomited and continued retching. He looked miserable. They gave him some coffee, bathed him, and put him to sleep. But when father found out, he was not happy and proceeded to warn Ignacito of the dangers of alcohol. Unfortunately, Ignacito did not heed the warning, and father saw his drinking as something beneath his own dignity, embarrassing and degrading, and as an indication of a lack of self-control and respect for the family.

Primary education for my siblings took place mostly at home, because there were no proper schools in the country. Father wanted the children to have a deeper and broader education than the one offered in Chambas. For a while, a group of prominent families in the town arranged for a well-qualified teacher to move into town and teach their children, but the experiment did not succeed. The teacher was a terror that applied excessive physical punishment to students. Nena told me that in his classes *no se podía ni respirar* (one could not even breathe). Ignacito got the brunt of it, of course. Once, he got such a hard *coscorrón* on the head that he fell off his seat. Another time, the teacher used a book to hit him. And Nena, who as a girl was generally not subject to physical punishment, was given a *galletazo de ampanga* (a hard slap of major proportions). Of course, Ignacito reported Nena's experience at home, and Nena reported his, but father always took the side of the teacher and ignored each of my sibling's complaints.

Matters changed, however, at the high school level. Father sent Ignacito to the Colegio Mimó, the school in Havana that father had also attended. That proved to be a disaster. When he arrived at the school, Ignacito joined a group of trouble-makers who were only interested in parties. Against regulations, they would leave school at night and spend the time drinking and carousing. Eventually, father had to take Ignacito out of the school. Then, he sent him to La Progressive (The Progressive), founded in 1900 as a liberal, Protestant school in Cárdenas. This was a well-respected educational establishment, both strict and known for the quality education it provided. But this did not work for my brother either. He failed miserably and after a time was sent home. This second failure was a painful blow for father. Not only had he to recognize that his son was nothing like himself, but also that he was an embarrassment to the family. The future looked grim, indeed.

Still, the attempt to at least graduate from high school was not abandoned. While in Chambas and Camagüey, Ignacito started taking classes from a tutor and taking the state examinations for each grade when he was ready. In time he was able to graduate from high school, but that was as far as he would go.

In father's view, my brother's job was to study, and if he did not want to work, he would have to work and earn a living and pay a rent for his wages. Obviously, it was not in the cards to throw my brother out of our home, so when father bought the orchard in Ceballos, he gave my brother a job in it which Ignacito was glad to take.

The work was manual. Ignacito labored along with other workers picking oranges from trees, putting them in wooden crates, and loading them on trucks. He also drove the trucks when necessary and did all the things that the other workers did: trimming, watering, and anything else required to be done. Ignacito was not lazy, and he worked very hard. He also saved his money and was responsible as far as his duties were concerned, even though he was still a teenager. He was a model worker by all accounts. The only problem was that on weekends he got together with friends and went out to have a good time with the ladies. He also drank and would come home late at night on the weekends with clear signs of inebriation. My parents would hear him come into his room and this riled father. He would get up and confront him. A fight would ensue. Mother would try to mediate between them and bring peace into the family, but she seldom succeeded.

Father was unhappy and so was my brother. As time passed, Ignacito got increasingly moody, avoiding father as much as he could, but clashes were inevitable. My brother wanted a car, but father would not let him buy one because he was afraid that Ignacito would drive recklessly and kill himself while under the influence of alcohol. There were also problems with women, and occasional scandals that embarrassed father. An impasse had been reached between father and Ignacito. They were very different men. My brother could not see the world in the structured way father saw it, and father could not understand why.

Chapter Thirty

A Philosophy of Underwear

Father was not a philosopher—I am—but he had elaborate philosophies for many things. One of these philosophies, perhaps more than anything else, reveals the source of the difficulties he and Ignacito had: father's philosophy of underwear.

A common memory of my childhood was to hear father complain to mother in the morning: "Niña, where is my B3 bottom underwear (or my A11 top underwear)?" and mother's answer: "It must be there, in the drawer of the wardrobe. The washer woman brought the laundry yesterday and I had her put and organize your things in it." "Well," responded father, "it is not here." "But it must be, look again," mother retorted somewhat irritated. And frustrated, father replied: "It is not, so what am I going to do now?" And mother: "You could use B4 instead." "That makes no sense, Niña, it would completely mess up the system. If I were to use the B4 bottom underwear, then I would have to use the B4 top underwear, and skip the B3 set altogether." "But Gracia," mother always called father by his last name, "why does it matter, aren't both bottoms?" "Niña, you do not understand. Why is it that a simple thing such as keeping underwear organized as I have them is so difficult to grasp? I just I don't get it! You know quite well that I like them organized in a particular way. Why can't it be done as I like it?"

By this time tempers were rising, and the argument was degenerating into the usual confrontation between two styles of living and ways of looking at things that were incompatible, but they had managed to survive together for years: his style was strict, methodical, systematic, scientific, and orderly, and her style was loose, erratic, unsystematic, artistic, and disorderly.

The conversation was about father's undergarments. He was a very methodical person, a trait he had inherited from the Gracia-Dubiés. They were all very methodical. Aunt Rosario, for example, ran her home with perfect order, according to a method that father admired and always mentioned to mother as a prime example to see if he could encourage her to change her disorderly ways, but he never got positive results. The meal menus at Rosario's home, for example, were arranged according to a master plan on a rotating bases for the week. If you went to dinner to Rosario's on Wednesday, you knew you were going to get chicken fricassee, and if you went there for lunch on Saturday, you would get *carne con papas*. The menu was set in stone, and changed only on very special occasions, such as a birthday celebration, for which of course, also a set menu was available. Her sympathy for improvisation or variety was non-existent. Order was the rule. I think Rosario must have secretly been a positivist!

The menu was just one of the many things that was regimented in aunt Rosario's home. Almost everything else was also regimented: the shopping, the washing, the cleaning (a day for this part of the house and another for that part, a day to polish the silver and another to dust the porcelains, and so on). Nothing escaped the master plan. Maids and cooks had a hard time with it, until they realized that such a system made things easier for them. The cook did not have to worry about what menus to put together, or what to buy at the butcher's, or if she ran out of something or other, because everything was planned and repeated every week. Still, most servants complied only grudgingly, and complained behind Rosario's back to anyone who would hear. This was a new world for them, accustomed as they were to a largely unsystematic and unplanned life. Rosario knew their feelings but, with a sense of proper superiority, ignored them although she often told father, and, after his death, me, that it was no wonder why they were cooks and maids. In her view, the secret of progress was order. (Surely, she was a positivist!) But then, what can we make of mother? She was a perfect counterexample, although Rosario would probably argue that the only way to succeed, if one did not have a method, was to marry someone who was a success, which is what mother did.

Mother used to complain that one of the greatest burdens she had in her life was planning meal menus every day. And it was one of the reasons she tried to convince father to live in a hotel rather than a home. Her ideal of good living was to reside in a nice hotel in Havana, where the family could go down to the hotel dining room to eat. Too bad for her that she never got her wish.

The first order of business for mother in the morning was to confer with the cook on what to have for lunch and dinner for that day, what to buy, where to buy the meat or the vegetables, and so on. It was a give and take, and it depended on what was available at the market, because the ingredients were bought daily even though as far as I can remember we always had a refrigerator, so the main ingredients could be bought on a previous day and kept from spoiling. But that was never considered a possibility because everybody thought freshness was essential to what we ate. After deciding on a tentative menu, the cook would go to the market to buy what was necessary. Often the cut of meat required was not available, and the cook would have to improvise, which was understood and allowed.

The planning of meals was difficult not just because there were two major meals a day, which had to be different—lunch and dinner (breakfast was always a simple affair of yogurt and honey, *café con leche*, and bread and butter)—but also because the same dishes could not be repeated within a week, and sometimes in two weeks. Variety was of the essence in a home like ours, where food was regarded as very important, and meals were an occasion for pleasure and conversation. Then there were the individual requirements each of us had, for we all had special dishes we liked and dishes we didn't like, and our tastes were regarded as sacred. Ignacito lived on filet mignon and French fries, but mother, coming from a vegetarian family, ate very little meat and certainly not those big, thick steaks he loved. So the butcher was instructed to save a full tenderloin every time a cow was slaughtered in order to feed my brother. The list of things I did not like was endless: tongue, liver, most vegetables, tripe, sweet potato, avocado, pigs' feet, and so on. If the main dish or dishes did not agree with the taste of any one of us, something different had to be prepared for that person. No wonder planning meals was such a burden! Our kitchen had to function like that of a Michelin-rated restaurant although it had only one cook and one meal planner.

When mother complained, father always brought up Rosario's method. Mother, of course, would dismiss this with a disparaging comment such as, "This is not an army," or, "Would you really like to eat the same thing every Tuesday?" The latter remark was usually effective, because father liked a well-set table, with variety and panache, and he preferred to be surprised. Still, he could not help expressing his desire for some order. Her chaotic ways resulted in wonderful meals, but the anxiety accompanying them went against his grain.

Father ran his businesses and daily life in the same orderly way aunt Rosario ran her household. He often referred to his stint in military school as the occasion where he had learned the value of order and discipline. The shoes must be polished, the trousers creased, and the coats carefully hung. But it was obvious that Rosario had never gone to military school and was as methodical as he was, maybe more! The source for the family penchant for order was the family, not the military. And I think it had something to do with our genetic make-up, because it was passed on to the children in different ways and proportions. A good example is the way I eat shrimp, something I had never realized and was not taught, but which an observant son-in-law noticed: As I eat shrimp, I arrange the uneatable parts of the tails along the border of my plate in a row, following the curve of the plate, perfectly aligned and separated by the exact same distance from each other. Why do I do it? No one else in my family does it, and no one taught me to do it. The sense of order and arrangement that this procedure illustrates comes from the Gracia-Dubiés. It is something that drove mother up the wall, to use a cliché! And such order is something I hope at least one of my grandchildren will inherit.

Just as important as meals was clothing to father, who was fastidious and meticulous when it came to his wardrobe. All his clothes were made to his specifications by a tailor that had worked for him for years—in fact, the man became his friend. Father was a sort of dandy, always well-dressed according to strict standards and circumstances, a trait the Gracia-Dubiés said he had inherited from his paternal grandfather. When he went to one of the plantations we owned, he always wore riding clothes—appropriate jodhpurs, gaiters, and even a whip, although he never rode a horse (he suffered from lumbago) and had his chauffeur drive him in our jeep. He also packed a gun when he carried important quantities of money with him, such as when he had to pay the workers, although I think this was more for show than anything else—I never heard of anyone being assaulted. He probably thought that carrying a gun was part of the appropriate attire for the occasion; I doubt he even thought about the possibility of ever firing it. Father could not abide shabby clothes and the idea that he would wear anything mended was anathema to him. He frequently remarked that a mended pair of pants indicated the beginning of the end of a man. So even when he was young and the family had scant resources, he told me he never wore mended clothes, not even socks. The best example of his obsession with order had to do with undergarments. He had these made to order of Egyptian cotton and in a set style. He always kept four sets of twelve bottoms and twelve tops each. They had to be made to his specifications—and he was very particular about them. Each top and each bottom was identified with an embroidered red letter and number. The letter, whether A, B, C, or D, was the same for all the members of each set, but the numbers went from 1-12 for both tops and bottoms. You ended up with a series of tops identified as, say, B1-B12 and a series of bottoms also identified as B1-B12. (I never found out why there had to be 12 in the series—perhaps he thought this was the perfect number because it is the number of Christ's disciples?) Of these sets, he kept two in use and two in storage at any time, so that when the two in use became a bit worn, he could switch to the two sets in storage, discard the worn two, and order two new dozens made. The purpose of the numbers that accompanied the letters was to wear down the sets uniformly and always have the tops and bottoms matched. He would wear top A1 with bottom A1 and top B3 with bottom B3, beginning the set of twelve with number 1 and ending with number 12. In this way, he argued, the sets would wear off evenly and he would get the most wear of them, barring accidents and other unpredictable events.

This was a tremendous ordeal for mother because it required an accounting system that was foreign to her nature. And it created problems when accidents happened, a piece was lost by the washer woman, or a piece got accidentally ripped. When this occurred father was torn about what to do, because the whole system would be threatened. The usual solution, since he would wear nothing mended and he would refuse to skip a numbered pair, was to throw out the entire set of underwear, even if most of the pieces were in good order. This solution hurt, though, for he loathed to throw out a good garment, and the entire purpose of the system, at least ostensibly, was to save money. Eventually, toward the end of his life, after Ignacito died, he finally gave up the system, but not without regret or struggle. Reality had finally defeated him.

Chapter Thirty-One

End of Paradise

Paradise is supposed to have been a garden where humans did not have to toil or experience pain, fear, suffering, or death. They did not have to worry about the tomorrow, about scarcity of food, bullies, crime, danger, disease, or work. Their existence was delightful, enjoying each other's company, blessed by God, and without cares and responsibilities. God took care of them. Their only duty was not to do something which they actually did and resulted, sadly, in their expulsion from the Garden of Eden.

I thought I lived in something as close as it could be to a paradise on Earth until school ended it on September of 1949, after turning seven on July 18. School meant responsibility, separation from my parents, attacks from bullies, and an existence where I was expected to toil. Although I had experienced good and evil before I went to school, after I started school my experience of them deepened, and both my innocence and happiness pretty well ended. The security of the cocoon where I had lived before ceased and I had to rely on my own resources to survive. My situation was similar to that of Adam and Eve, although, unlike them, I had done nothing to deserve it.

The Marist Brothers in Cuba devoted themselves to the education of boys from first grade all the way to the end of the equivalent of high school in the United States. They had one of their schools in Ciego the Ávila where they enjoyed a virtual monopoly on the private education of boys. Apart from the Marists, there were other religious orders that had schools in Cuba. In Havana, La Salle and the Jesuit Belén in particular were major rivals of the Marists. Very few other private schools of note functioned on the island. Colegio Mimó in Havana, where father had gone and he had sent Ignacito, La Progresiva in Cárdenas, which my brother also attended as a last resort. The Ruston Academy, and the Edison Institute were some of the most prominent, but none of these were run by religious orders.

Chapter 31

I ended up going to the Marist Brothers because it was the only private school near Ceballos. My first experience with school had ended in failure. My parents wanted for me to learn to socialize with other children, so at four they sent me to a kindergarten, but matters did not go well. I would not stop crying, and after trying all sorts of enticements, the effort was terminated. Schooling was postponed as long as it could, so I stayed home and continued my usual happy existence until I was seven years old. By then I had already learned the rudiments of writing and reading from mother and sister, who had taught me at home.

The building of Colegio Champagnat (the official name of the Marist Brothers School) was an impressive structure done in a neo-classical, with a touch of baroque, style and with fine materials. It had been built to last for generations. The school had all grades from first to fifth, with a sixth grade for students interested in commercial subjects. Each class had around thirty students and all the equipment required at the time in a good school. My parents talked to the principal, a tall, athletic brother, known as El Tigre (The Tiger) by students, and universally feared by them, and were favorably impressed, so the decision was taken that I would enter first grade there.

In order to make that possible, *Abuelita Belé* and aunt Maruca moved from Camagüey into a house father bought for them in Ciego de Ávila, just two blocks away from the Marist school. This allowed me to walk to school.

I was very apprehensive about these developments, particularly because no one consulted me about them. They were all in cahoots, trying to convince me of how wonderful school was going to be, which made me highly suspicious. I had never been outside the home for any period of time and the idea of being in a school, surrounded by children I did not know, and taught by men dressed in black skirts, was frightening. Preparations began weeks before the first day of classes. Nena stayed away from her school so she could help—yes, I was considered that important, but not important enough to ask me what I thought. We had to go shopping, buying the paraphernalia that children in first grade buy: pencils, paper, notebooks, color crayons, a work book, and so on. The uniform was a particularly important item. Stores carried these in various levels of quality with the result that, contrary to the equalizing intention of the uniform, it was clear that some students were better dressed than others, even though the colors of the uniforms were the same: blue shirt, white tie, khaki pants, and leather shoes.

The first day of classes was a disaster, at least for me. Nena walked with me to school. She carried a camera with which she recorded every part of the process, except when I was crying, which was often enough. Just thinking about being left alone, away from my family, made me cry, but I was able to hold back the tears until I got to school and I was taken to the classroom where I was supposed to stay and Nena left. Well, I did put on a show, I began to cry and would not stop. Nothing would console me. I wanted to go back to my sister, my mommy, and my home. I was in a panic. But what else could have been expected under the circumstances and the fact that I was the grandchild of *Abuelita Belé*, who shed tears on every possible occasion? I lived in a family where tears were as frequent as smiles, perhaps more abundant, and grandmother had made a career out of them. So, I did my part to maintain the family tradition. No one should have been surprised at the spectacle I put on. Besides, I had never been in a room with thirty kids and a male teacher dressed in a black skirt. To make matters worse, the other kids had attended a preparatory grade, so they were used to the school routine, while this was the first time I attended school.

I stopped crying only when the Tiger came and got me out of the classroom. He led me to his office, sat me on his lap, and consoled me. This big guy, strong and affectionate, was a refuge to which I clung. He talked to me for a long time, and eventually convinced me to go back to the classroom, where Brother Felix, who reminded me of Ignacito, took over the job of making me feel safe. He was a most gentle man, with great experience dealing with small children. Perhaps it was the soothing way of the Tiger and Brother Felix that did it, or perhaps it was that they both wore skirts, so that they looked to me like someone half way between a man and a woman. Strong and masculine as could be, but dressed like females. I was not used to seeing priests or members of religious orders, since my family did not frequent churches and I had lived in the country from age four to seven. In any case, I felt sufficiently safe to stay in school until lunch time. In the afternoon, children attending the first day of first grade were excused from class, so the shock of going to school for the first time would be tolerable. I walked happily back to grandmother's house with Nena, who had come to fetch me. The next day I was also upset, but not as badly, and in a couple of days, after I had made some friends and had become attached to Brother Felix, I felt reasonably well.

Still, primary school was never happy for me. I had lived a care free existence, surrounded by adults who catered to my whims, and now I had to compete for attention with other children, who had their own idiosyncrasies and needs. It was frustrating. And there was homework to be done. I did not relish the homework, or learning all the things I was supposed to learn. I was an indifferent student, not particularly interested in doing well, or in learning. I did my homework, helped by aunt Maruca, but there was no pleasure in it; it was more a matter of duty and avoiding embarrassment. At the time, my parents did not particularly encourage me to do well, or to concentrate on school work. In fact, since I saw them only on weekends, it was especially Maruca to whom I related. My interest in learning had to wait much longer to develop.

For many children, attending school is a great experience that they look forward to and enjoy. For me, it was the end of Paradise and the beginning of pain on Earth. I was a spoiled child not in the sense that I behaved badly in front of strangers or even friends of the family. I was always a model of behavior outside the home. Nonetheless, I was terribly spoiled in that I was pampered and allowed to have my way, and most of my behavior was excused. Things were even more so after I fell from the horse and developed a stammering which lasted for more than a year. This was mistakenly identified as a result of a spanking by mother. Mother was terrified that the stammering would not go away and felt guilty that she had been the source of it.

Making matters worse was that I had lived surrounded by grown-ups who celebrated everything I did. Indeed, I wonder how I could have turned out anything but a monster given the way I was raised. But I have come to think that what really damages children is not permissiveness, provided it is filled with love, but injustice and harshness. From a very early age, I had a keen sense of injustice, and to this day I remember when others wronged me unjustly. The bitterness of these experiences can never be forgotten even when one forgives the affront.

Chapter Thirty-Two

The Bully

The sense of injustice caused by bullying was perhaps the most traumatic and frustrating experience I had in school. I had never encountered bullying until I went to school. Bullying in the four different schools I attended before I entered the university was endemic. Physically stronger students bullied weaker ones. Athletes bullied non-athletes. Richer kids were bullied by poorer ones and sometimes vice versa. Good-looking kids were bullied by bad-looking ones and vice versa. Older kids bullied younger ones. Anyone who did not swear and was not constantly interested in sex, was regarded as a sissy or, worst, as gay—to be gay in Cuba was the ultimate insult and *pájaros* (birds), as gays were known, occupied a particularly despised status in a society where *machismo* was the rule. Bullying, mocking, and both verbal and physical abuse were part of school life. Generally, any one that differed from the patterns taken as the norm established by those with power was bullied. For some children, life was a continuous misery, and for many others that did not enjoy to bully, it was only tolerable. School life in Cuba could be, and often was, miserable. Don't believe a word of what anybody else, influenced by nostalgia, tells you.

    I came to school from a sheltered background; I was better off economically than most of my classmates; I was dressed better; I was timid about discussing sex; I was good looking as a kid; I was more carefully groomed than most other kids; and in time I became a good student favored by my teachers. These were enormous handicaps in the eyes of many of my classmates. Some tolerated me, and many were my friends, but there was always one particular kid in each school I attended who devoted some of his time to bullying or trying to bully me. Serious bullying began in second grade, as far as I remember, when I was eight. Some of the bullying was in school and some outside school. The bullying outside school took place in the neighborhood where I stayed with *Abuelita Belé* and aunt Maruca. Most neighborhoods in Cuba, as happens in most of Latin America, are mixed in terms of social and economic classes and this provides fertile ground for bullying.

The guy that took upon himself the task of making my life miserable had a face of a boxer that, from that moment on, I came to associate with a bully, no matter how hard I have tried to convince myself of the irrational nature of my reaction. One of its most prominent features were the lips; they were fleshy and lacked definition. Some people would probably consider him handsome in a rough sort of way, sexy perhaps. I had no opinion on his looks when I met him, but after he subjected me to torture, I came to despise his appearance and subsequently have intuitively avoided anyone who even remotely looks like him. He was also one year older than I and, unlike me, who at the time was wiry, he was built like a premature bodybuilder and, more pointedly, a boxer. Massive legs and arms, a thick cylinder torso, and a protruding chin. The guy inspired fear on everybody in second grade, but he had chosen me for his victim.

During school hours he behaved fairly well because our teachers kept an eye on us and tried to prevent any abuses, even during breaks. Unfortunately for me this guy, whose name was appropriately "Leon" (Lion), lived near my grandmother's home, and so we ended up walking to school together. It was painful. Of course, if that had been all and I had been able to escape from him after school, things would not have been as bad. But he could not leave me alone, and was always trying to find me after school hours to play. Play for him meant torturing me. I was very unhappy.

I confided in aunt Maruca, because I trusted her not to say anything to my parents or sister. I was ashamed, like many victims are, of being bullied and not being able to end the intolerable situation. Her typically Cuban advice was that I had to teach the bully a lesson. She said I had to beat the guy up. The only way he would stop would be if he had to fight me, even if he won the fights, because he would eventually get tired of fighting. I understood what she said and even agreed with it, but I felt I would get a thorough trashing if I followed her advice. Sure, I was a chicken! But what could one expect of a kid like me, who had been treated always with love at home, and was as skinny as could be, when confronted with a kid that had it rough from the very beginning, had become tough and unkind, and was built like a boxer?

I spent a good deal of my time fantasizing about the horrible things I would do to this bully. I would smack him on the face and break his nose. I would make him trip and fall on his face. I would grab him by the head and push my fingers into his eyes. I would kick his crotch and make him double over in pain. I would twist his arm and make him beg for mercy. Oh, the tortures I made-up in my mind to teach him a lesson! I applied to him some of the tortures they told us in school the martyrs had suffered. How about toasting him on a fire grill? Wouldn't it be great to see him on a Procrustean bed with his limbs cut off and bleeding? What about the water torture or the rack? Quartering sounded particularly appropriate for him!

The problem was that all this was unreal and I needed to solve the problem I had in a realistic manner. But how? I was mentally ready to do something but I had no idea of what. I was handicapped because, in spite of all my ruminations and imaginations, I was not violent by nature and was unaccustomed to fighting. I needed motivation, a provocation that would raise my anger to such a pitch that would make me take an action that was against my nature, upbringing, and the fear I had of the guy. For him, on the other hand, abuse was his modus vivendi and he felt confident that he could win any fight, thus he always took the initiative when we were together.

The matter got resolved eventually and unexpectedly, however. One day I was out playing when Leon came to torture me as usual. I had recently received as a gift a magnificent double barrel pirate gun of which all the kids in the neighborhood and school were jealous. Leon came to see if he could take it away from me, maybe to try to tease me and even to break it if possible. He had already broken some of my other toys before. But by this time I had had enough and when he approached me and tried to wrest the gun from me, instead of letting go or running away, I took it by the double barrel and hit him on the head with the butt, with all the force I had. The skin broke on Leon's forehead and blood poured out freely. At first, he did not know what had happened. After all, he was not expecting this kind of response from the wiry wimp he had been torturing for a couple of months. But soon enough he understood because the blood was flowing into his eye and the pain intensified. Then, shocked and scared, he whined: "You broke my head!" All of a sudden, he was not a formidable enemy, not master of the situation, but a scared little kid who turned around and ran home crying and screaming. I was exultant and went into grandmother's house and told aunt Maruca. I was afraid of what would happen next, but she told me not to worry; she would take care of the aftermath. "You stay put, keep your mouth shut, and don't mind what I say!"

Shortly after the bully's mother came to complain. She was a bully herself who thought her child was Jesus Christ on Earth and could do nothing wrong! Poor little baby, being abused by the wiry rich kid! I loathed her even more than I loathed her son. I do not know what she expected, but what she did not know is that in Maruca she would meet her match. Maruca, with her suave and gracious manner, agreed entirely with the woman, but pointed out that there had been many provocations. All the same, Maruca chastised me in front of her, sending me to my room and promising that she would deal with me later, while unobtrusively winking at me to let me know she was putting on a show. After the bully's mother left, Maruca came into my room laughing and kissed me, saying: "You'll see that he never bothers you again! But if he ever does, repeat the treatment. Some people need repetition to learn a lesson. In fact, I think you should carry that gun with you every time you play with him as a reminder of what you did to him, and a warning that you can do it again." The next day she cooked tamales for dinner, which were my favorite dish.

After this incident, Leon and I became relatively good friends, and let me emphasize "relatively," because old habits are hard to overcome, but he generally behaved well. This taught me a lesson, an unfortunate one perhaps. From then on, I became very sensitive about responding with all I had, anytime that anyone tried to make my life difficult or tried to take advantage of me. Rationally, I have never been able to reconcile the lesson I learned from this event with my belief in harmony and peace. To this day, I cannot satisfactorily answer the question of whether and when the use of force is justified. My heart tells me one thing, whereas my brain tells me another. Perhaps this is one of the reasons why, as a philosopher, I have stayed away from issues that have to do with war and peace.

Chapter Thirty-Three

First Holy Communion

I became seriously aware of faith only when I started at the Marist school. Before then I had a vague sense of religion. Most households in Cuba had some small statues or pictures of Jesus, the Virgin Mary, various saints, and plenty of crucifixes everywhere. Most of the pictures and statues were rather gruesome and unappealing. Instead of attracting they repelled. You might have one of the many likenesses of the Virgin such as *La Dolorosa,* in which her heart appears outside her chest. It is pierced with daggers, with blood dripping from the wounds. The suffering Virgin was present in almost every household. Or you might have a picture or a statue of the patron of Cuba, *La Virgen de la Caridad del Cobre*, or of the Sacred Heart of Jesus Christ. In the last case the heart would also be presented outside the chest and illuminated in various ways. The gruesome character of some of these images was sometimes more evident than others, but they were frequent enough in keeping with the traditions of Spanish art, where the suffering of Christ, the Virgin, and the saints are central elements in depiction.

Religion, like sex, was never far from your thoughts in Cuba. The society lived immersed in symbols associated with Catholicism, although the most popular images were those identified with African deities, as was *Santa Bárbara,* identified with *Changó Santería, San Lázaro* with *Babalú Ayé,* and *La Virgen de la Caridad del Cobre* with *Ochún.* The Catholic clergy seldom made an effort to get matters cleared up. They let Cubans believe what they wanted as far as these religious syncretic associations was concerned, concentrating their efforts in keeping people in church, not in making sure their beliefs were orthodox. More upsetting to Catholic clergy than these African associations were Protestant inroads, which they combated fiercely and tried to undermine at every turn.

It was impossible for anyone to grow up in Cuba and be oblivious to the religious context that permeated the island's culture. As a young child I was aware of these practices, but I had very little knowledge of what they meant or sympathy for them. I knew mother prayed, as did my grandmothers and other female members of the family, but the males never paid any obvious attention to religion. Religion was supposed to be for women and sissies, not *macho* men. I was aware of the images that were on display in our house and those of our extended family and friends, but I had no sense of religion or faith, even though I was made to wear medals and engage in some religious rituals.

I first became explicitly and systematically introduced to religion when I began attending school. The Marist Brothers had a routine that included going to Mass first thing in the morning, prayers before and after each class period, a daily class period devoted to teaching religion beginning with the Catechism, saying the Angelus at noon (this is the prayer that recounts the Annunciation, when Archangel Gabriel is supposed to have announced to Mary that she was going to give birth to Jesus), and saying the rosary first thing in the afternoon. It was a heavy schedule of religious practice and indoctrination, and the last word correctly describes the procedure, because doctrine was being pressed upon us throughout. I do not remember that anyone ever objected, but why would they? I never met anyone in school that was not Catholic, whether from a practicing family or Catholic in name only.

Religious instruction was adapted to the audience. We were small children and like all children we loved stories, so instruction was peppered with tales about Jesus, the various apparitions of the Virgin Mary, and the saints. The Marist Brothers were particularly devoted to the Virgin, whence their name, so the Virgin predominated everywhere, including the chapel, where the Virgin occupied center stage. But the stories came from all over. Catholic lore is rich and extends for more than two-thousand years, so there was plenty to tell and to hear. Many of the stories had to do with the Eucharist. Stories of sacrilege and blasphemy produced effects that clearly showed that the consecrated bread was actually the Body of Christ and the wine was His blood were favorites. Blasphemers and perpetrators of sacrilege, we were told, would pierce the bread with a nail or a knife and the bread would bleed. The wine would run like blood if spilled.

Not to mention the stories of martyrs and how they experienced the most horrendous tortures for the love of Christ. Sitting on scalding iron chairs, being quartered, their flesh being cut slowly, and bodies pierced by arrows. The Coliseum and the enjoyment of Roman mobs of Christian martyrdom loomed large in these accounts. Those of us with a strong imagination vividly pictured these horrible events, which were presented as true and accurately described, so that we could realistically imagine the screams of the tortured in our minds. At night, I had nightmares, but I never dared say anything about them to mother or father, and least of all to my teachers. I loved my teachers, and perhaps I loved them more because they had introduced me into a terrifying new world that I had not known before.

All this instruction was preparatory to First Communion. This was the great event in first grade and involved elaborate preparations. First, we had to confess our sins and receive absolution. We were supposed to have reached the age of reason, seven, and, therefore, were made aware that all the nutty things we did were sins, mortal or venial. I had a great deal of difficulty distinguishing between mortal and venial sins. I tried hard to have something to say when I was asked what sins I had committed and I made extraordinary efforts to find something that was so horrible as to qualify for a mortal sin, so that my soul could be washed clean again and I could be in a state of grace. It was all very stressful.

The stress was made worse because boys had to meet the confessor face-to-face. Girls had the advantage that, out of a sense of modesty, they only approached the confessional through a screen located on the side of the confessional, so that they were not seen and the confessor did not look into their eyes directly. But boys did not have this advantage. We had to face the inquisitor face-to-face, although it was a benevolent inquisitor who took the place of Christ, always absolving our sins, and gave us very minor punishments.

One serious problem was that, although one confessed one's sins and was absolved of them the day before Communion would take place, it would be always possible that one committed a mortal sin between that moment and the moment of Communion. This was particularly worrisome because it meant that one could not have Communion. To have Communion being in a state of mortal sin was a sacrilege, it was like putting Christ in a soiled vessel, an insult to His benevolence and divinity.

To take care of that possible situation, our teacher told us that there would be a priest hearing confessions at the church earlier that morning, so any of us who fell into mortal sin would be able to receive proper Absolution before having First Holy Communion. But imagine the humiliation of having to confess that day, an acknowledgment of having sinned mortally, in front of everybody, including our parents. This was too much to bear. It felt as if I was in a state of complete inertia from the time I confessed until Communion, in order to make sure I would not have to confess again. Only after I had First Holy Communion did I feel liberated.

There were also practical preparations for First Holy Communion. We had to learn to take the Host in our mouths and eat it—at that time no one touched the Host, you could only eat it. We were warned, though, not to let it fall, because this was the Body of Christ and letting it fall was a horrible thing. Besides, even a tiny piece of the bread that fell on the floor would have to be picked-up since the Body of Christ was in every part of the bread, but of course not with the hand. Whoever let it fall would have to lick the floor to make sure no particle remained on it. Imagine if a particle stayed on the floor and someone accidentally stepped on it! That would be a sacrilege and would have enormous consequences, almost as bad as the crucifixion itself! To step on the tiniest piece meant to step on the whole of Christ. Never mind that no one understood how the entire body could simultaneously be in every part of the bread and in every piece of consecrated bread everywhere. That was a mystery we were not expected to understand. Mind you, not a contradiction or an unintelligibility, but a mystery. Our business was rather to prevent an accident that would cause someone to step on Christ.

This was not my only worry about First Holy Communion. The whole idea of eating the Body of Christ worried me to no end. If piercing the host with a knife was sacrilegious and the host bled, what would happen if I bit into the bread? Would the host bleed? Would the blood come out of my mouth? Did Christ feel the bite? No one explained to me why this would not happen and I was too afraid to raise the question. One solution would be not to bite into the bread. But how could one not bite it? It would not dissolve by itself, and if one tried to swallow it whole, one would surely choke, maybe spitting it on the floor. That loomed like a horrible prospect.

We had to dress in white for the first time we had Holy Communion, symbolizing the state of grace in which we were supposed to be. Apart from the white suit, there were other special accouterments we had to carry. A bow decorated one arm, and a candle was lavishly carried on the hand. A mother of pearl rosary (for those who could afford it) was carried in the other hand, and a little book of prayers, beautifully illuminated and bound in a cover of mother of pearl and gold was held with the rosary. The white silk bow ended with gilded tassels. Of course, the shoes to match the attire, and the socks, were also white.

Strict fasting (no food or water) was required from midnight until after Communion was taken on the following morning—it was deemed unseemly to mix Christ's body with food in your innards. A clean digestive track was an indispensable requirement—never mind that the Apostles ate the bread Christ offered to them after they had eaten the meal at the Last Supper. But then, the Apostles were different from us. What no one explained to me was how this abstinence forced on us would prevent remnants of the bread, even if modified with gastric juices, from mixing with bodily refuse in the intestines. Shouldn't we be given a purgative every time we had Communion? This was just one of what seemed to be many inconsistencies that were not explained to communicants and about which no one dared to talk.

The morning arrived, I was dressed and ready in my new, specially tailored white suit. Fortunately, Communion took place early in the morning so that, although I was famished, I lasted well without eating or drinking anything. I remember the moment in which it was my turn to go up front and receive the Body of Christ. I was trembling, it was such a momentous event in my life, from what my teachers had said! This was the first time I would be in physical touch, indeed united, with Christ himself. God was entering my body and it would be like a light entering a dark room. Life, light. Two boys at a time went up, everybody looking at us in a church packed with family and friends. The emotional mothers with tears in their eyes, and the proud fathers, happy for the moment! Of course, some fathers, like mine, regarded the whole rigmarole as ecclesiastical theater, but what the audience thought did not count. I remember vaguely that there was music in the background, but I could not tell what. I stole a furtive glance at mother, and she smiled, resplendent as usual.

I knelt and opened my mouth, putting my tongue out as I had been taught. The priest blessed me in Latin, and, after I said "Amen," he put the Host on my tongue. I expected something to happen, the world to shake. But nothing did except for the racing of my heart. The flat, unleavened bread tasted just like the unconsecrated one I had been given before at the rehearsal. I closed my mouth and chewed on it as gently as I could. This was the Body of Christ! I did not want to hurt him. "Please, Jesus, understand what I am doing!" And I swallowed it. I could hardly walk back to my seat—I was so moved—but I did, looking pious, overwhelmed by what was happening. God was in me in a way that He had not been before. He was becoming part of me. I felt unworthy. I took my seat and knelt, praying, thanking God for this enormous gift. Communion took a while longer, and then the mass was wrapped up and we were taken to the big breakfast served for the communicants. It was as expected, hot chocolate with delicious sweet buns and butter, cookies, and other delicacies. I got my fill.

I had anticipated First Holy Communion to change my life, but it did not. Life went back to the ordinary. I had to live just like before. And although I was a little more reverent in my prayers, at least for a while, nothing was different. I began to wonder whether anything had really happened.

Chapter Thirty-Four

Summers at the Beach

Summers at the beach became an institution in our family beginning when I was four years old. It was an escape from the unbearable heat of July and August. This was a time when air conditioning did not exist. As soon as classes had ended for Nena in June, we got into the jeep we had bought when father acquired the farm in Ceballos, and we traveled to the shore. Generally, Ignacito did not accompany us, except for short periods of time. He stayed at the farm and, being a young man, had plans of his own. The troop that went to the beach was composed of my sister Nena, our parents, and I. The whole family loved it. Even the road trip was an adventure. We would send some of the luggage ahead of time, but the family drove in our jeep so that we could have it at the beach. Usually father and Nena would take turns driving, so it took one or two days to get here, depending on where we were going. We would stay in hotels on our way, something that could also be enjoyable. The cook, a maid, and perhaps an errand boy would join us later, traveling by bus.

At first, we went to places on the north shore of Camagüey or Las Villas provinces. These were closer to Ceballos and made it easy for father to go back home and check how things were going in his absence. But mother was attracted to Havana—she detested the provinces and wanted to be close to the city so she could go shopping and visit friends and family. Also, the accommodations available in these places were not to father's liking. He required good food cooked as he liked, for example. The coup de grâce was that the last time the family tried to go to a beach on the provinces was a disaster, and made us finally decide in favor of beaches closer to Havana.

Father had found out that the family of one of his friends who had died suddenly had settled on the shore of Caibarién, a presumably picturesque town on Cuba's northern shore. The widow had bought a large house and had made it into a kind of hotel that provided full pensions. Father reserved rooms for our family for two months. When we got there, however, the first impression was negative. The place was supposed to be quaint and attractive, but it was nothing like that. Things started to fall apart immediately.

Proper renovations had not been done on the house, which was old and smelled of humidity and mold, as wooden houses by the sea tend to do. It was a two-story monstrosity furnished with heavy, dark mahogany pieces, some no doubt valuable but belonging to a different era. The rooms did not have enough windows, but even those that did covered them with frilly curtains of various patterns that impeded the light from coming in. They felt like caverns and the entire structure resembled the kind of Victorian mansion associated with horror films. I was small and the place struck fear in me. Were there ghosts? Did monsters lurk in corners, under beds, behind locked doors? Mother hated it from the moment she laid her eyes on it. She generally hated anything that was old, preferring the new and avant-garde. She also liked light and simplicity, and the Victorian and Rococo styles favored so frequently by the Cuban bourgeoisie were anathema to her.

After our luggage had been brought in, we went outside to check the beach, reputed for its sand, but that turned out to be another disappointment. This area of Cuba's north shore is peppered with keys, sand bars, and small islands. It is pretty, except that the sea is often enclosed and has no movement, there is no sound of the breaking of the waves, a rhythm that is so dear to those of us who love the ocean. The whole area gave a sense of decay and stagnation, and the water did not look particularly clean. A couple of dead fish lay on the sand, and algae and garbage were not far away. How were we supposed to play in the ocean without waves and in a place that looked like this? Nena and I were sorely disappointed, and mother was alarmed.

To top it all, dinner was not just a disappointment, but a disaster. The food was served improperly, piled up on serving dishes without the least attempt at making the meal appealing. The rice was sticky, the meat tough, and the vegetables overcooked. There was no fresh green salad. And the dessert was a flan full of holes that tasted like raw eggs. We ate in silence and then retired to our rooms. Mother, as usual, was the first to say that the lodgings were inadequate. I was too small to have an opinion or know what to say, but Nena chimed in, complaining about the beach. Father could not disagree after the meal he had been served, although it had been his idea to come here. To make matters worse, during the night a crab tried to get onto Nena's bed and scared her out of her wits. She first heard scratching sounds coming from the back of the bed. She got up and went to tell mother, but mother told her to join me in bed and leave the matter alone. Not happy with that, Nena called the person in charge of the inn who came and discovered the crab.

Each of us had a particular complaint. But how to tell these people that we were leaving? A commitment for the entire summer had been made, and it would be difficult for them to get guests to replace us at this late date. Moreover, they were supposed to be friends and to be in financial difficulties! We should have followed one of father's favorite rules: Never do business with friends!

It was a terrible bind, but we all agreed we could not stay. Father would go downstairs and tell the owner that we were leaving. I never found out how he managed it or what excuse he gave. I am sure he paid the woman a good portion of what he had arranged to pay for the summer, maybe the whole of it, but all the same the deed was not a pleasant one. Rejection is never pleasant and for these people it was particularly significant because they had placed their hopes on this venture. Our departure was a bad omen for the future. Next morning everybody was very quiet at breakfast, after which our bags were loaded on the jeep and we left.

Happy to leave, we now faced a new problem, for we had no reservations anywhere else. Imagine trying to find a place to rent on some beach we had not decided on at the height of the summer season! Still, we were lucky. We drove to a beach all the way west of Havana, Santa Fe, and there we fortunately found a house for rent that was adequate. It was not on the water and the beach was rocky, rather than sandy, but the house was only a short walk to the ocean and the ocean was active, the water clear, and the rocks full of shells which I would spend hours collecting throughout the summer. The house, although too small, was modern and cheerful. For me it was a wonderful place, and the rest of the family adapted to the new circumstances.

Life on the ocean was special. We had a well-set routine. My parents would be the first to get up and go swimming at seven in the morning. Both of them had very fair skin and neither of them tanned. Father would get red like a lobster, and mother got blotches anywhere exposed to the sun for a prolonged period of time. This is why they swam only very early or very late in the day, when the sun was weak. He wore a hat because he was bald and she wore a hat to shade her face, in addition to a scarf and a blouse. Both wore dark glasses. This was not my idea of a swimming outfit; they looked like different versions of the Invisible Man. Nor did Nena and I like the cold water and weak surf in the morning or late afternoon.

After my parents came back from the swim—they never stayed longer than half an hour—we had breakfast and then Nena and I went to the beach. By this time there were other people there and we played and talked for a couple of hours before getting into the water. Swimming before two hours had passed from a meal was strictly forbidden because of the belief that it might cause cramps and thus drowning. At around one o'clock, we went back home, washed off the salt in a shower, and had lunch. Games or visits to friends followed lunch. Then, at four o'clock, it was time for the second swim, which took us up to dinner time. After dinner we walked the beach to watch the sunset. Then perhaps a game of cards while listening to the radio and to bed. This routine repeated itself every day, except that some days we explored other beaches, deserted places with clear waters, full of turtles and crabs. Often, we fished for crabs on the piers of a small bay, and other times we snorkeled, although I don't remember having had masks with respirators. We just held our breath while we looked down.

Frequently, we invited friends who were also staying on one of the beaches in the area to go places, or visit and dine with us. On weekends, family and friends from Havana would come. *Arroz con pollo* was de rigueur. Beach life was a relaxed, wonderful existence. Nena drove the jeep everywhere, becoming known throughout the area as "*la rubia del jeepi*" (the blonde of the jeep). Her hair became bleached with the salty water and the sun, turning almost white, as mother's hair had been when she was a child.

The summers at the beach were something special for us, and mother, Nena, and I longed to have a permanent place on the beach to which we could go not just during the summer, but throughout the year. That dream was never completely fulfilled.

Chapter Thirty-Five

Yearly Audit and Crocodile Tears

One of father's yearly rituals was the audit of the family expenses. In preparation for this event, he kept a detailed account on a ledger of all expenditures that went beyond the allowance he gave mother to manage the household. The allowance was generous, because father wanted a well-set table and a well-dressed family so, as much as he disliked spending money, he was resigned to these expenses; these were priorities for him, and he understood that both required funds. The servants were paid separately, insurance was also separate, and he took care of his own expenses, including his clothing. Also left out were car costs, medical and vacation expenses, furniture replacement, and other larger items. Furniture, however, could become a sore point because mother insisted on having the house furnished according to the latest trend. She couldn't stand old things because, she claimed, they depressed her. We lived in a constant process of furniture change; nothing lasted for more than a couple of years.

She also wanted to be *au currant* concerning the latest appliances, one of the things that father refused to pay for because he thought they were unnecessary. Why did we need a gas stove when coal worked as well as gas, it was cheaper, and the cook did not care whether she cooked with coal or gas? In his mind, there was no reason to spend money on a gas stove. He complained bitterly about what he considered to be a waste, and often refused to pay for what he regarded as extravagances. In those cases, mother had to pay for the purchases from savings she made in her household allowance if she wanted the object bad enough. And she did, often engaging in creative accounting practices behind his back. Fortunately for him, credit cards had not been invented yet. I can only surmise what life would have been like if mother had access to a credit card with a generous limit!

I remember well one particular purchase against which father was dead set. This was our first TV. Television had come to Havana in the early fifties, and when we moved there in 1954 all of us except father wanted a TV. A good set cost nearly four hundred pesos, which was no small change and therefore should be taken care of by the general budget. But father was very much opposed, first because of the price and, second, because he thought the TV programs were awful. He certainly was right concerning the second point, and so he drew a line in the sand and said he would not contribute a penny toward that purchase. Well, of course, mother went ahead and bought a set, and of course he refused to pay or watch it. But, as the sly dog he was, father sat on a chair in the living room with a view of the TV while he kept an open book on his lap in case any one of us would accuse him of watching television!

Mother received a personal allowance, which father often complained was too generous. The non-working children—the only working issue was Ignacito—also got allowances. Since Ignacito worked in the orchard, he received a salary and his household expenses were not deducted from it. He also took care of his clothes, which, because he resembled the older Ignacio in this respect, involved considerable expense. Nena got an allowance and so did I. With me, father negotiated special amounts that, beginning in fifth grade, depended on the quality of my school performance. I remember when I first got a twenty pesos-bill. It was a lot of money for a kid, considering that some middle class families paid a cook and maid half that amount per month. I felt rich! I used it all to buy comic books, to which I had become addicted and of which in time I had a large collection. They cost between 25 and 50 cents each, depending on the number of pages.

What was covered and not covered by the general household allowance in particular was supposed to be very clear, but in fact the demarcating lines were not very strict, and they were a constant source of friction. Mother kept asking for more money, and so were we. Father resisted many of our requests, but gave-in to others. Negotiating with him about money was a permanent condition, particularly for mother whose view was that the purpose of money was to spend it. She often said, "Coins are made to roll and paper is meant to fly." She complained regularly about the size of our allowances. In her case, it certainly was insufficient for what she considered her needs. As far back as I can remember, she liked to dress elegantly, something father appreciated, and she also dressed me fabulously. I recall mother going to El Encanto in Havana, then under the influence of Christian Dior, and drop 80 pesos for a dress for herself, and 40 pesos for a pair of pants for me, without a second thought. I had linen shirts that cost 20 pesos. Shoes and purses especially were obsessions for mother. She did not at any time keep large numbers of shoes or purses, but she had the best and the latest one could find in

Cuba. She always said that shoes and a purse were the secret of dressing well in a woman.

One area on which she saved was jewelry—she practically wore none. She considered most jewelry vulgar. Apart from the wedding band and the emerald ring I mentioned before, the only bauble she wore was a silver bangle. Her ears had been pierced as a child, as was customary at the time, but because she never wore earrings, the piercings had closed. I saw her wearing earrings only once—a moment immortalized in a photo, which she did not like precisely because she was wearing earrings.

The lack of interest in jewelry, however, did not make finances easier for mother. Expenses were always too high in father's estimation. One way in which he tried to keep a handle on what he deemed to be her extravagances was by going through a yearly auditing process. At the beginning of every fiscal year, he would open the leger in which he had kept a minute record of the expenses for the previous year, written in his uniquely beautiful hand. These were accounting books, long and narrow, with places for dates, figures, and descriptions of items. Only expenses that were not part of our personal allowances were put down, although father also noted the overall amounts of the allowances.

He would carefully pour over his annotations on the ledger and then called mother for particular explanations and justifications. "Niña, what is this expense here? Why did you buy that chair? Was that set of glasses really necessary?" And then he would complain: "This cannot go on. We have spent thousands of pesos on items that are utterly unnecessary." And on and on he went. Mother did not sit with him throughout the process. She stayed at a distance, fluttering around like a butterfly looking for a place to rest, busy, avoiding questions, being vague. He was merciless.

Eventually the process came to a head, always in the same way. It was a ritual that we were accustomed to. At some point, in response to some comment father made, mother would come in, sit down next to him, and burst into tears. This was more than he could tolerate. He was miserable, torn between what he considered necessary and what he could not tolerate emotionally. He would try to calm her down, but she would not allow him this triumph. To save face, he would, weakly and despondently, try to get some answers from her, a small concession if you will, but she was uncompromising; until he closed the accounting book, she was inconsolable.

Father didn't gain anything by this process. He certainly didn't change mother's habits or her view about money. I am sure he must have known it, so why did he do it, year after year? One possibility is that it made him aware of the need or desirability for saving in other areas that were more under his control, such as the cars we had or the places where we lived. But the reason may have been deeper than this. One possibility I surmised was just that he needed to go through a process that established a sense of financial order in his life. It did not change anything, but at least it did succeed in making him aware of where the money was going, even though he could not control its destination. Another was that the lean years after his father's death had marked him for life. This limited control over family finances gave him a hope that what he and our family would be spared the unpleasantness he and his family had suffered.

And mother? Well, tears have always been a way for women to get their way in societies in which they are at the mercy of men. An appeal to a man's feelings of compassion has frequently been effective, and mother was not shy about using whatever weapons she had at her disposal to get what she thought she needed or wanted. She allowed father to have his game of auditing, but in the end, her tears, whether of crocodile or not, always triumphed.

Chapter Thirty-Six

Lean Years

Things, in fact, had been going well for our family in the thirties and forties. In spite of the financial difficulties that both the paternal and maternal sides of the family had to endure before then. Father had been extremely successful and had accumulated a respectable fortune. And we had not suffered death or sickness for a number of years. Then, the first setback took place at the end of 1949, when father had a heart attack. I recall quite well the anxiety I felt when I saw father crippled by pain. One of the most terrifying things that a child can experience is the danger of losing a father. Although a mother is usually loved more than a father, in a Cuban family the father is traditionally regarded as the support and foundation of the family. He is a pillar of strength on which everything depends. And to see a father in serious peril is to experience an abyss of insecurity. Everything seems to be in danger of crumbling and the future looks uncertain. This is what I felt when father had his first heart attack. I was six years old.

I remember mother's agitation. Ignacito jumping in the jeep and driving like a madman. Father, lying in bed, speaking very little. The doctor's arrival after what appeared to be an eternity. The examination, with everyone in the room, looking anxiously at what was happening. The doctor's diagnosis was that the problem was father's heart. To our relief, he said that it looked as if father was going to be all right. He prescribed some medications and told father to continue bed rest for a few days, after which he should travel to Havana for a more thorough examination by a specialist.

Father seemed to recover and, as prescribed by the doctor, left for Havana with mother. There, he was thoroughly examined by a top cardiologist, Ramón Aixalá. I stayed in Ceballos, with Ignacito and aunt Maruca. Nena was in school and missed most of the agony we were experiencing. She was kept from learning the details about what had actually happened. Nena believed that father had only experienced a collapse due to exhaustion.

Father's heart attack was the first of a series of events that were devastating. The death of grandmother Dubié, whom we all loved dearly, followed a few months later in 1950. She was eighty at the time and had been in good health, so her death was unexpected. That same year aunt Maruca was burned very badly, although she miraculously survived. Next came a serious case of food poisoning that affected all of us, but to different degrees. Some of us were very sick for at least two weeks and had resulting symptoms for years afterwards. The poison came from a fish father had bought. It had been sick with *ciguatera*, a disease that comes from fish eating certain sea plants that grow in coral reefs and become contaminated. The fish gets sick and then passes on the disease to those who eat it. Years later, I read in the United States that the effects of *ciguatera* can last as many as twenty years after the initial poisoning occurs and includes both stomach and neurological problems. It is often misdiagnosed as multiple sclerosis, and flare-ups of the disease can be triggered by a variety of causes. Perhaps *ciguatera* was the cause for a serious case of eczema I suffered for several months that year. It affected my left foot and the place between my upper lip and my nose. It started with painful blisters and spread rapidly. Eventually I was unable to wear a shoe on the affected foot. Everything was tried in Ciego de Ávila but nothing worked. It was only after we consulted a specialist in Havana who put me on a strict diet, and prescribed calcium and a topical cream for the affected area, that the condition began to improve. This was bad enough, but the worst was yet to come.

The following year, in 1952, just before father bought the sugar plantation after selling the orchard in Ceballos, we were living at the beach when aunt Carmen died of cirrhosis of the liver after a long and painful agony. Nine days after her death, we had the news about Ignacito's fatal accident. This raised the stakes to a dimension that was almost unbearable for us, particularly for mother.

A few months later, in 1953, uncle Jaime died of a ruptured aorta. He had just awakened in the morning and was sitting on the side of the bed getting ready to get up, when he fell back vomiting blood. When the doctor arrived, he was already dead, having bled to death. Both he and grandmother had been staying at aunt Maruca's home in Majagua. According to Maruca, the scene was harrowing, with blood everywhere and grandmother, splattered with blood, holding Jaime in her arms, and crying hysterically.

Next, after a brief lull, our sugar plantation burned down in 1955, causing considerable damage to our finances. And less than two years later, in 1957, father died of a heart attack. I was fourteen, Nena was twenty-six, and mother was fifty-one. We had reached a point where we feared thinking about the future. What more could be in store for us? Little did we know that after a short reprieve, Castro's Revolution was going to bring a different sort of chaos into our lives, leading us into a state of need and depravation, and separating us from each other for years. But that did not occur during the seven years of disease, death, and pain; the Revolution happened one year and eight months after father's death, which closed what I have called the lean years. The damage that the Revolution inflicted on us was nowhere near what we had suffered before, nonetheless its financial impact was devastating, and the emotional price we had to pay was unbearable. But the lean years had prepared us for practically anything, strengthening our will and resolve to survive.

Chapter Thirty-Seven

Written in the Stars

Ignacito's tragic destiny seems to have been written in the stars, for it is not clear that any of the factors that brought it about depended on any one in particular. His small bouts of drinking were occasions for argument and quarrels with father, who regarded his behavior as intolerable, a source of great grief to him and to all of us because father's dissatisfaction spilled over into a general malaise that infected the entire family. To complicate matters, Ignacito also had a weakness for women that he had inherited from our maternal grandfather and which was fueled by the overcharged sexuality of Cuban culture. He was handsome, came from a good family with resources, and obviously had a strong libido. Years after his death, I found a friend of his who told me that, by age sixteen, Ignacito had gone through many women, married or unmarried, in the little town of five thousand people where we were born and he had lived until he was seventeen. These affairs gave rise to confrontations and scandals. While we were living at the orchard in Ceballos, he took up with the bailiff's wife—a woman much older than he, with children, but obviously still young and restless. Ignacito was just a teenager! When the bailiff discovered the affair, there were threats, guns were pulled out, and angry encounters ensued. The matter could have ended in tragedy had father not settled it quickly by letting the bailiff go with a generous compensation. It was a miserable affair, father was furious, and mother was afraid and sad.

The scandal with the bailiff's wife was so traumatic for our family that Ignacito felt he had to leave home. He got a job as a salesman in Havana, and was thinking of emigrating to the United States. Things would have turned out quite different, not just for him, but for the family as a whole, had he done that. But a rapprochement was negotiated by father's family, and Ignacito came back to Ceballos. The experience of being away from home had been good for him. Indeed, he had changed in many ways, becoming more mature and deliberate about his actions, and father began to give him increasing responsibility in managing the sugarcane plantation.

Father's heart attack made clear that he had to slow down, and it made sense for Ignacito to fill the vacuum. After the farm in Ceballos was sold and the sugarcane plantation was bought, father put Ignacito in charge of the everyday management. We moved to the beach near Havana, with plans of staying there for a while before moving permanently to the city. Father traveled to the plantation only once a month to check on things.

In spite of the changes, however, father still hesitated in allowing my brother to have a car; he was afraid that Ignacito would kill himself in an accident. Father wanted him to get married first, settle down, and show that his new ways were not a mere passing phase, that he had stopped being a wild teen and was now a sensible man. And there were signs that he was on his way. Ignacito had become serious with his latest girlfriend, Nieves, and it looked like they might become engaged in the not too distant future. Unfortunately, fate was not to be thwarted.

On a holiday, the workers at the plantation wanted to go into town, and Ignacito offered to take them on one of the plantation trucks. It had been raining, the dirt road was bad, and my brother had a very heavy foot. Driving to town, the truck hit a stone and was about to turn over on the driver's side when Ignacito opened the door, and jumped out. The truck fell on him. Ignacito stayed alive only for a few minutes. His chest had been crushed. His last words were "Call father." No one else suffered any injuries in the accident, not even minor ones, and there were rumors that someone had pushed him out of the truck. He was twenty-two years old.

Was my brother marked from birth for the fate that awaited him? The Greeks believed that our destiny is in the hands of the gods, who manipulate human existence capriciously, at their whims, for diversion and pleasure. No one takes this view seriously today, but some might argue that this would be as good an explanation of my brother's fate as any other, his death was that meaningless.

Chapter Thirty-Eight

A Night to Forget

We all loved the beach. The summer father sold the orchard in Ceballos he decided that the best thing for us would be to move to the beach near Havana where we had been vacationing recently. It had the advantage that we had family in the capital, and it was always fun to visit them and to enjoy other amenities the city provided. East of Havana a series of beaches extend for miles. Santa María del Mar, Celimar, Boca Ciega, Guanabo, La Veneciana, and others. Some of them are rocky, but others have fine white sand.

I was enrolled in third grade at a school which was part of the *Escuelas Pías* run by Piarist Fathers in Guanabacoa, a city closer to the beach than Havana. The grueling trip to and from school every day was long and painful. The tunnel that crossed the entrance of Havana bay had not yet been constructed, so in order to get to the beach it was necessary to go all around the very large bay, through small streets and considerable traffic. Guanabacoa was one of the towns that one had to go through. For anyone coming from the beaches, it was the closest town where one could find an acceptable private school.

I did not adapt very well to the school. All I remember about it was being bored to death throughout the day, food that I could hardly tolerate, and the boy who sat next to me in class who would not talk of anything but sex. About the food, one particular dish stays with me to this day: *arroz con camarones* (rice with shrimp). It sounds sophisticated and yummy, but it was disgusting. I could smell it from far away on the days it was served, always on Fridays for lunch, and it stank because, instead of fresh *camarones,* they used dried up ones that develop an awful taste and smell. School was an overall unpleasant experience. The homework was exhausting, and I needed help from my parents and Nena in order to complete it.

The trip to school every day took so long that I had to get up at 5:00 a.m. to take the school bus at 6:00 a.m. It took that long because the bus picked up kids from all the beaches before it got to the city of Guanabacoa. School began at 8:30 a.m., which meant that I spent at least two-hours every morning going to school and two-hours coming back home. Classes ended at 4:00 p.m., and I arrived at home after 6:00 p.m. hungry and exhausted from the long day and trip, and frustrated because there was another day ahead. Then, I had to take a shower, eat, work on homework, and go to bed.

All this was made worse because I was not doing well in school. I misbehaved by talking in class while teachers were speaking. As punishment I was assigned to write hundreds of lines (*No hablaré más en clase.*), which eventually, because I was never on time for turning them in, reached into the thousands. I figured some shortcuts that helped. For example, I put a very long "No" on the left side of every page so that I would have to write only one "no" per page.

Still, the rewards of living at the beach compensated for school inconveniences. I loved it and on weekends we could still swim, the water continued to be warm and inviting well into December. The house we rented was not on the water. We had not been able to find an acceptable beach front property to rent. Available waterfront properties were too close to the water and in areas that were commercial. My parents liked the natural landscape, away from the bustle of public beaches. It was a four-bedroom house on a second floor, with the garage and a service bedroom on the first floor and a terrace above, from which we could see the ocean and the sunset. Watching the sunset at the beach or on the terrace was a daily ritual that we all enjoyed. The heat of the day had passed and soft ocean breezes caressed us into a state of pleasant reverie. Father smoked a cigar, while mother and Nena chit-chatted. I mostly stayed quiet, taking in the reds and purples, the oranges and blues, of the setting sun. The entire family loved the house and its location and the year promised to be especially pleasurable. Father had recovered well from the heart attack he had suffered. Ignacito was taking care of the sugarcane plantation in the country and he could stay with us most of the time. What could go wrong? Destiny had other plans. This idyllic situation came to a halt when Ignacito was killed and we had to hurry back to Ciego de Ávila.

On March 2, 1952, a Sunday, father had put a deposit on a corner house next to the one in which we had been living since the summer, a much larger and comfortable place. It was nine o'clock in the evening. We had finished dinner and were sitting in the living room. I was doing some homework and Nena was helping me. Father was reading the newspaper. And mother was talking to María, the cook, in the kitchen. The phone rang and father picked it up. I heard a tone of concern in father's voice. *"Si . . . ¿un accidente? ¿Como está? ¿Puedo hablar con el medico? Ya veo. ¿En Ciego de Ávila o en el Central? ¿En que clínica?"* Mother came in as father hung up. Nena and I were now paying full attention. He explained. There had been an accident at the plantation and Ignacito was seriously hurt. She had more questions than he could answer. We had to leave for the country immediately. The important thing was to pack and leave as soon as possible. But what to pack? How long should we plan for? Do we need to take something for Ignacito? Will he need medications? Clothing?

Mother set out frantically to pack everything she thought we would need. Nena took care of herself and me. María Picadillo helped, preparing some sandwiches and coffee for the trip. We would be traveling by night and it was not clear we would find places to buy food on the way. But who was thinking about food, or clothes? The thoughts were on Ignacito. We knew nothing and the image of him, hurt, perhaps unconscious, played tricks on our imaginations. Each of us working out superficial details in an effort to change reality and have him back to us as he had been.

Transportation posed a problem. We did not have our car with us, just the jeep. Nor did we have a driver who could take us—our chauffeur had gone back to Ciego the Ávila. It was winter and so the beaches had mostly shut down. Summer tourists had left and the number of businesses, including transportation services, had ceased to operate. It took a great deal of effort to find a limousine with a driver who could take us to Ciego de Ávila. We left at midnight.

The limousine was a large affair, and for a child like me it looked foreboding—more like a hearse than a car—but it did accommodate all of us. Mother sat on the back seat and I laid across it, resting my head on her lap. Father and Nena sat on the middle seat. María, the cook, who had come to the beach with us, stayed at the house to wait for our instructions. I slept on and off. Every time I woke-up I heard mother's prayers, the anxiety and pain, the hope. Promises, if everything would be all right. . . . There were no tears, just a stream of bitter anguish. Nena trying to contain her emotions. This was her brother, her pal for over twenty years. She consoled herself by hugging me. Father keeping a hermetic silence. What was going on inside his head? Was he thinking about his conflicted relationship with Ignacito, about the disagreements and quarrels they had? Was he resenting not having been more tolerant or strict? Was there guilt, regret, sorrow?

We arrived at Ciego de Ávila around ten in the morning. The main highway, Carretera Central, runs through the town. I did not know where we were headed in the town, but father must have known because we stopped in front of the main private clinic in Ciego de Ávila, Clínica Olazábal. But my brother's body had already been taken across the street to a funeral home. Father understood right away and I clearly remember him saying: "The people are already here." Yes, the people who had come to pay their respects. I will never forget those words

Chapter 38

    The funeral home belonged to one of Ignacito's friends, a young man like himself. I have always wondered whether father already knew that Ignacito was dead and kept the secret for mother's sake. Whether he had been told the truth in that terrible telephone conversation and kept it to himself to spare the rest of all. Why had he not asked whether Ignacito could be flown to Havana to receive proper care? Yes, he must have known, although I never had the courage to ask him.

    I remember only moments, vague snap-shots of the cataclysm that followed. Mother's controlled cry of pain, her desperation. Nena holding my hand. Father opening the door of the limo. The crossing of the street, oblivious to the traffic. People everywhere. Bearing, pressing on us, offering words of comfort, the usual banalities. "I am so sorry." "He was so young." "You must pray." "It's God's will." Mother's tears, her distraught sorrow. Crossing another street. I do not quite know how we got to the funeral home, but I remember entering a room packed with people, overflowing, stifling. The smell of sweat and the heat of bodies. People sitting all around. In the middle of the room a very large casket with an open lid surrounded by people standing. Too high up for me to look into it. Mother's wailing. "Oh, my child, my sweetheart! Oh, the light of my life, my love!" People crying around us. Mother leaning over the casket, someone holding me up so I could see. My brother laying there. Eyes closed, with a fixed, expressionless countenance. Some cotton on the side of his face, traces of blood. The mother caressing the bruised face of the son, and kissing it. The pain. My own tears, the confusion. Leaning inside the casket and kissing him. Cold. Cold. Cold. Father serious, as I had never seen him, a marble statue with clenched jaws to prevent desperation. Acknowledging people. Holding up. Impeccably dressed. The face of death. Is there a proper way to describe it accurately? The difference between death and life. Inert. Rigid. Like stone. What is the difference? A mystery. How can something alive die? From one moment to the next. In a second. And yet an abyss between the two. There is no death without life, and no life without death. I did not understand. Was this Ignacito? Was this the brother that loved me, the brother that I loved? What was in the coffin? What was it that I had kissed? Where was the brother I knew and loved? Years later, when my young daughter, Clarisa, had gone home to find a dead gerbil and called me on the phone to ask me what it was, I told her that it was dead. She responded in a plaintive voice, "But he is so hard!" Yes, hard and cold. That is death. Life is soft and warm. The moment she said it my thoughts went back to that moment of horror in Ciego de Ávila. Cursed town, to which our pain was forever joined.

    I don't remember how or when we left the funeral home. I was placed in someone's charge. We were entering grandmother's house. Aunt Maruca was always there for us in moments of crisis. And this time also *Abuelita Belé*, and uncle Jaime in the background, void of the usual irony and sarcasm. The suffering was excruciating, unbearable. Hugs. Kisses. More tears. Mother going to the bedroom and throwing herself on the bed in utter desperation. "How can I live now?" Grandmother remembering her ordeal with her own son, José María, also lost in the prime of life. Maruca managing, comforting, helping others, forgetting her own suffering to palliate that of others. She was Ignacito's godmother. I, lost among them, not knowing what to do or where to turn. Eventually, mother coming to me and holding me tightly, consoling herself consoling me.

Ciego de Ávila is an ugly little town. Even the parish church on the main square is a tasteless building without style or grace. There are only two structures in the town that are worthy of note. One is the Colegio Champagnat run by the Marist Brothers, where I went to school; the other is the Centro Asturiano. The school is a neo-classic building, with granite floors and large windows. The style of the Centro is eclectic, with gracious pillars and attached columns, generous balconies and fine arched doors on the second floor. It is located on the main square, at the corner of Calles Independencia and Máximo Gómez. It was there, on the second floor, that my brother's wake took place. Since then it became unforgettable. One enters the building through a large door that opens onto a grand staircase that goes up half way and then branches out into two other stairs on opposite sides before it reaches the second floor.

The provisional casket in which Ignacito's body had initially been placed had large containers on the sides filled with ice to preserve the body. Now the body had been moved to the casket in which it was going to be buried. Made of bronze, with a magnificent cross on the lid, it was open and had been placed at the top of the stairs; it was the first thing one saw when coming up. Behind it a red velvet curtain, with gold trim and tassels, served as a backdrop. A red rug underneath it and four large lighted candelabra guarding it. A place to kneel and pray had been provided at the foot of the casket so that people could do so if they wished.

The room extended all the way to the front and sides of the building, but the large doors to the balconies that overlooked the main plaza were closed. Wreaths and other flower arrangements had been placed on the opposite sides, and there was a smaller room on one side of the staircase where our family gathered. Chairs were placed all around the entire floor to accommodate family and friends. What seemed to me an endless line of visitors came to express their condolence. Every time a friend or even an acquaintance arrived, the wound of the tragedy would be reopened, new tears would be shed, and consoling but meaningless words would be spoken.

Ignacito's body was kept there until the following morning. I was taken to grandmother's house for the night, but early the next day everyone was back at the Centro Asturiano for the trip to the church where a solemn funeral Mass was to take place, and from there to the cemetery for burial. The casket was taken down to the first floor with difficulty because of its heavy weight. Pallbearers carried it down the stairs and placed it in the hearse to be driven first to the church and then to the cemetery. At the church our family sat in the first pew, the coffin in front of the main altar down a few steps. The ceremony was long and the music soothing. When it ended, we followed the coffin until it was loaded onto the hearse for the trip to the cemetery. Then the procession began.

The trip to the cemetery was slow and deliberate. A band playing funeral music, on foot. The hearse crawling slowly. Father and the adult males, on foot, behind the hearse. Mother, sister, and I in the back of the limousine, and María Picadillo sitting on the front seat, by the driver. María had arrived and was helping in the commotion, keeping us fed and properly dressed. Aunt Maruca did not go to the cemetery, she was still recovering from the effects of the flames that had nearly killed her, and grandmother was too distraught to come with us. As usual, she needed more attention than we could give. Then other cars. All of this followed by five trucks full of flowers, wreaths with purple satin bands and golden legends—*"Para mi querido Ignacito, de su amigo . . .,"* *"Con amor de su abuela . . .,"* *"Te queremos, familia Suárez . . ."*.

At an appropriate fork in the road, the funeral procession stopped, and a friend of my brother's mounted a platform to give the eulogy. I could not hear what he said. Then again, after the eulogy was concluded and at a slow pace, the procession proceeded to the burial vault. The final stop. The casket was taken by the pallbearers to the vault where it was to be interred. We gathered around the casket, and then it was opened again for the final farewell. Mother was inconsolable. The last kiss. The last time she would hold Ignacito's face in her hands. I was propped up so I could also kiss the body one last time. Since then, I have had to kiss two other corpses, father's and mother's, and it has not been easy. Then the lid was closed, and the casket was lowered slowly, by hand, into the tomb. The impact of this moment cannot be described properly, only experienced. This is finality. My brother, with whom I had played and laughed. My brother, who had given me my horse, and had enjoyed my tricks. My brother, never to be seen again, never to be touched, never to be kissed, never to be hugged.

I don't remember what happened afterwards. But two years later mother and sister had the casket opened so that Ignacito's remains could be placed in an ossuary, as was the custom. This was very hard on mother, but she would not hear of anybody else doing it. His bones, she told me, were completely clean. Nena tells me that she gathered them, with tears in her eyes, and placed them in their new resting place, after having kissed them.

The summer after the accident, instead of renting a house, we lodged at the Hotel Miramar in Guanabo. Mother did not have the fortitude to manage the household, even with the help of a cook and a maid. In the hotel, of course, we ate in the dining room, and everything was taken care of by the hotel staff. The place was comfortable, located about five blocks from the beach, and had a very good view of the ocean from the upper floors. It was full of people who stayed for the entire summer, so my sister and I made many friends, and were never bored. In spite of our family's grief, it was as good a summer as it was possible to have under the circumstances.

The following year, the family decided to rent a house near the hotel so we could enjoy the company of the friends we had made the previous summer, and this worked out well. But the year, after we permanently moved to Havana and this disrupted our summer plans for the first time in several years.

Chapter Thirty-Nine

The Refuge of Faith

After Ignacito's fatal accident, mother was distraught, dwelling in a foreign land of desolation and despair. Can anyone who is not a mother understand the sorrow of losing a son at the height of his youth? Can anyone realize her regrets from not having done so many things she now imagined she should have done? Could she do anything to make up for missed opportunities to kiss and hug him? To please him? To make his life better? How to counter the regret of having been too strict and harsh on some occasions, of not making his life more pleasurable and rewarding?

There is no consolation for a mother who has lost a son. For a while, as many families who experience similar losses do, mother tried to build a memorial to my brother, to keep him alive somehow and to atone for past guilt. Ignacito's tomb became a place to embellish, a garden of flowers and memorabilia to connect with him, to visit and remember him, to recall happy times. But in the end this did not satisfy her. The garden was empty, without its main host. It dried out. The flowers withered. The tomb silent. The marble white with gray strains, the granite gray. Solid, impersonal. There was no movement, no play, no laughter, no response. The benches remained cold, colorless, and lifeless. Visiting Ignacito's memorial did not answer the many questions that his death had raised for mother.

Why had he died, so young, full of life and with a generous heart? Was there any explanation? Could there be a reason for his premature demise and her desolation? Where could she find relief? The Catholicism that she knew offered little consolation. Yes, there were masses for his soul, with all the magnificent pomp and beauty of centuries-old liturgy. Otherworldly Gregorian chanting momentarily helped assuage her grief. Prayers were said for his soul. Priests told her what they are used to saying, but what they said had no connection to my brother. They spoke in generalities, empty formulas that applied to everyone, universally, and not to *her* son. She needed more: she needed to know why *he* had suffered this unintelligible fate and to understand the source of her own destiny and sorrow. And she needed a credible reference to the future. She tried to wrap herself in her pain and the signs of grief, ready for a life devoted to death, but this did not help her either.

Part of the routine that follows tragedies, such as Ignacito's death, is a process in which the living try to connect to everything that remains of the deceased. Even scraps of what they did or owned become important links that help with the grief. They allow the bereaved to find solace, to understand the dead, to make them alive in some sense, bringing them back into their desolate existence, talking to them, connecting with them through memories and what they left behind. A process of reconstruction slowly takes place in which the lives of the dead are put back together and become the source of meditation and solace.

Mother also did it. She went through Ignacito's things—his fashionable suits and ties, his fancy shoes, among which was the pair I had ruined by painting them all black, and from which he had not been able to part, preserving a memento of mirth caused by his nutty but beloved little brother. The tailored shirts, embroidered handkerchiefs, the discreet tie clips, the shaving cream and the pomade for his hair, the clippers he used to trim his nails, his undergarments, his work clothes, some still unwashed, preserving the smell of his sweat. Men in my family do not wear jewelry, so my brother had none, but in his short life he had accumulated a collection of paraphernalia, some useful and some commemorative of events deserving remembrance. They now became sacred to mother. Letters from his loves and friends. Papers, accounts. Everything he used and collected while alive. Every one of these remnants brought him back and released new tears, but none helped. None explained anything. And none gave a greater understanding of his death. In her search, mother eventually turned to things less physically connected to him, the books he had read, and here it was that she unexpectedly found what she was looking for.

Roaming through bookcases to which she seldom paid any attention before, looking for my brother's school books, she found a Bible from his days at La Progresiva, the school to which father had sent him after he had been taken out of Colegio Mimó. This was a Protestant school, Presbyterian, and there he had been taught the Christian Scriptures. Ignacito's little Bible had passages he had underlined in school. Mother eagerly read them, thinking about their meaning and what Ignacito would have thought in reading them. There she found unexpected solace in the words of Christ, his gentleness and wisdom. She thought these words had been underlined for her. God had anticipated her pain and had seen to it that, through my brother, He would communicate to her and provide contentment and peace. It was a miracle of Providence. Mother did not stop with the underlined texts, she went further and read every page of the Bible, not once, but many times. In it, she discovered a message of comfort and life, while in fact she had thought her future was all about death. She found the promise of life everlasting in Christ. Ignacito was not dead. He could not be dead. He had been a good son in spite of his minor faults. He had been the love of her life, and he would be waiting for her, next to Christ, and thanks to His mercy, in Paradise.

The biblical text has had similar effects on others who have read it, as the example of St. Augustine shows. For mother, just as for him, the sacred words were the key to her survival and salvation. From the moment she discovered and read the biblical scriptures, her life changed. Not that she converted to any particular established version of religion based on the Bible. She converted to the book, the Word she believed to be the Word of God, and until her death, she looked to the book for satisfaction of her spiritual needs.

From her reading of the Bible, she eventually inferred that she should join a spiritual community, with whom she could worship. Christianity was a community, the people of God, it was not an individualist faith. So, she began to search among different Christian denominations for one that resembled more faithfully what she read. She did not considered Catholicism because it was too different from anything she found in the Old or New Testaments. The rejection of idolatry in particular weighed heavily against it in her judgment. Something was wrong with the Catholic interpretation of the biblical message insofar as the Church had distanced itself so much from its scriptural commands. She visited Baptist, Presbyterian, and Lutheran churches, but finally decided to join an Assemblies of God church because of the warmth of its pastor and the joyful quality of the message to which it subscribed. In this church she faithfully remained for many years, becoming a pivotal member of the congregation.

In Cuba, these churches attracted simple people with few financial resources. Because mother had those resources, she was able to do much for the church and its successive ministers. But eventually she became dissatisfied with the radical departure of this Christian denomination from the message of the Old Testament. The more she read the Bible, the more she believed that the regulations of the Old Testament had not been completely superseded. The Bible was God's revelation to humanity and no part of it should be discarded. The biblical regulations about food in particular fit well with the naturalist regime under which mother had been brought up. Eventually she withdrew from the Assemblies of God and joined the Seventh-Day Adventists, who in her judgment were the only Christians that took the Old Testament seriously.

It was not until she had lost her mind due to senility many years later that mother gave up on the strict regulations on food found in the Old Testament. These regulations were an enormous burden to her and to those around her. She developed a legalistic attitude that made her a slave of Old Testament rules, to the point that it was impossible for her to eat outside the home, and it became difficult even to meet her dietary needs in the home. Freedom eventually came, but it came at the cost of her mind.

Mother's conversion relieved her from the unbearable pain that Ignacito's death had caused. At the beginning it was a liberation that gave meaning to her life and made her again a useful member of society. With time, that same religion enslaved her. The fundamentalism and intransigence she eventually developed became a prison from which she could not be freed. Her life focused exclusively in the effort, first, to proselytize so as to bring others to her faith and, second, to satisfy the rules she thought God had stipulated for His community. In the process, she made life very difficult for herself and for those around her. Nothing had meaning for her but the fulfillment of her religious goals. In the end her situation became deplorable. Somewhere on the way, she had lost the proper understanding of the biblical message, a message that, as that of all worthy religious faiths, has to do with human liberation and happiness, but which is so often used to cause slavery and misery.

Chapter Forty

The Consolation of Giving

One of the things compassionate people with means do is to help those who are less fortunate than themselves. Helping takes many forms. There is lending money. Those who have accumulated some capital are constantly beseeched by others for loans which they generously provide. The money is ostensibly borrowed, and therefore is supposed to be returned, but the unspoken understanding is that lent money is lost money. Father was regularly pestered by acquaintances and friends asking for loans. He dutifully kept a list of the sums he lent, but the money was never returned while he was living. After he died, we found the list of loans and timidly tried to pry some of the money out of borrowers who appeared to be in fine financial circumstances. The result was not only that we did not get any of it back, but our relations became cold to us, and in some cases picked a quarrel so that they could feel justified in not returning any of the money they owed us. Never mind that some of the borrowed money involved substantial sums; most debts to father were in the thousands of pesos, which at the time was significant.

Another way of helping the needy is in response to occasional requests from the poor that appeal to pity. Father was quite hard about these. His idea was that if you give money to the poor, they often use it for purposes other than buying food and the things they need the most. And there is some reason to what he believed. Father and mother had arguments about this frequently, because mother could not resist helping anyone in need. And when father complained that the money was not being used properly, her answer was that making sure the money was used properly was not her responsibility. She saw her responsibility as responding to a voiced need, how the money was used was someone else's problem.

The worst abuse I know of mother's generosity occurred one time, after father's death, when she had hired a cab to take her from Havana to our sugarcane plantation. Mother was traveling with Nena, and carrying a substantial amount of money to pay the wages of the workers at the plantation. From her talk, the cab driver realized that she had cash with her and that she was vulnerable. So he made his appeal. His sick child needed surgery; his wife had abandoned him; there was no work. The usual con stories. Having gathered that mother was a very pious woman, he threw in some comments about his prayers for divine help.

Mother could not resist the appeal, particularly because she felt that God had brought her to him in order to help. Nothing in her world happened by chance, everything was part of God's Providence. Nena told me that the driver asked mother for the cost of the surgery which turned out to be 1,000 pesos. So, when they arrived at their destination mother took out the cost of the fare and added 1,000 pesos to it. This was a very large sum at the time. Consider that the rent for a recently built one-bedroom apartment in a middle-class neighborhood in Havana was 40 pesos a month! Actually, mother was lucky, she got away with merely a loss of money. She could have had a serious scare if the driver had decided to steal everything she had. Nena was shocked at what mother had done, but had been unable to stop her.

Part of mother's reaction to the death of my brother was a desire to do some good for others, and in Ciego the Ávila that was easy, because there were many beggars. The town was not particularly poor, since it was a center of sugar production and the first town of note in the Camagüey Province when one was driving from Havana. Camagüey's landscape was flat and mostly uninteresting, but rich in agriculture and cattle. Still, beggars were abundant—some sick, some lame, some mad, some marginal, some drunks, some drug addicts, and some crooks. Regardless of their plight or scam, the word spread that there was a lady at Calle Independencia that was generous and asked no questions. The result was an increasing stream of beggars at our doorstep. Everyone got something, but a select few were encouraged to come back. And come back they did at regular days, times, and intervals. Mother kept a mental schedule of appointments for their visits. Some came early in the morning on Mondays, and some came late at night on Wednesdays. There were the ones that always came at lunch time, and others at dinner time. Some came for food, others for money, and still others for clothing or paper or what have you. She kept the particulars of their situation in her head and was prepared for their arrival. She also learned about their lives and circumstances from what they told her and often helped with these when she thought it was called for.

Mother gave the beggars descriptive names to remember who they were. In line with her family custom, their original names would not do. One was called *el cojo* (the lame), another *el loco* (the nut), still another *la señora de las berrugas* (the lady with moles), another *el caballero* (the gentleman), and so on. Many epithets derived from idiosyncratic behavior. The guy who stammered became *el gago*, the woman with a nervous tick *la nerviosa*, and the one who was always in a hurry *la apurada*. Of course, mother did not use these names when they were present, but it was a way of communicating to the rest of us something unique about them. At one point, we counted more than thirty beggars who visited our home every week. When one of them happened to miss an appointment, mother was extremely concerned and tried to determine the cause of the absence by questioning other beggars. It got to a point that it was becoming difficult to have visitors in our home because mother was constantly being interrupted by beggars knocking on our door, for although the maid was in charge of answering, mother insisted on seeing the beggars herself and giving them what they expected.

This went on for the entire time we lived in Ciego de Ávila after my brother's death. It stopped only when we moved to Havana where there were no beggars in the area where we resided. Father occasionally grumbled, but mother needed the diversion. Getting to know a bit about the misery of others helped her perhaps unconsciously to deal with her own pain. It was also a distraction and something to do on a regular basis. It filled her empty days and kept her from brooding about our recent tragedy. Father must have understood because, although he disapproved, he generally looked the other way.

Chapter Forty-One

An Interim Abode

After Ignacito's death and our move to Ciego de Ávila, mother was completely distraught by the tragedy and left every decision to others. Nena was merely twenty years old, but a great deal of the responsibilities resulting from the move fell on her. We needed to rent a house and to buy furniture. Our plans had been to live at the beach while we looked for a place to buy in Havana, but everything had changed because of Ignacito's accident.

Ciego de Ávila did not have much housing that could satisfy our needs. After considerable effort, father and Nena found a place that would do for the moment. There was never any idea that we would stay for long since I needed to go to high school and my sister had to go to university. In Ciego de Ávila there was no appropriate high school for me, let alone a university for Nena. The house they chose was located on Calle Independencia, half a block from the main plaza and just around the corner from the Centro Asturiano, where Ignacito's wake had taken place. The first block of this street had a smattering of better houses than the ones in the rest of the town and, fortunately for us, one of them was available for rent. The landlady was a widow who lived next door with her married daughter, and supported herself mainly from a pension, some money her late husband had left her, and the rent from the larger house we ended up renting.

The house was typical. It had a porch with Corinthian columns and at the top a balustrade that went along the width of the house. The floorplan was standard, and not very different from our house in Chambas. The style is often called *casa chorizo* (sausage house) because it consists of a long structure of room after room with a narrow plan. The lay-out goes back to Roman times, a courtyard surrounded on four sides by rooms, although it is only half of what a Roman house would be: a smaller courtyard at its center surrounded by rooms on three sides, which if added to another similar structure would result in a standard Roman house.

The living room and a generous *zaguán* (foyer), a smaller version of the entrance for carriages in grander houses, occupied the front. The foyer had a large double door to the outside whose design was repeated three times in the living room. One entered through the foyer, which had an opening to the living room covered with a grille, and a door, also covered with a grille, which led to the *saleta*, a more informal living space used by the family for receiving friends and spending time together. The formal living room was separated from the *saleta* by four pairs of presumptuous Doric columns whose shafts were painted with a faux finish imitating colored marble. The ceilings were very high. From the *saleta* you could go through the courtyard into the dining room, which was at the back of the house, next to the kitchen. Along one side of the courtyard were the bedrooms, which you could access from one another or through the courtyard. The kitchen was built to operate with coal, although we added a gas stove and other modern conveniences when we moved in. Beyond the kitchen and the dining room, a porch overlooked the backyard. This and the courtyard were the only parts of the house in which mother showed any interest. Following Spanish custom, she filled them with flowering plants, mainly geraniums, pansies, roses, and a large variety of carnations.

Mother was despondent: she did not want to think about furniture. So, father and sister went to a local store and got whatever they had available. Even though mother had little interest in it, when she saw what they had bought for the living room, she was appalled. The ensemble included two enormous chairs and a sofa, with a disgusting fake brocade on a dark lavender color. The tables were cheap, and the lamps did not give out any light. The furniture for the *saleta* was more acceptable, made of rattan with green cushions covered in vinyl which was all the rage in the fifties. The bedroom suites were ordinary but acceptable, although not aesthetically pleasing. A few pieces were brought from the plantation, where Ignacito had lived. The only furniture they purchased that mother liked was the dining room set, which was painted in a combination of dark red lacquer and a contrasting very light beige. It was pleasant and cheerful.

When father and Nena saw mother's reaction, they started blaming each other. Nena said that he would not let her choose any of the better-looking furniture because he said it was too expensive. And we believed her; she was no match for father; only mother could deal with him when it came to money. The furniture was horrible, but under the circumstances it had to do. We had no choice but to settle in with ugly things and hope that we would not have to live with them for very long.

Chapter Forty-Two

Long Journey Into Darkness

The owner of the house we rented in Ciego de Ávila lived next door. She was old and had every disease that a child of my age could possibly have heard of, including high blood pressure, a hearing condition, diabetes, liver problems, allergies, rheumatism, and so on *ad infinitum*. She looked very sick, indeed. Her face was so pale that she appeared never to have been out in the sun, which led me to conjecture, at first, that she may have been a vampire. Her skin was so wrinkled that one couldn't see any flat surface anywhere on her face. She gave the mistaken first impression of being obese, but when one looked at her more closely, it was clear that she was not. Rather, she was bloated, particularly her face, swollen unpleasantly, with big flaps for cheeks, and puffy eyebrows falling over the eyes. Below her chin hung a thick set of rolls that extended in waves through her neck all the way down to her chest. Although her body also looked bloated, particularly her belly. Her arms and legs were very thin, like sticks belonging to someone else that had been glued to a foreign torso. She resembled a kind of Humpty Dumpty, which would be funny if the reality had not been so sorry.

Given her condition, it was not surprising that she seldom got up from her rocking chair, but she kept her front door always open, an invitation to any passerby to come in and entertain her. She was profoundly bored because her ailments prevented her from engaging in any activity. Her eyes did not tolerate prolonged reading, her arms were too weak and arthritic to make knitting or drawing possible, she was irritated by the radio in part because of her impaired hearing, and her legs could barely support her, let alone allow her to take walks. Her only activity was conversation, and converse she did, although even that she did with difficulty.

The landlady's name was Generosa, which means "generous." She and I became pals right away. Shortly after we moved next door, she lured me in with candy and stories about old times, and, from then on, I spent long hours in her company. She lived with her daughter, who had married a man Generosa considered a gutless and useless wimp, a spineless leech without prospects or initiative, a kind of Tennessee Williams character. He had a minor job as a traveling salesman and could not afford to live elsewhere else with his wife. To make matters worse, he listened to the radio whenever he was at home, disturbing Generosa's tranquility and desire for conversation. He never dared to sit in the living room, of course—that was Generosa's kingdom—preferring the *saleta* and scurrying in and out as inconspicuously as possible. This made the old lady despise him even more, and her daughter for marrying him. She frequently, and openly, abused them verbally or behind their backs, and I heard a lot of it because I became her confidant.

Generosa resented her daughter in part for marrying him and also for not devoting herself entirely to her mother, as she should have done if she were a dutiful daughter. Remember, in Cuba it was the job of the youngest daughter to take care of her mother in old age, and she was Generosa's only living offspring. Obviously, Generosa was not very generous with her family, but she was very generous with me, always welcoming and telling stories that entertained me and helped her pass the time. I was eleven then.

I loved Generosa's laugh. When she laughed, which was surprisingly not infrequent considering her misery, her belly would go up and down. The sound was a loud cackle that appeared great to me, because it changed her regular suffering appearance into a radiant moment of mirth. In my visits, I would sit opposite her, on the second rocking chair in her favorite part of the living room, and we would rock away in a world of narratives, some sad and some happy, which she told in a mellifluous voice. The saddest of them, and the one that explained much about her and her bitterness, concerned her deceased son.

Her first child had been a boy born with what was called at the time the blue disease (*mal azul*). His heart had a hole in interior wall that separates the atria, allowing the blood from the veins to mix with the oxygenated blood that came from the arteries. There was no remedy for this sickness at the time, and those children who had it slowly withered, until their bodies could not resist any longer the progressive poisoning of their blood, and died. The child had died at eleven, just my precise age when Generosa met me, and so I surmise that she saw in me the child she had lost, the one she could have seen grow to maturity. The loss itself was tragic, but it was not as terrible as the long agony she suffered, helplessly watching him die slowly for years. At the time I did not compare her tragedy with my mother's, but in time I did, understanding that as bad as Ignacito's sudden death had been for mother and all of us, Generosa's agony was vastly worse. That thought has never consoled me—I don't believe sorrow or pain can be good at all, or that one sorrow or pain can be better than another, they all appear to me to be equally bad and gratuitous, although they may vary in intensity—but it did make me realize that some of us are luckier than others, even in our misery, and for no apparent reason at all.

Chapter Forty-Three

Bicycles Are for Boys

Apart from mother and aunt Maruca, my sister Nena was the most important female in my life. She had grown up in Chambas and the country life that was prevalent in the town and its surroundings. Father had horses on his farms, and Nena and Ignacito were almost born on the back of horses. She probably learned how to ride before she learned to walk. School was mostly by tutors and so it involved a limited amount of time. She spent her days on top of her horse, exploring the countryside with other young children. The town and its surroundings were safe and there was little control that was exercised over Nena or Ignacito. She was a tomboy, and could do almost everything our brother could do—he was supposed to be wild—but she could come close. However, her position in the household was different from his or, for that matter, from the one that I came to occupy after I was born. The reason is obvious, she was a female. In Cuba, daughters occupied a different place the family than did their brothers.

This involved both a few pluses and many minuses. As a girl, she was supposed to be pampered and treated nicely. She was never punished harshly, no matter what she did, and certainly she was never spanked or anything of the sort. Our parents tried to tame her wild instincts and to make her a lady, but that is not exactly what she had in mind for herself. She was an Amazon, not a society girl. But then society was not something our parents cared for, so there was no opposition to her tendencies. Social climbing or social position were completely foreign to the family's way of thinking.

Nothing could reveal better Nena's status in the family than an incident that she experienced when she was a child. When Ignacito turned seven, father bought him a bicycle, which was the natural thing to do from his perspective. After all, he was a boy, and not only that, but he was the family heir. Nena was just two years younger than Ignacito, but father never thought of buying her a bicycle, even when she turned seven. When Ignacito outgrew his bicycle, he got a new one and father sold the old one. This was a great disappointment for Nena, who had been hoping she would get Ignacito's bike, even if old and beaten down. Naturally, she complained to father, whose response was that if she wanted a bicycle she should save her allowance to buy it herself. This was hard and it took time, because Nena's allowance was two pennies a day, which she forfeited if she did not ask for them. (She told me that she always remembered to ask for her allowance, unlike Ignacito. He seldom bothered to ask for it, probably because he was able to get money in other ways.)

After almost a year, having saved her entire allowance and not spending additional money gifts she had received, Nena thought she had collected enough money to buy the bicycle, but in fact she had only eleven pesos and the bicycle cost twenty-five. So father told her that he would make up the difference if she gave him the eleven pesos she had saved. This is how Nena got her bicycle. Whereas Ignacito got his bicycle free and several years before her, she had to purchase her bicycle almost entirely. Nena resented father's double standard. Of course, this had nothing to do with father's personal prejudices. The stark fact is that sons and daughters were not treated equally in Cuba.

Another sign of the difference between sons and daughters became clear to us after father's death. He had made provision, through the purchase of an insurance, for the completion of my studies both at high school and university levels, but he had not made any provision for Nena. He had also purchased two other insurances for mother that were quite generous, but Nena got nothing, even though she had not yet finished her studies at the university and had no independent way of supporting herself. In father's mind, I needed to have a career and he was going to do all he could, even after his death, to see that I did. But for his daughter a university education was secondary to her main goal, which presumably was to get married. Father was very progressive both politically and socially, but he was Cuban and so he often acted according to Cuban values.

When I was born, Nena was twelve, and she looked at my birth as a great event in her life. She was of an age in which dolls were still important, and at which some maternal instincts had started to reveal themselves. I was perfectly located between these two drives. I became a living male doll that she could dress and fuss over, and also in a sense her own child. Her devotion to me had no bounds and continued until she married and had children of her own. Indeed, even after that she has always reserved a part of her heart for me. Even today I think one of the things that she enjoyed the most was a phone call or a visit from me that allowed us to talk and reminisce about the past.

When she was still a girl, the intensity of her affection for me was especially deep. She saved from her allowance to buy little things that she thought I would like. She always had time to play with me, and hugged and kissed me constantly. Indeed, when I became an older child, and in line with our family tradition of giving names to people, I baptized her *"la besucona"* (the kisser), because she was always trying to kiss me and I thought it excessive.

The photographic history of my life in Cuba is largely the history of the pictures Nena took of me, walking, playing, and doing the ordinary things that children do, which she thought were worthy of being preserved in photographs. In one of these pictures in which I must have been two or three, I am dressed in a pair of overalls with one hand in my pocket, looking seriously and intensely at the camera, with utmost concentration. The concentration was because I was trying to get a candy out of my pocket. Nena tells me that she spent a long time trying to get me to pose in that way, putting candy in the pocket and asking me to look at her so she could take the picture.

Like Ignacito, Nena was mainly educated at home by tutors that father hired, but when high school came around, he sent her to *La Inmaculada*, a well-known school for girls in Havana. Unfortunately, instead of boarding at school, she stayed at aunt Rosario's home. That was a great mistake and Nena always resented it. Being accustomed to unfettered freedom and mother's tender, although chaotic, ways, she suffered dearly under Rosario's strict and insensitive regime. Nena particularly objected to having to sleep in the same room Rosario's step-daughter slept just before being sent to a sanitorium. This woman had been mad and, after her death, her room had been kept exactly as if she were still alive to the extent that all the large armoires were kept full of her things and Nena had no place to put her own clothes. The room was like a funeral memorial that would inspire fear and disgust in any young girl.

Nena also disliked the food at Rosario's, and she did not tolerate well the restrictions imposed on her. She particularly resented that she was not allowed to touch anything that belonged to Marta, our cousin. As mentioned before, the house looked like a museum of paraphernalia collected over the years by Marta. Above all other curios, Nena loved a little piano, but when aunt Rosario discovered that she had been playing it, the piano suddenly disappeared. Most of all, however, Nena missed me. And in fact she had been saving part of her allowance to buy me trinkets that she thought I would love.

After a year and a half of a very unpleasant stay at aunt Rosario's, Nena insisted on returning home and my parents relented. The following semester she and my brother were assigned a tutor to prepare them for the national high school examinations. In Cuba one need not go to school to earn a high school diploma. It was sufficient that one take and pass the national examinations for each grade. Both Nena and Ignacito, for different reasons, were forced to avail themselves of this program while we were living in Camagüey. They began to take the examinations in Ciego de Ávila and stayed in the home of some friends who had moved from Chambas.

Once we moved to Ceballos, Nena was enrolled at a school of Teresian nuns that was located in Ciego de Ávila. She would stay at the school during the week and come home most weekends. She had always intended to study pharmacy, like father, uncle Carlos, and other members of our family. Accordingly, after she graduated from high school, she entered the university, this time staying at the Teresian residence for young ladies in Havana. But this was not going to last long. Grandmother Dubié's death so shook Nena that she decided to quit her studies and go back home to Ceballos. Father was not happy with it, but much less disappointed than he had been with Ignacito.

All along Nena was turning into a very nice young woman. Had she lived in the United States she would have been a hit with American young men. She was blonde, had honey color eyes, and always maintained a lean figure. She was a preppie through and through. Interested in swimming, horseback riding, and other physical sports, she never rejected her tomboy image. Her favorite clothes were jeans, a shirt, and penny loafers. Mother insisted on dresses, skirts, and blouses, of course. And there was always some seamstress creating an outfit for her. But Nena thought these things superfluous and a hindrance to her physically active life. This attitude did not make her popular with young men, who were interested rather in fleshy body of the milkmaid type with the mind and behavior of an ingenue, quite the contrary of what Nena was.

Mother never ceased in her attempts to fatten Nena up. All kinds of concoctions were tried. Since I was also a stick, we were both subjected to the same sort of treatments: glasses of milk at all times of the day, raw eggs in sherry to be swallowed whole, condensed milk with Coca Cola, wheat meal balls (*gofio*) with milk, *chocolate con leche* and *tostadas con mantequilla* (chocolate milk with buttered toasts) for *meriendas* (snacks between meals, particularly in the afternoon), and so on. But nothing worked for us. Nonetheless, occasionally males became interested in Nena. I remember a very serious one she met at the beach. He was not only handsome and agreeable, but he had capital. He was serious, and so was she. After they met, he began to visit her regularly, and when we returned to Ciego de Ávila, he came to visit.

On that trip, he arrived well stocked with gifts for the family, and for Nena he brought a pendant consisting of a cross studded with very large diamonds. Could there be a better suitor? This looked like a match, but it was not to be. Naturally, father wanted to know something about the young man and since he was from Havana, he asked his family to inquire about him. It turned out that he was separated from his wife and in the process of divorcing her. For our family, this was enough reason to reject him. Nena returned the diamond cross together with all the other gifts she had received from him, as well as his letters to her.

When we moved to Havana, Nena went out with various young men, but she was disappointed in them. They seemed to be interested only in one thing, and she was a proper young woman.

Chapter Forty-Four

Nena's Insistent Gay Suitor

Probably few things were worse for a male in Cuba than to be, or to be thought to be, gay. Calling someone gay was one of the worst insults you could throw at a male. There was a pathological hatred of gays among most straight men, and in school there was a constant fight to keep anyone from questioning your heterosexuality. From very early on kids had to be on the alert about accusations of being gay, which often were based simply on the clothing worn, certain mannerisms, or even being different from the mold which every male was supposed to fit. Even being particularly studious or appearing intelligent could be reasons for accusations along these lines, and those of us who were academically inclined had to work hard to appear to be *muy machos*. The kids that got stuck with the gay label were miserable because no one wanted to associate with them so as not to be accused of being gay themselves. True gays had to keep their sexual orientation a carefully guarded secret. Indeed, I am told by the few gays I met in Cuba, that gays were quite common in the country, but they were generally in the closet.

One of the closest friends of our family was "in the closet." His mannerisms indicated that he was gay, but he never revealed this to anyone in the family other than me. He told me many years later, outside Cuba, when I met him in New York. He was on one of his trips to the United States from Venezuela where he had settled. I was twenty-one years old and in college.

The interesting thing about this man, whose name was Alfredo, and to our family Alfredito, is that he tried for many years to become engaged to my sister and marry her. His family and our family were friends from before the time when either of them was born. His father had been father's tailor when they lived in Chambas, and his mother worked for father. They were humble people. The father had come from Asturias. He was fairly well educated, but the mother, Gumercinda, was a simple woman who worked very hard to give everything they wanted to her two children. Father established a close friendship with him. Indeed, as a wedding gift, he gave the couple a sterling silver set of flatware. It was very heavy and completely out of place in a modest home, but that did not seem to matter to anybody. For them it was a great gift and they showed their appreciation by using it every day in spite of the incongruity of having sterling silver on an ordinary tablecloth and next to ordinary ceramic plates. After father died, we found out that Alfredito's father owed several thousand pesos to father, which of course he never repaid.

The family had two children, Alfredito and Olga, and their dream was that Olga would marry my brother and Alfredito would marry my sister. Olga was a very nice girl, but she was far from attractive. She had a receding chin with a couple of hanging folds under it that made her look like an old lady, whereas my brother was a handsome Don Juan. Alfredito not only wanted to marry my sister, he was also in love with my brother. In his mind, heaven consisted in having children with my sister and having my brother as a lover.

Alfredito was not handsome. Indeed, none in the family were. One of their problems about which Alfredito complained bitterly was the huge nose, which was his family trademark. It dominated their faces. Apart from being too big, the nose was too thin, and had a large bump at the point at which it started to go down. Alfredito talked about having plastic surgery done, but to his credit he never did. I believe that secretly he was proud of the trademark; it was a character nose that distinguished him and his family. Indeed, there was an aristocratic dimension to it that set the family apart and traced their ancestry to Asturias. But then, I am not sure Alfredito's aesthetic sense was well developed. He was very concerned to be on the chunky side, but perhaps this was a way to look a bit soft and feminine. Although he was gay, he did not appreciate traditional masculine features on himself.

Alfredito never lost hope that my sister would come around. Nena never encouraged him in any way, although she was always polite, even in response to his several declarations of love. His behavior was very effeminate and my sister liked masculine men. How he thought he could convince her to marry him was beyond me. Indeed, I couldn't understand how, even decades after, he still clung to the idea that such a marriage would have been possible and a good thing.

Alfredito was one of the standard fixtures in our home. He would come to visit at least once a week and was full of stories and gossip. He was up to date on everything that was happening, had the latest news about male and female fashion, and dressed impeccably, although not quite in a style I favored. A great part of his conversation had to do with his attire, of which he took extreme care. Everything was deliberately arranged and the colors matched perfectly. The ties had to go with the shirts and the shirts with the socks, the belt and the shoes had to be of the same leather and color, and the handkerchiefs were elaborately embroidered. In time, his clothes began to look extreme and some of his choices moved in the direction of a kind of Liberace aesthetic—he began to wear a gold ring on his finger and a gold chain around his neck. Cuban males generally liked to dress up and wear jewelry, but he went well beyond anything that was common.

We often heard of Alfredito's travails at work. He worked as a bookkeeper and rented a room in a *pensión*, which he shared with other young men in similar situations. When I met him in New York, he told me that he looked on this as a great opportunity for recruitment, and claimed that he had affairs with all the men who had been his roommates, including those who presented themselves as heterosexual and who later got married. His view of sex had much in common with the prevailing customs of ancient Greece. He thought erotic love was truly a matter for men, and women were mere instruments for having children. He idolized women but, like proper idols, their place was on an altar, to look beautiful and be nice. Passionate sex would mar their virginal aura. Accordingly, he worshiped his mother, in part because he recognized the privations she underwent while her children were growing up, and the hard work she endured to give them what she thought they deserved. But there was more to it than this. He felt sorry for her and hated his father, whom he thought had always exploited her. At the same time, he was embarrassed by her simplicity and lack of proper manners and education.

As far as I know, Alfredito always kept his true sexuality secret, although his mannerisms and way of talking suggested it. Eventually he emigrated from Cuba to Venezuela, where he secured a lucrative job and lived a pleasant existence. When we met in New York he confided his sexual preferences to me because I was a mature young man who showed no signs of homophobia. Indeed, he asked me to have sex with him, to which I responded by declining as delicately as I could.

I never saw him again, but a few weeks after we met he sent me a pair of gold cufflinks which I still own, but have never worn. They are made of two gold coins set in a rather elaborate setting which I find garish. In the accompanying note, he said that the gift was a token of his appreciation for the many attentions he had received from our family over the years. I took this to refer to the debt his father never had paid, and which had come up in passing during his visit. A few years later I heard he had died, still single, and in his fifties.

Chapter Forty-Five

Looking for Domestic Help

Cuba was a colony of Spain until the beginning of the twentieth century. The rest of the Spanish colonies had achieved independence at the beginning of the nineteenth century. This is why Cuba has always been considered the faithful daughter of Spain, the *madre patria.* This meant that colonial ways were still well entrenched in Cuba in the 1940s and 1950s. One of these was domestic service, which was widespread among the middle class. It was not necessary to be rich to have at least one servant. The salaries that were paid for these services were generally very low. Some cooks in Havana, which was the most lucrative employment market for service, were paid as little as ten pesos a month. Maids were paid a similar amount, but chauffeurs got a bit more. Part of the compensation was food, or meals and lodging, and often there was an unstated understanding that food extended to the family of the employee. It was expected that most employees would leave every day with left-over food for their families. Of course, some households were more generous with salaries, but they were rare, and some were less generous with food for the families of the employees.

The domestic service system made it possible for middle class families to enjoy leisure and not to have to engage in manual labor. Manual labor of any kind was looked down upon in Cuba, something well entrenched from colonial times. No males of any middle class family ever did any repairs in their homes, contrary to the situation in the United States. The idea of taking a brush and painting a wall, of fixing anything, was anathema. But domestic service was not a panacea by any means, and it did not insulate members of the family from some responsibilities. For example, although we always had a cook, mother considered the task of deciding on the daily menu as one of her duties as mistress of our home, and she often took care of special desserts.

Perhaps as bad, or even worse than deciding menus, was hiring, firing, and dealing with domestic help. At various times we had from one to five people working for us: a cook, a maid, a chauffeur, a gardener, a general errand boy, and when we had the farm in Ceballos, a stable hand who took care of the family horses. The task of hiring all these people was not easy. Fortunately for mother, she only dealt with the cook, the maid, and the errand boy. Father took care of the others. But dealing with the cook and the maid was enough to periodically send mother into bouts of grief, particularly when it came to hiring a cook. In one case she felt so terrible that, even though work was anathema to her, she actually went into the kitchen for a while and cooked for us. It took a whole month for father to bring her to reason and do a search again.

As I remember, the worst time for finding a proper cook was after my brother's death. We had settled in Ciego de Ávila and María Picadillo, the cook that had been employed by the family for over twenty years, had decided to join a lover in a far-away town, leaving us in a lurch. This was nothing short of disaster! We were new in town and had no friends who could help mother find a suitable replacement. The task was very difficult. The result was that we had a procession of cooks and maids some of whom lasted only a day, others lasted a week, and none more than a month.

One of them came highly recommended, probably because the previous employer wanted to get rid of her quickly. She was a young woman, clean and apparently resourceful. And indeed resourceful she proved herself to be, particularly when it came to dressing herself in enticing and provocative clothes. Mother objected to the custom of having the cook and the maid dressed in uniforms supplied by the family. She thought this was demeaning to them. But there were some good reasons for doing it. A uniform is always presentable, it identifies the person with certain duties, and it relieves them from having to spend money on clothes for the job. Mother was to regret her views on this matter, particularly with the new cook. She wore low-cut dresses that revealed enough of her natural endowments to get the masculine imagination racing. I liked her well enough, although at the time I was too young to be interested in what grown males found attractive in her.

The masculine reaction to this cook was most obvious in uncle Carlos, who had come to Ciego de Ávila to help father take over the running of the plantation after Ignacito's fatal accident. His routine until that time had been to come to visit twice a week and stay for dinner. But now, with the new cook in the house, he started coming every day. Something similar happened with Jaime, my maternal uncle. He seldom came to visit, but the moment he met the new cook, well, he became very attentive with us. We never found out whether something developed between either of my uncles and the cook because mother acted quickly. The moment she realized what was happening, she dismissed her, although she was very generous with the severance pay. This was cruel and unfair, because my uncles were out of line, and we did not know the role the cook had been playing. But mother did not think she had a viable alternative. She could not very well fire my uncles, could she? That's what she answered when Nena objected.

Father liked to keep a good table, a hangover from the French branch of the family, which meant that finding a cook that satisfied his requirements was especially difficult. Most of the time mother had to train whoever she hired before she was deemed acceptable. But there were some cooks that either could not or did not want to learn. One of these had worked for friends of the family for many years and they swore by her. Her name was Lucinda. She lived in another town not very close to Ciego de Ávila, so bringing her was an involved process. She had to resign her current position and resettle near us with her family.

The first day she came to work, mother gave out a sigh of relief, but the feeling did not last long. When we sat down for the mid-day meal and Lucinda brought the food to the table, father's expression spoke clearly. This was unacceptable! A major problem was the way she had served the food. An appealing presentation was part of what father required. Food, he often said, is a matter of taste, smell, and sight. Lucinda had piled up the food on serving dishes in a manner that father described as worthy of a hog. Before he reached a final conclusion, he forced himself to put some of the food in his mouth—I remember it was chicken fricassee—and tasted it. That was enough for him. He pushed the plate away in disgust. He would not eat anything and mother had to go into the kitchen and ask Lucinda to fry a couple of eggs for him.

Detailed instructions to the cook followed, and the quality of the presentation improved, but the taste was ordinary, and ordinary was not good enough for father. Besides, Lucinda was one of those arrogant people who felt that she knew what she was doing, and she did not want to hear complaints or recommendations. After two weeks of hell, in which most times father found excuses to eat out, she was dismissed. The dismissal in this case was particularly painful, because the woman and her family had to be sent back to the town where they had come from. The issue was not the money, but the humiliation. Mother suffered deeply having to break the news to her. Then there was the problem of the friends that had recommended her highly. How were they to be dealt with? The family had deep discussions about elaborate ways of breaking the news to them, but I never found out how it actually was done.

The case of a new maid was even more dramatic. This was a relatively young woman, well-dressed and appointed. She looked not very different from my sister and she was very sweet. At first, mother was pleased that we could have her. She was in charge of cleaning, dusting, making up beds, and similar tasks. Things seemed to be going very well, but a few weeks after she had started with us, all of a sudden there was a vile smell of excrement coming from one of the bathrooms. Nena was commissioned to find the source of the odor, but she could not figure out where it was coming from exactly. The smell just inundated the bathroom, but the toilet looked clean. Mother thought that it was perhaps related to the sewer, so she made an appointment with a plumber. In the meantime, Nena did some additional detective work and found the source of the effusions. Under the claw-foot bathtub, someone had defecated on newspapers and pushed the mess under it. We assumed it was the maid. Maybe she had an emergency. She had been with us for some time, so it was difficult to understand the problem.

The next morning when the maid came to work, mother dismissed her. If she did not know what toilets were for, or she did not want to use ours, or she was crazy, what else did she not know or not want to do or be ready to do? Mother did not have the courage to tell her the reason for her dismissal; she was too embarrassed or afraid to bring the matter up. Instead, she found some convenient excuse and gave her three months of severance pay, which appeared to make the maid extremely happy.

One cook, Julia, turned out to be very good, clean, and relatively knowledgeable about food, but she had a nasty disposition. Julia was a no-nonsense, efficient woman. She considered herself a professional, and she had a lot of pride. Although we had a good relationship with her, it never developed into the sort of friendship that we had with María Picadillo. I do not remember ever teasing her, as I did María, or vice versa. She always treated all members of the family as her employers, and we never found out much about her, her background, or her family. As most cooks did, every day when she left for home she would take bags of food with her for her family, but we never learned any details about them. It was unclear whether she had a husband and the number of her children.

A story Julia did tell us, about the birth of her last child, confirmed our judgment that she was efficient, tough, and independent. She was always ready to do what was necessary under the circumstances without weakness or whining. According to her narrative, she knew that she was due to give birth at any moment, but she could not turn down the opportunity to earn some much-needed cash for picking vegetables in a field. Her time came when she was working, and she was alone, far from any place where she could ask for help. So, she squatted on the dirt and pushed vigorously until the baby came out. When she was done, she tied the umbilical cord and cut it as best she could, using saliva as disinfectant. Then she wrapped the baby in the bag she was using to gather the vegetables she had been picking and walked to a bus stop, where she took a bus to her mother's. No one paid any attention to her and she asked for no help. Both she and the baby did well and in a couple of days she was back in the field, picking vegetables.

In spite of her many virtues, Julia's generally nasty disposition did not endear her to the family. In particular, given father's expectations about meals, no cook could go without instruction. But Julia got mad any time anyone suggested anything. We had to live with angry looks and impertinent comments, and this was unacceptable; she could not take any criticisms of how she did things, no matter how gently they were presented to her, so she had to go. Mother did the deed in the kitchen, and on her way out the front door of the house Julia grabbed one of mother's favorite porcelains, and disappeared.

Eventually a maid was found that was halfway acceptable, but no cook seemed to measure up. This was the time that, in desperation, mother went into the kitchen. This lasted a month and the search cycle began again. For a while we had a restaurant cater our food. This lasted for a week. Father made an effort, and would say that the food was satisfactory, but he hardly ate. The restaurant was given instructions about how to cook this dish or that one, but nothing worked. Everything was fried and soaking in pork fat, which was forbidden after father's heart attack. Obviously, this was not going to work out. The ordeal ended when my parents convinced our long-time cook, María Picadillo, to move back to Ciego de Ávila and work for us again. Her love affair had by now ended and she was ready to return to us. What a delight her arrival was for everyone! She was with us until we moved to Havana.

Complete satisfaction with a cook in particular was never possible as long as father lived and María did not cook for us. He was the type of person who always sent dishes back to the kitchen when we were eating in restaurants, so it was to be expected that at home he would also be difficult. But he was happy with María.

Chapter Forty-Six

María "Picadillo"

María was our cook, on and off, for over twenty years. She was given the surname "Picadillo" by father because when she first came to cook for our family, the only thing that she knew how to cook was *picadillo*. This is a very common Cuban dish made up of ground beef, garlic, onions, tomatoes, peppers, and spices. Many recipes for it exist, but generally they are all quite good. María was one of the first cooks the family hired.

Mother was twenty-one when she married father in 1927; he was approximately nine years her senior. In the first few months of their married life, they regularly ate out. Chambas had very little of anything in the way of restaurants, but the town's single hotel, if it could be called that, had a small restaurant with a decent cook and father liked the idea of eating out because he could choose from a different menu every day. Indeed, I am told that the restaurant's cook made every effort to satisfy his exacting standards. This was a special challenge he enjoyed, being otherwise bored to distraction by the mediocrity of local taste. He prepared special dishes for my parents and discussed the menus for the week with mother to surprise father. He also learned a lot about setting a proper table and humored mother's taste for vegetarian, wholesome meals. Mother also loved eating out, because she did not have to plan meals or deal with a cook, and being young she did not feel well prepared to manage a kitchen.

However, her vacation from kitchen duties ceased earlier than she expected, because she got pregnant, apparently on the wedding night or shortly thereafter, and when her womb started to grow, it was not comfortable for her to go out both for lunch and dinner. After a few disastrous trials with various cooks, María interviewed for the job, at which time mother asked her if she knew how to cook. Her answer was an unambiguous "yes." The thing she neglected to add was that she knew how to cook only one dish: *picadillo*.

The first day she cooked for the family, she made *picadillo* for both lunch and dinner, and then she made *picadillo* for lunch and dinner the next day. The differences among the three were that one had garlic, which the other two did not, another had tomatoes, which the other two did not, and the remaining one had red peppers which the other two did not. By the third day father sent her an ultimatum via mother: either she cooks something else or she goes!

This was a major crisis for mother in that María had told her the truth—she knew how to cook. Lost as to what to do, she asked grandmother for help. She came right away and gave María a crash-course on cooking, from which mother, who was no dummy, also learned a lot. Grandmother had considerable experience in what was needed because she had run a home with several children and various other dependents, and she also had supervised the preparation of food for the workers at grandfather's tobacco plantation in Vuelta Abajo.

María never lived in our house. She had a mother and a common-law husband who came and went as he pleased. She knew that she could not keep her mother with her if she moved into our house, and she also knew that my parents would not tolerate visits from a wayward lover. Moreover, she had a daughter, Mariíta, with whom she wanted to live in the privacy of their home.

Occasionally, after María had been with the family for many years and we were living in Ciego de Ávila, she would take me to spend a day with her mother and daughter. The old woman was full of narratives, some funny, but most sad. She had lived a hard life, a life of struggle, but she still enjoyed being alive and she was not bitter. Her life gravitated around María and Mariíta. She loved the radio father gave her, and would listen to it constantly while she was taking care of her house chores. I enjoyed listening to her narratives. She looked very old and weathered, although probably she was younger than *Abuelita Belé*.

Her stories dated back to the times of slavery, stories of blacks, abuses, and catastrophes, although she had not been a slave herself. Slavery in Cuba ended in 1886, but it began to disappear after the *Guerra de los Diez Años* (1868-78) and the *Tratado de Zanjón*, and she had been born after that. But her grandmother and grandfather had been slaves, and they had related tales of those times to her. Some of these tales were about injustices committed by white owners against black slaves, about the abuses, unwarranted punishments, and generally bad treatment they had to suffer. I realized that the stories put us whites on a bad light, but this did not bother me, for *Abuelita Belé* also told similar stories and had no qualms about calling an injustice by its proper name, no matter who committed it. They were very human stories and we all knew that slavery was a great evil, but María's mother did not narrate them with rancor. This was one of my first introductions to a dark side of Cuban history. It also made me think about the role that some of my ancestors may have played in that history. María was a *mulata,* but María's father had been white, so María's skin was lighter than her mother's.

I had a love/hate relationship with Mariíta. She usually outsmarted me, and she never treated me as the boss's son. It particularly infuriated me that she would squeal on the nutty things I did. In retaliation I would pull her long tresses, which would prompt more squealing. But I did like going to the place where they lived both because of the old lady and Mariíta.

They lived in a shack, with a thatched roof made of *guano* and a dirt floor, in one of the several shanty towns that sprawled irregularly around Ciego de Ávila. The clay dirt floor had been built up to prevent rain water from coming into the house, and pounded vigorously with ashes so it was very hard and even. They had practically no furniture and kept the place in perfect order and cleanliness. When I went there, I would spend the whole day with them. Apart from hearing stories from the old lady, Mariíta played various games with me, some previously unknown to me, and probably made them up for the occasion—she was very smart—and frequently a few neighboring children joined us. I particularly liked the game of *Chucho* (whip), not because *Chucho* was my nickname, but because it involved a lot of running around. I looked forward to these visits, and I think María and her family encouraged them. Mariíta, I believe, enjoyed them as much as I did, although she did torture me frequently by mocking me or showing her superior intellect and physical prowess, even if she was only a year older than I.

When we moved to Havana, María moved away to stay with her beau. Shortly after this, father learned that she was having some money problems, so he went to Camagüey, where she was living. She told him that she was pregnant, but when father saw her condition, he knew better. Although he did not say anything to María because he thought her case hopeless, he told us when he got back that she was very sick and would not last long. She died shortly after from a large, malignant tumor. She was still a young woman.

María was a significant member of our family in many ways. She was always cheerful and funny. She smiled frequently and had a contagious laugh. I can never forget that when she opened her mouth to laugh, several teeth were missing, and when she talked, the missing teeth caused her to make an idiosyncratic, lisping sound. Father had given her money several times to get her teeth fixed with some dentures, but the money always ended up elsewhere, buying something for Mariita, her mother, or her lover. This infuriated father who complained bitterly about it behind her back, but he respected her too much to say anything to her face-to-face.

María was very affectionate with me. I knew she loved me and I loved her. When father brought the news of her death, I insisted on knowing every detail about it, and what would happen to Mariíta and her mother. But what could he say? I am sure he did not want to tell me the grim details of the disease, and he did not really know what would happen to María's mother or

Mariíta. But he made something up that satisfied me. That night, when everyone had gone to bed, I cried myself to sleep, and to this day, my heart still aches when I think about María. Mother trusted her completely, in fact we all did. Apart from her many virtues, she knew many things of which the rest of us were ignorant. I am told that one time, when I had yet to be born, the family was deep in discussion about something or other, puzzling about some subject of concern, and my brother said, "Well, why don't we ask María, she knows everything!"

Chapter Forty-Seven

"¡Yo soy muy macho!"

Cuban males are supposed to be super masculine, *muy machos*, an expression all male children are told to repeat from very early on in their lives. *¡Yo soy muy macho!* The fear that they might have feminine proclivities, that they may not be willing to fight against other *machos* for their territories, is consuming to the parents. Like Italian males, they are also encouraged to be constantly on the alert for females. These are regarded as their natural prey. Even serious, older men, feel the call to prove their *machismo* by having relations with younger women and flaunting those relations. Sex occupies a substantial part of their lives, and in some cases it appears to be the major part, if not all of it. As soon as boys go to school, they begin to hear about sex from older boys, and this continues and increases as they grow. Matters are ironically made worse because of the general puritanical pretensions of Cuban society—I'm speaking of the bourgeoisie in particular, where sex is not discussed among family members, as it was not in our family. No member of my family ever had a conversation with me about sex, and most girls learned about menstruation outside the home, as did my sister.

    The street was the place where children, particularly males, learned about sex, although some Catholic schools made the effort to teach boys about sexual functions and organs. Most boys learned about sex in the gutter, literally, while they were playing with other boys on the street. The street was the social center of children's universe in town. It was where most of them met and played. So it was appropriate, in a convoluted sense, that children learn about sex there. Of course, schools were another propitious place. Those breaks between classes were the perfect location for salacious talk. Sex was ubiquitous. When boys got to the age when their libido became active, there were very few conversations among them whose topics were not sex. No wonder a good-looking woman, and even some not particularly good-looking ones, could not walk by and pass some men without eliciting comments from them—the so called *piropos*—which sometimes were tasteful and even poetic, but at other times gross and explicitly sexual. Men had been kids, and kids had been well trained to think in erotic terms.

Amorous affairs, keeping mistresses, and engaging in all kinds of bawdy behavior were also frequent and condoned, or even encouraged. Males were expected to brag about their exploits with women and engage in "dirty talk" to demonstrate their masculinity. Failing to do so could carry serious consequences. It could be considered a sign of homosexuality. To make sure boys learned what they were supposed to do, many fathers entrusted their older sons to prostitutes, who ran a well-known bordello in Havana. Their sons could be initiated in sex by an experienced teacher. You had to be, and prove that you were, a real *macho man*. This entailed talk and action.

Father was a very proper man. Although he occasionally used bad language among men, as most Cubans do, he never engaged in conversations about sex or sexual exploits—at least I never heard him do it. However, he did have an eye for the ladies, and at least on two occasions that I know of, mother claimed to have caught him at it red-handed. In one case their marriage almost ended. Of course, it is difficult to blame father for having these lapses considering the weight of Cuban culture. The pressure the culture placed on men, and particularly men of means, with a respected position in society, and with a distinguished presence, was overwhelming.

Father had married mother for love. He loved her dearly all his life. She was a beautiful and elegant woman and he doted on her, allowing her to get away with murder, to use the cliché. But there were temptations. Most of these never came to fruition, and if they did, they did not amount to much, or I never found out about them. Mother's greatest complaint was that father always managed to have her find out about any affairs, or budding affairs he had outside the marriage bed. She would say, "Why can't he have his affairs and keep me in the dark? What I don't know doesn't hurt me!" But obviously, for whatever reason, mother always found out, maybe because father wanted her to do so and become jealous. Most of the time nothing came of it. I remember the last instance, in which father apparently had a fling with uncle Carlos' former mistress. Mother found evidence in father's wallet, and she put two and two together. So they had a spat, but it was not significant. Either he became extra careful and terminated the affair, or the affair had never begun.

The most serious situation occurred a couple of years after Ignacito's death. This tragedy had been a devastating blow to the family, and certainly to father, but it was particularly hard on mother. In Spanish societies the first born, especially if male, has a unique place in a family and accordingly Ignacito was a favorite of mother. What made this more significant was that, because of his disagreements and even altercations with father, his failures in school, and what father considered objectionable behavior, she pitied him. Love tied to pity is a very strong bond. When Ignacito died, mother was inconsolable. She felt that an important part of her life had ended, and she had difficulty coping with living. She used to say that her heart had been equally divided into three parts, one for each of her children, but now one part had died and the heart had become partly paralyzed. She continued to be her usual affectionate self with Nena and me, but the joy of life had gone out of her.

Father had also suffered greatly by Ignacito's death. I am sure that there were feelings of guilt involved and of frustration in seeing that his oldest son and heir was no more. He needed his wife's support and love, and even more, her understanding and affection. But part of her had been buried with Ignacito and she could not give what she did not have.

We were living in Ciego de Ávila, and close to us lived a middle age woman, quite handsome, with a seriously handicapped daughter. She was well educated, had a strong personality, and a sad story. Like father, she needed love and affection and he took notice of her. How far their relationship went, or even if there was really a romantic relationship at all, is difficult to ascertain. Mother was convinced of it, and gave Nena and me details about what was happening, when, and how. However, we could not be sure, and we did not see anything suspicious. Indeed, Nena always believed that, in fact, father was using this woman to make mother jealous and force her to be more attentive to him.

Once mother was convinced that father was being unfaithful, she decided that she would abandon him and move to Havana, which was after all the place where she had always wanted to live. It was as simple as that. We were to move. Was she using the excuse of father's affair to accomplish something she always had wanted? This sounds callous and manipulative, and mother would have been horrified to hear me even consider this possibility. In fact, I don't think she calculated and managed the move in a cynical and conscious way. Most likely she was acting impulsively, as she often did, propelled by her unconscious needs.

The time was fortuitous in that I had finished fifth grade, and there was no school in Ciego de Ávila where I could continue my studies. Instead of sending me away to boarding school, or having me tutored, mother thought we could accomplish several things with the move: get me to the school I needed to go; save her own self-respect; and, punish father for his presumed disloyalty. We would move to Havana and father could stay in Ciego de Ávila by himself, alone, and suffering.

I was quite frightened, but I said very little against mother's decision, and I think Nena also kept quiet. Mother was a formidable woman when she made up her mind to do something. In a difficult situation her solution was always to force the issue, bring it out into the open and force the other party to back down or live with the consequences. She was never afraid that such a move would result in penury for her. She was sure of herself, of her power over others. One of her favorite sayings was *"Del cobarde no se ha escrito nada"* (Nothing has ever been written about a coward.) But I was not sure at all, and my insecurity made me suffer intensely. How would we live? Who was going to support us financially? And would we ever see father? What would life without father be? The prospect was new and scary to me.

Father could not think of anything to do other than try to persuade mother to abandon her plans, but that she would not do. I think he was as frightened as I was, albeit for different reasons. He had recently lost his older son, and now he was going to lose the rest of the family. His health was questionable, and he liked having a family life. He surely loved us, although he was not the type to be telling us that he did. This love talk that is so common among Americans and even in Cuba in certain families, was not used in our family. In response to mother, he thought his only alternative was to cooperate and see that everything went smoothly.

We left Ciego de Ávila and arrived in Havana at the end of August, 1954. I had turned twelve two months before. After staying at a hotel for a few days, we rented an apartment a few blocks from the Marist Brothers school in La Víbora, a nice neighborhood of Havana. We moved into the apartment on September 4. This would ensure as little disruption to my schooling as possible since the school I had attended in Ciego de Ávila was also run by the Marist Brothers. Mother, as was her custom, had discarded most of the furniture we owned before we left Ciego de Ávila and used the opportunity that the move provided to buy new furniture. She furnished the new apartment in the latest trends, with the kind of modern furniture she liked, and so the place looked fabulous.

It was a three-bedroom apartment, on the third floor of a three-story duplex, with the garage on the ground floor, where we kept the family sedan—father kept the jeep in Ciego de Ávila. The living room was all glass and overlooked one of the most beautiful churches in Havana, belonging to the *Padres Pasionistas*. It was a kind of white neo-Gothic extravaganza that attracted weddings from the highest levels of the power establishments in the country, particularly the army and air force. We would sit at the terrace and watch the newly-weds walking out of the church in a tunnel formed by the swords of an honor guard.

In the meantime, father stayed in the country. We received missives, which mother did not answer, while Nena and I kept mum. We knew who was in charge of the situation. There is no power greater than love, and father loved mother in a way few husbands love their wives. Finally, after it was clear that we were living as mother thought we should, that is in proper style, she allowed father to visit. He came like a dog with its tail between its legs, contrite and miserable. He had been staying at a hotel in Ciego de Ávila, eating poor food, badly served and cooked. He had lost weight and was clearly in distress and ready to do penance. This was all to our advantage because mother proceeded to extract all kinds of promises from him about our future.

The main promise was that, if she took him back, we would buy a house and settle permanently in Havana. So, my sister and I started salivating about the place where we would buy the house. Should it be in El Vedado, an older, established and somewhat stodgy neighborhood? Or should we go to Miramar, a newer area where things seemed to be happening? Of course, nothing could be done until I had graduated from secondary school. We had moved to La Víbora so I could attend the Marist school, and moving far away would mean a change. This played into father's hands, who was a sly dog and never liked to spend money on things that did not turn into an investment. While mother and Nena were thinking about a house, he found a three-story apartment building that happened to have a nice apartment on the ground floor and was sufficiently close to my school for me to continue going to it without much difficulty. Without saying anything to anybody, he bought it at the end of 1954.

This was disappointing to the rest of us when we learned about it, but father's strongest argument was about my school. It would be better for me to live close to the school I attended, at least for a few years until I graduated from high school, while we looked for a place, and perhaps—here was the carrot—we could buy a lot and build a new house.

We moved into the apartment in January of 1955. It was pleasant enough, and mother turned it into a very swank place. Indeed, when grand-aunt Mina came to visit with her daughter Baby and grand-daughter Cucha, Cucha said that the place looked like what you see in the movies. That made mother's day, because the Dubiés were the arbiters of taste in her estimation. That is how father got his way, how mother was mollified, and how we ended up living in a provisional place for the rest of our stay in Cuba. Father died before we bought the lot to build our dream house, and then the Revolution turned everything upside down. As the saying goes, *"El hombre propone y Dios dispone"* (Man proposes, but God disposes).

Chapter Forty-Eight

Teenager in Havana

My first year in Havana was full of surprises and adjustments, some pleasant and some not so pleasant. It was not easy for a twelve-year old to leave the world to which he had finally acclimated after the shock of gigantic proportions that had shaken our family and whose after-shocks we were still experiencing. A change to a new school is always traumatic, and it was no less so in this case, even though the school was also Marist and followed the same pedagogic methods as the school in Ciego de Ávila. But the school in Ciego de Ávila was small in comparison with the very large establishment the Marist Brothers kept in La Víbora. True, the brothers were quite similar, Spanish and Marist with a small sprinkling of Cubans, but Havana was a large and complex city and the students that attended the school were accustomed to a way of life that was quite different from the one I had lived in the country and a country town. As in Ciego de Ávila, I was able to walk to school, but the similarities between the two situations stopped with that. The school building was enormous and divided into two parts, one occupied by grades one through six, and the other by the grades in high school and commerce.

    Most of the students in my grade knew each other from previous grades and had formed cliques that stuck together and ignored newcomers. As a new arrival, and being of a rather shy disposition, it was difficult for me to make new friends. In fact, I do not recall that I had a single new friend in sixth grade. Some of my classmates lived in the neighborhood, but I was unable to join the groups to which they belonged. Most often I walked the few blocks to school and back alone. This had been the fourth time in six years that I had to go to a new school in which I knew no one. The first time was in first grade. There, the transition from no schooling to schooling had been traumatic. Then, in third grade, when we moved to the beach, I attended the Piarist

Fathers school in Guanabacoa, a place far from where we lived and with a population quite different to the one that lived on the beach or in Ciego de Ávila. Then we moved back to Ciego de Ávila when Ignacito died. And now, I had to suffer still another change, this time to Havana. These changes were made worse because I had no one with whom I felt I could talk about my situation. I was embarrassed about it. Ironically, the recurring change did help me in that I knew what I was in for. I grit my teeth and went on.

Still, four home and school changes in six years were four too many for a kid at my age, and the results became evident immediately. In Ciego de Ávila in fifth grade, I had been at the top of my class, but in Havana in sixth grade I fell back to the middle of the pack. This was quite frustrating to me. If I had done well and stood out, perhaps I would have been less unhappy, but being socially alone and performing poorly in academics was adding insult to injury. There was nothing to celebrate, to be proud of, or to enjoy.

I was going to experience still another move to a new neighborhood. This time, father invested in an apartment building, and the following year, we moved into one of those apartments. Because I was in sixth grade, there were no school buses to take me to and from school. So, I had to use public transportation. This was not difficult insofar as we lived a block away from a bus route that took me close to the school. That this bus was taken also by other students in my grade turned out to be both good and bad. Good because I liked some of the students and we became friends of sorts, and bad because others were often not nice to me for various reasons. One student in particular was jealous because in the first year of high school he had been the uncontested first in his class and in second year we were put together in the same classroom and I challenged his position. There was also the issue of social status. He came from a lower middle class family, with very limited resources and he envied the situation in which I lived. Naturally, I would talk about what I did on weekends, about the club, and similar things, that frustrated him and made him angry. And yet, I enjoyed his company because he was very smart and there is nothing so attractive as a bright intellect. Indeed, we did some things that were fun. Apart from reading forbidden books, like Malaparte's horrific novel about World War II, we devised a code for verbal language that made it possible for us to talk among ourselves without being understood by others. It was a simple code, but quite effective.

I was miserable on and off but, as the saying goes, *no hay mal que dure cien años, ni cuerpo que lo resista, ni médico que lo asista* (there is no harm that lasts a hundred years, no body that resists it, no doctor to assist it). I survived once more, partly because Havana had incentives that Ciego de Ávila had not had, and which in time fascinated me. One of these was the club, which made it possible for me to enjoy the beach year around. I loved the ocean, and the beach facility of the Casino Español was superb. Havana had many movie theaters, stores, and all kinds of things to which one could go and activities in which one could participate. At first, I was shy about these, but slowly I started to enter the life of the city. I made friends and my grades stabilized, meeting my academic expectations. My teachers recognized my efforts and bent over backwards to help me, encouraging my participation in school activities. For a while I played basketball, until I realized that it would take too much of my time and would affect my performance in academic subjects. Practice every day after school was just too much to keep up with academics. I also joined a Catholic Action group, of which I became president, and joined a gym close to my home where I worked-out regularly.

Havana was nothing like Ciego de Ávila. It was a great metropolis, full of people and variety. Just going to the Malecón and walking the streets of Old Havana was a treat. This was a new world for me, full of possibilities and endless avenues of exploration. At the center of many of my activities was the club.

Chapter Forty-Nine

The Club

When we settled in Havana, we realized that we were largely alone in the city. We needed friends and what could be better than the Casino Español, one of the oldest gentlemen's clubs in Havana, having been founded by loyalist Spaniards as a club for gentlemen of Spanish ancestry to meet, socialize, and conduct business. Records show that it was functioning and advocating political views in the nineteenth century during the wars of independence Cuban patriots fought beginning in 1868 with the Ten-Year War. It began in a gracious building on El Prado, the genteel thoroughfare of the city going back to colonial times. Eventually the club added a beach house in a row of buildings that included the Havana Yacht Club, the Army Officers Club, and the Club Náutico, all along the public beach, La Concha.

    The Havana Yacht Club was the most exclusive club in Cuba. Yes, exclusive, which, as the word suggests, means one that excludes. Indeed, I think its main object was to keep as many people out as possible in order to make those few who were included to feel special: they were the select few. Joining it was not just a matter of money, although its entrance fee was substantial for the times (if I remember correctly, it was something like 1500 pesos) and the monthly charge was also quite high; it was a matter of pedigree. The Club Náutico was a middle class enclave that charged only a 60 pesos joining fee and a very modest monthly charge, and accepted almost everyone that applied for membership, including light mulattoes that passed for white. The Army's Officers Club, as its name indicates, was restricted to Army officers, their families, and their guests and occupied a narrow strip of land and beach between the Casino Español and the Havana Yacht Club. Farthest to the east was La Concha, a public beach that charged a small entrance fee per day. Everyone "who mattered" looked at La Concha with horror, for it allowed blacks in. Yes, such was the Cuba of the fifties!

These clubs were located in a safely secluded bay, with a barrier reef at its entrance. The water was very clean because the bay opens to the strait that separates Cuba from Florida where there are strong currents, but the beaches along the bay only receive mild waves. The bay was excellent for swimming, row boating, and sailing. Ironically, the best beaches in it belonged to La Concha and the Club Náutico. Both had very long stretches of sand at the opposite ends of the bay. The three other clubs were squeezed in between these two, with the Army Officers' Club being the one with the smallest beach. La Concha and the Club Náutico were also the most populated clubs. Very few people were ever seen at the Army Officers' Club or the Havana Yacht Club, but the Casino Español had a good number of members who enjoyed its excellent facilities.

The proximity between the clubs encouraged exploration by those using the public beach and the Club Náutico. It was a struggle keeping them out, and the Havana Yacht Club and the Casino Español had guards posted on their piers, the area where the interlopers got in, to prevent them from swimming in the club's private beaches or from using their facilities. The guards had no difficulty spotting interlopers because of their skin color or the cheap swimming outfits they wore. Of course, members of the Casino Español also liked to explore the other clubs and use their beaches and facilities. La Concha and the Club Náutico did not mind, but the exclusive Havana Yacht Club did. Many a time my friends and I were asked to leave the Havana Yacht Club beach, even though some of us had been guests in it at some point.

La Concha had a superb diving platform with several diving boards, one of which was very high, and my friends and I loved to swim there and use it. The building for the Officer's Club was small and somewhat insignificant, but the Havana Yacht Club had an impressive building, with richly appointed salons and dining rooms. Next to the Havana Yacht Club, the Casino Español had the best grounds, very large, with tennis and racket-ball courts and even a baseball field, in addition to restaurants, salons for playing table games, lockers, a gymnasium, a swimming pool, and other dependencies. The ballroom, a large round salon with an impressive ribbed dome (which collapsed after the Revolution failed to keep the building up), was used for formal parties. The Club Náutico had the most modern and exciting architecture. A very large area facing the beach was used for many purposes, including dancing and eating. It was covered by large, airy arches in the style made famous by the Tropicana Night Club.

The other two major exclusive clubs in Havana located on the coast were the Biltmore Country Club, and the Miramar Yacht Club. The Biltmore was located west of the bay where most of the other clubs were found, and the Miramar to the east, on a little bay near the shore of the neighborhood that gave it its name. The Biltmore was notorious for its nouveau riche membership, and people such as the dictator, Fulgencio Batista, belonged to it. It accepted anyone who had sufficient money, provided that the person did not look perspicuously black and a black grandmother was not known to be kept in a closet. Batista himself was a mestizo/mulatto, and had been denied membership in the Havana Yacht Club, but had no trouble getting into the Biltmore. The Miramar was a non-Spanish version of the Casino Español, although neighborhood centered; it specialized in yachting. All the private beach clubs had sailing and boating facilities, and I spent many pleasant hours sailing or boating in the bay at the Casino Español when the sea was calm—for I have always been prone to seasickness.

These clubs provided a way to divide Cuban society according to strata of social standing and wealth before the Revolution. The first division was between those who belonged to a club and those who did not, that is, between those who went to the clubs and those who went to a public beach such as La Concha. The second division was between those who belonged to the top club, the Havana Yacht Club, those who belonged to the least discriminating club, the Club Náutico, and those in between who belonged to clubs that were discriminating but were not the top club, namely the Miramar, Biltmore, and Casino Español. Club membership was pregnant with meaning and social significance in pre-revolutionary Cuba. Some people would kill to belong to the right club. And not be belong to a club carried a social stigma.

No one in my family ever gave a hoot about "clubs" or "society." I grew up in a family atmosphere in which to engage in social posing, climbing, and name-dropping were thoroughly ridiculed. Father in particular thought of most club members as leeches, parasites that lived thanks to the efforts of their ancestors, but had no merit or ambition themselves. He had a sense that he came from solid stock, and that social climbing was for people who came from weaker strains. The important thing in life was true merit, be that excellence or money. Father could not forget his personal history.

Mother also was not interested in the sort of thing that went on at the clubs—the ritual card games, tennis matches, Sweet Fifteen celebrations, or gossip and boasting. Before Ignacito's death, she had been interested in showing-off her beauty wrapped in proper attire. After his death, her interest shifted entirely toward religion. And before and after, she despised the superficiality of society and social clubs. The Gracia-Dubiés were intellectual people who liked to read and prized excellence. And although mother's family was not on the same intellectual level as they, after the death of Ignacito, her attitude changed drastically and she became interested in serious subjects. A club did not figure importantly in that scheme. The empty chitchat among club ladies was intolerable to her. What meaning could that have for a woman who had lost a son in the prime of his life and was consumed by questions about the ultimate meaning of human existence? She also bristled at the name dropping and boasting that is typical of the ladies that play cards at the clubs. Could they possibly understand a woman who read the Bible, Khrisnamurti, and Amado Nervo? In the years that we were members of the Casino Español, I recall only a couple of times in which she visited the club.

We had moved to Havana in the early fifties, and although father's family was originally from the city and its members still lived in it, the rest of us did not know many people there. More important still, Nena had to find a husband. Indeed, that was the main concern at this stage of life, according to aunt Rosario, who also had a marriageable daughter in the same predicament. How little had matters changed from the times described so accurately by Jane Austin in *Pride and Prejudice!* Finding a husband for their marriageable daughters was the primary goal of Cuban matrons.

Rosario convinced father that the girls, particularly, needed exposure. How else could they meet the "proper" young men among whom to choose a husband? Both of them were getting desperate; it was a case of spinster's panic. They were both over twenty-four and ready to *agarrarse de un clavo caliente* (hold on to a hot nail). My cousin's long engagement to an Air Force pilot had ended, probably because he was searching for fortune and she did not have enough money to satisfy his ambitions. Nena was too much of a tomboy and too thin to fit the popular female paradigm in Cuba. Her type would have fit perfectly in certain circles of American society, but we lived in Cuba, where women were supposed to be brunettes and 'full-figured'.

We had no difficulty joining the Casino Español, for it turned out not only that we had the right credentials (Spanish background, education, and enough money) to qualify, but also that my paternal great-grandfather had been a founding member of the club. From then on, I spent many weekends there, at the beach, during the school year and many week days during the summer. I had a reasonably good time and I enjoyed most of my summers at the club house on the beach. I would drive there, change, and go swimming. Then, I had lunch at the cafeteria, the fashionable blue plates had recently been imported from the United States—and then I drove back home, unless there were plans for something in the evening. I kept a variety of clothes in a locker and so I was ready for any eventuality. Cousin Marta (as the daughter of a qualifying widow, Rosario and Marta were entitled to be members of the club as part of our family) did their duty, trying to get husbands, although neither of them succeeded. And father occasionally visited the main club location on the Prado.

As a student at St. Thomas Military Academy, the club provided a venue for me to bring girls to dance, lunch, and swim. Many of my classmates and their friends belonged to the Miramar or the Biltmore, and others from lower grades to the Havana Yacht Club. It was a pleasant, superficial existence, where life was secure, predictable, and enjoyable. The future looked like more of the same, although it was all a bit too stuffy, uneventful, and at times deeply unsatisfactory. Yet little did I know that in a very short time, life was going to change drastically and adventure was entering my existence.

Chapter Fifty

Another Call

Another call. Another night trip. Another death, alone. After our move to Havana, father spent most of the time with us in the city, but he also traveled frequently to Ciego de Ávila to take care of the sugarcane plantation. He had a driver who took him back and forth to Havana, and also drove him from the town to the farm and back. One fateful day in April of 1957, however, his chauffeur got sick and father decided to drive himself. The roads were bad, and when it rained, as it had the night before, they became as slippery as soap. On the road, he lost control and the car turned violently around, forcing him to strain and make a strong effort, too strong for his heart. He immediately felt a sharp pain in his chest. After his first heart attack, he always traveled with nitroglycerine pills, so he took one and, after a while, the intense pain subsided. But he knew that something serious had happened and he needed to look into it. As soon as his immediate business was done in Ciego de Ávila and he could get away, he returned to Havana and went to see his cardiologist, who informed him, that Friday, that father was in great shape. In the doctor's own words, he would die "of anything but his heart." Father was cheered by the news. On Sunday, his chauffeur drove father back to Ciego de Ávila to some business he had left unfinished. On Tuesday evening, we got the call that father had suffered a cardiac infarction.

As with Ignacito, we had the hope that father would still be alive when we arrived at Ciego de Ávila. But, also like my brother, father had died before we were notified. He had felt sick after dinner and had called for help to the front desk of the hotel where he was staying. Help came, and a physician was called, but it was too late. We never learned the details of what happened. No one wanted to discuss father's last moments. There would be recriminations. We were told that he knew he was in trouble, and that his last words had been, *"¡Dios mío, Dios mío!"*

Another night I would like to forget. History repeating itself, but this time I was older, fourteen rather than eight, and uncle Carlos accompanied us. We left Havana in the very early hours of the morning and reached Ciego de Ávila by mid-morning. Father's chauffeur was waiting for us and he led us to where the body laid. The doctor had put the time of death after midnight so that the body need not be interred immediately. This gave us time for a proper wake. The Centro Asturiano, where Ignacito's wake had taken place, was not available, so the body was laid-out at a funeral home near the train station. I remember getting out of the car and walking into the room where father's body laid. Mother again in pain, moving ahead with my sister, and I following, with Carlos, his arm around my shoulders. The coffin. The face. And a kiss. Cold, the stiff frigidity of death with which I was now familiar. He looked old, withered, exhausted, like a soldier who had fought a battle and had been defeated. Wrinkles of frustrated speech around his mouth. This was not my father; it was a shadow of what he had been, a remnant that had little to do with him.

The funeral was similar to other funerals, but I do not remember as much of it as I do of my brother's funeral, although I was older. I can't recall the procession to the cemetery, or the eulogy, or even who delivered it. This time there was no solemn funeral mass, since father would have disapproved. I have no image of the coffin, of the people present, of words exchanged. I cannot remember the moment of internment that had terrified me so much in the case of my brother. Surely there were flowers, father was an important man, but I can't even picture in my mind where they were in the salon where the wake took place. Everything is vague, unclear. It is as if my memory had stopped working in a bout of amnesia. Perhaps it was too much to ask of it to relive what it had witnessed already once. The same experience could not be repeated.

After the burial, lawyers and bureaucrats accosted us, hoping for instructions none of us could give. Father's will, the finances. Immediate problems. The sugarcane plantation. The bailiff was an old and trusted friend, but he was a drunk. The lawyer that had handled father's business for years turn out to be a crook. He was just one of the many that behaved like vultures preparing for a banquet. We were vulnerable. Trips to the sugarcane plantation. Trips to the lawyer. Nena and mother stayed in Ciego de Ávila to follow-up on all the inheritance business. I was fortunate to have to leave for Havana to go back to school. Uncle Carlos accompanied me. It fell upon aunt Maruca to look after me in Havana.

I was fourteen when father died. I had been much younger when Ignacito died. There was a great difference between the two experiences. At the earlier age, I was crushed both by my personal pain and the family pain, but I did not dwell on death. At the later age, I had already begun to read extensively and to think about faith. Mother had experienced a conversion and there had been much talk in the family about the meaning of life. After father died, the first questions I asked myself were about the significance of death. The notion of a benevolent God receded in my estimation. How could I believe in such a God when we had been repeatedly beaten, mercilessly, for the past seven years? Had we done anything to deserve such a fate? What had I done? Sure, I was nutty here and there, but my minor sins could never motivate a judgment as harsh as the one that seemed to have been passed on me and the family. I felt like Job. God was supposed to be our Father and care for us accordingly, but I could not imagine a truly benevolent and caring divine Father punishing His children as He was punishing us. If there was a God, He must not be benevolent or caring. Logic and empirical experience had begun to challenge faith.

More important still, the question of human existence took up most of my attention. What is the meaning of it? These seeds of a philosophical attitude eventually led me to philosophy as a profession. Socrates said that philosophy is the study of death, and I must agree with him to this extent: Death leads us to ask questions that most humans are afraid to ask. Yet, regardless of whether we do or not, the questions are inescapable, if ultimately and paradoxically unanswerable.

Chapter Fifty-One

The Cursed Plantation

Some people believe that certain places—houses, lands, farms—are cursed. Something surrounds them that attracts evil. They also believe that only some people can tell. I don't believe in cursed places, except insofar as they might be cursed in the sense that someone did in fact curse them. This, indeed, is the case of the sugarcane plantation we owned, because after the suffering we experienced connected with it, some of us did curse it. In spite of mother's newly found religion after the death of my brother, she had a premonition of bad things happening when father bought it. She often had presentiments and premonitions. And when father closed the deal on the plantation, mother felt apprehensive, and warned us that something bad might come of it. And indeed, many bad things did occur.

Father bought the plantation after he had sold the orchard in Ceballos in 1951. The only fault with the farm had been its isolation since it was in the country and, after father's heart attack, the location and the intense attention it required made it impossible for us to live there and for father to manage it. But we had loved the place. After we moved to it, we seem to have fallen into place, perhaps because of the surrounding beauty. Not that nothing bad ever happened while we were there. There were the quarrels between father and Ignacito, and the romance between him and the bailiff's wife. And it was there that father had his first heart attack. But somehow these things did not count, or not count as much perhaps, compared with the death of both Ignacito and father. Besides, the garden in Ceballos was enchanting and when you are surrounded by beauty you tend to focus on the good rather than the bad.

From the very beginning, mother said that there was something wrong with the plantation, although it was not until after Ignacito's death that she called it cursed. After father sold the orchard in Ceballos, he started looking for something to invest in, which for him meant land. He could not give up his love for growing things. Because sugarcane appeared to require little attention, father thought that my brother could take care of the plantation while he spent more time with us in Havana. Originally, he had decided on a farm that grew sugarcane and raised cattle before he changed his mind.

Cattle were the love of my brother, who thought of himself as a cattle rancher, a kind of Cuban cowboy. The farm was similar to one of the three plantations father had purchased before. I never saw it, but apparently the place was charming. An old colonial house, like those one thinks of in an Argentinian *estancia*, was surrounded by mature fruit trees. Mother, thinking of Ignacito, figured he could be happy there, marry and manage the farm. A river crossed the property, pretty much like in El Anoncillo in Chambas. Everyone was enthusiastic about it and father gave his word to the owner. Then the owner of the sugarcane plantation turned up in the evening and talked father into buying it instead. No one knows what he said, but he convinced father. This created an embarrassing situation, because father had given his word to the other owner, who understandably became quite agitated about it. But somehow father, who was so strict about his dealings with others, and so careful with his word, dismissed all of Ignacito's and mother's objections. Thus, the plantation was born in distress and as a result of a dishonorable deal, and mother always said that the devil had gotten his hand into it.

Within a year after Ignacito died, the plantation was destroyed by fire. And some years after that, father died. Perhaps mother was right, the place was cursed, although to say so is nonsense. But it is true that father's decision to buy the plantation changed the course of our lives in ways that no one could have anticipated, opening the doors to tragedy and pain. This cannot be forgotten. If the plantation had not been bought, things would have been very different. It would not have stopped Castro's Revolution from eventually turning everything upside down, but had Ignacito and father been alive when the Revolution took place, the whole family might have moved to the United States early on. We would have settled in Miami and prospered as other Cubans have, without suffering death and separation. Would our lives had been better? We can only speculate as to details, but surely they would have been very different. All of this because of the wrong decision by one man who broke his word and paid dearly for it.

Chapter Fifty-Two

Sugar and Slavery

The raison d'être of the cursed plantation was sugar production, which in Cuba was inextricably associated with slavery from the very beginning. First the island's Amerindians were given away to be exploited to *encomenderos* who were supposed to take care of them but, instead, used them as de facto slaves. As the Amerindians began to die-off because of excessive work and the diseases the Spaniards brought with them, Africans were brought in to take their place. They became slaves both de facto and in name. By the time independence came at the beginning of the twentieth century, slavery had been abolished, but sugar production had continued to foster a kind of slavery, although with a different name and under different conditions.

In the fifties when father bought the sugarcane plantation, the sugar industry was heavily dependent on manual labor. No one had yet invented a machine that could cut sugarcane without damaging the plants. The cutting had to be done by hand with *machetes*. This cutting occurred only during a short season in the year. Most of the year sugarcane needs relatively little attention; just de-weeding, watering, and fertilizing, which are done with minimal manual labor. Large numbers of workers were hired only for the cutting season called *la zafra*. When *la zafra* came to an end, they had nothing else to do and no way of earning any money. Because very few other jobs, let alone well-paid ones, were available for unskilled workers, the workers had no alternative but to come back to cut sugarcane.

The needs of workers—food primarily, since most of them dressed in rags—created a great opportunity for enterprising plantation owners to make extra money. In order to provide what the workers needed, they set up stores where they would sell to them what they required, on credit and sometimes with interest and for a fee, which varied from owner to owner. No one else, of course, would do this for workers, because no one else could be sure that they would return to pay their debts. The condition for the credit extended to workers by plantation owners was that they would pay it back during the cutting season. In principle, the workers could choose not to return to pay back what they owed, but this meant that they were out of work for the working season. They had to come back, whether they liked it or not.

At the beginning of every *zafra*, workers began to pay the debts accrued during the time they were laid off. Very little was left for them afterwards, to use for the coming months in which they were not working. So again, they borrowed from the plantation owner's store, and the cycle would be repeated. The system turned them into virtual slaves, tied down to the land and unable to liberate themselves from the vicious cycle in which they were entangled.

For owners the system worked well. First, they were assured that they would have workers for the cutting season. Second, they had a hostage clientele to whom they could charge whatever they wanted for the goods they sold in the stores, in addition to charging them interest and fees for giving them credit. Since most workers could not read or write, and thus could not keep track of their debts and payments, which owners jotted down in little note books they kept, the system was perfect for unscrupulous owners who wished to cheat workers. Of course, not all owners, perhaps not even most, were scoundrels, but for workers the system was dehumanizing, even when they worked for decent landowners, in that it took away their freedom and tied them to a way of life from which they could seldom liberate themselves. They became indentured to the land, de facto slaves, while the owners accumulated capital.

Yet, no one questioned the justice of the system. Owners were largely insensitive to the miserable and unjust existence of workers. Indeed, they were even insensitive to the physical conditions in which they lived. They provided sleeping quarters for workers which even generously did not deserve that name. Mostly the places where workers stayed during the *zafra* were shacks, with dirt floors that flooded when it rained hard, rotten wooden walls that could not keep bugs and the weather away, and primitive cooking conditions. To make matters worse, workers were separated from their families.

One of the first things that Castro's Revolution did was to establish requirements for the living quarters of workers in sugarcane plantations. Good walls, cement floors, beds or hammocks to sleep on, and appropriate cooking facilities were required. Many owners complained bitterly about these requirements, but I remember that mother, Nena, and I were ashamed that we had not thought before of remedying the situation in which workers lived on our plantation. This was the first time I realized how insensitive one can become to the misery of others, and one's own responsibility for it when a society as a whole turns its back on part of its population. Our family considered itself moral, just, and even generous, while workers were living in subhuman conditions on our plantation. Why did we not notice it when the conditions were quite evident, and we certainly would not have tolerated those conditions if applied to any of us?

There was irony in the lives of sugarcane workers. Lives spent in the process of creating sugar, something very sweet, but such existence was sour. Yet, they managed not only to survive, but even to have some fun in spite of the dire conditions in which they lived, a testimony to the resilience of the human spirit. I never spent time on the plantation, but father did and he told us of a custom among black workers that illustrates that resilience.

At dusk, after an exhausting day of work, they would go into their quarters to rest and eat their dinner. Then, as they smoked tobacco, they would slowly drift toward the rails of the trains that carried the sugarcane to the mill, *el ingenio*. They would bring metal objects with them, perhaps a spoon with which they ate, a knife, an iron rod, a piece of broken machinery, or a *machete*. The first to arrive started playing a simple rhythm on the rails with the metal object he had. Then came another who added a variation to it, and then another, until there were thirty or forty workers banging away at the rails. Sometimes one of them would sing a plaintive song that sounded more like a lament, and others would join. According to father, the complex rhythms that mixed-in both expected and unexpected ways were full of energy, variety, and creativity; the rhythm stuck to your body and made your feet move.

Dusk gave way to the darkness of night when the faces, arms, and legs of the men became indistinguishable, except for the big white eyeballs, concentrated on the music, blending into the night. Above, the shining stars in a clear sky, uncluttered with smog or pollution, matched their eyes and the purity of the music. The men would play for a long time, until it was late and they began to drift away, as they had come, to their shacks. Tomorrow there would be another day of heavy work, and at dusk they would return to make music. There was no radio, no TV. There was only the night, their hands, and their soul. This was their pastime, their entertainment, a sweet moment in an otherwise sour existence.

Chapter Fifty-Three

"El Marañon Aprieta la Boca"

After father's death, the most important financial matters pressing on our family were the settlement of the estate and how to deal with the sugarcane plantation. The settlement of the estate was supposed to be a simple matter because father had left a will with standard provisions. Unfortunately for us, in spite of all of father's planning, he had overlooked an important factor. Ignacito had died intestate, and so father's estate could not be settled until my brother's estate had. This meant that the entire process of determining heirs for someone who had died without a will would have to be undertaken. This created an opportunity for our unscrupulous lawyer who saw this as a way to get hold of a profitable plantation for a bargain price. Here was a widow without any knowledge of financial and business matters, with a fourteen-year-old son who was just a stupid kid, and an older but inexperienced daughter who was not sufficiently savvy to deal with the situation. The trick for the lawyer was to drag-out the process, and thus to put pressure on us to sell the plantation for a fraction of what it was worth in order to get money to survive. He was efficient at it. Months passed and nothing happened about the settlement. There was always some paper or other that was required, and we were told that the wheels of the government bureaucracy were not moving. Fortunately for us, and unknown to the lawyer, father had left two substantial insurance policies for mother, and another one to cover my expenses while I was studying. This money, which was paid immediately, not only kept us in good shape, but could continue to fund our needs for a substantial period of time.

Eventually, in spite of our naiveté, we realized what was happening, but we were not experienced to know how to deal with things. We could not openly accuse the lawyer, who had been father's legal counselor for many years, of doing anything illegal or unethical. That would backfire since he had all the papers and the connections to make life even more difficult for us. So, what to do? Mother realized she had a powerful weapon that women usually have in societies where they do not enjoy the same power as men: tears. After all, she was grandmother's daughter and had seen that women's tears, at least in Cuba, had power. So, she made an appointment with the lawyer and we all went to see him.

I remember the event well. We went into his very stodgy office in Ciego de Ávila, with law books lining the walls, and leather and mahogany furniture. After the proper courtesies, mother came to the point. We needed money, it had been a year since father's death, and she could not understand why the legal proceedings concerning the estate were taking so long. The lawyer, like the good snake he was, tried to blame others and to wiggle out of his predicament, but mother would not let him escape and eventually started crying, begging him to do what he could to help us—all the time knowing that he was the cause of our situation. Well, the man became increasingly uncomfortable and finally realized that he had lost the game and that he better come clean or face not only a continuous uncomfortable situation, but perhaps even some serious accusations if mother realized what had been going on. Not that he thought she would, although there was something about her that made him uncomfortable. Prudence made him relent, and so he said he would help. Mother played the part of the gracious lady until we were in our car, then she gloated. The lawyer did what he promised and the matter was resolved within a month. I guess he was not such a snake after all if my mother's crocodile tears influenced him so much.

Another one of the difficulties we faced was the managing the plantation. After Ignacito's accident, father had brought the bailiff of one of the farms he had owned in Chambas to help him manage the plantation. He needed someone he could trust to take care of the day-to-day details. Although he visited the plantation every day, there had to be someone *in situ* to supervise the operation even at times when there was little to do and he was not present. He chose a good man, a Spaniard known for an unimpeachable morality. He had been bailiff in El Anoncillo, where he had taken over the administration after uncle Jaime had failed to do the job properly. Even his name, *Prudencio,* suggested trust. He could be trusted implicitly to do what was right and not to cheat. Still, father kept money matters in his own hands; he always paid the workers himself and handled all the accounts.

Subsequently to father's death, the only alternative we had was to increase the bailiff's responsibilities, and continue going to the plantation to pay the workers and do some occasional supervision. Because I was still in secondary school, this was done by mother and Nena. The logistics of all this were cumbersome and made us think about buying a place around Ciego de Ávila that would allow us to stay near the plantation for longer periods of time when it was necessary to do so. Mother and I did, and for a time it seemed that we had succeeded in finding a way to keep the sugarcane plantation going. At some point we had thought of selling it, but the yield was so good that we changed our minds. Of course, we had no idea that within a short time Castro was going to come to power and confiscate all lands and eventually all private property. This took time and we still had to face another serious crisis on the plantation.

A couple of years after father's death, we realized that the bailiff's initial drinking problem had become so serious that he was not managing the plantation properly. In fact, a couple of times we found him completely drunk when we visited. It was clear that he could not take the stress. But getting rid of him was not realistic, and as the saying goes, *más vale mal conocido que bueno por conocer* (better the devil you know than the devil you don't). Given the importance of the plantation to our financial future, something had to be done to exercise control, but there was no immediate solution we could think of. Eventually, in the storm unleashed by the Revolution, this was a minor inconvenience in comparison with everything else that was happening in Cuba.

Chapter Fifty-Four

"I Believe in God"

While all these events were changing our family, I was undergoing individual changes in my personal life. One of these concerned faith. A good number of Cubans I know, regardless of whether they are Catholic, Protestant, or something else, believe in spirits, ghosts, magic, incantations, and the occult. Cuban society is flooded with stories, personal and common, about happenings of this sort. Many Cubans visit spiritualists, mediums, and everything else that comes with the territory. Many keep altars and shrines in their homes, hang pictures of saints and deities on their walls, and offer food, drinks, tobacco, and even sacrifices of animals to various deities and spirits. Indeed, at the time pertinent to this narrative, all sorts of rituals were performed in front of the images. It was customary in many households for the lady of the house to light up and puff on a cigar, enveloping the images in the smoke, while uttering prayers and to burn incense throughout the houses to get rid of evil spirits. Most people wore medals of their favorite saints, the Virgin Mary, as well as crucifixes and scapulars. Children had black amber pinned to their clothes to guard against the evil eye, and everyone was encouraged to venerate relics of saints, to kiss the rings of bishops which presumably enclosed pieces of Christ's cross, to use blessed water, and to attend processions.

Many of the religious entities venerated by Cubans were mixes of Catholic and African saints or deities, but no one was bothered by these facts and beliefs, and the Catholic hierarchy turned a blind eye to the proceedings, as long as the people stayed in the fold. From the very beginning of the conquest and colonization of America, the Catholic hierarchy encouraged practices that, intentionally or not, favored a syncretism between Catholicism and African or pre-Columbian religions. For example, following a long tradition of religious imperialism, the Church built churches to Christian saints on places where pre-Columbian temples had existed, with the result that the population was prone to identify Amerindian deities who had been worshiped at the temples with Christian saints to whose veneration the Christian church was dedicated.

In Cuba there were no pre-Columbian temples, but Africans brought with them religious deities, spirits, and rites, and these became identified and mixed-in with Christian ones. And who is to criticize the attitude of the Church toward these practices? The people had faith and they needed it after the brutal conquest and colonization by Iberians. Why not allow them to expand their faith to include Christianity rather than abandon their original beliefs without a raft to maintain them afloat? Expediency was not in the minds of most friars and priests that evangelized Amerindians. Probably foremost in their minds was to ameliorate the impact of the conquest and colonization. Why pay attention to fine points of doctrine when there are more important things to worry about? Why go to war on whether an egg should be eaten from the pointed end or the rounded end? Indeed, the Gospels are full of examples in which Christ appears to place compassion over doctrinal precision or orthodoxy. Isn't love the foundation of the Christian faith?

My family was no different in this than other Cuban families, except that most of its members were highly educated and thus their attitude was rather paradoxical. Among the Gracia-Dubiés, the only unbeliever was father. He styled himself a *librepensador*, a free thinker, a Mason and Rosicrucian, who paid no attention to goings-on of spirits. But uncles Julio and Carlos, and aunt Rosario were believers of one sort or another.

At home, mother had also had experiences that she considered to be spiritual and supernatural. One of these struck very close to home. She told us that when Ignacito was a small child and had been sick, one morning he told her that his uncle Carlos, who was his godfather, had spent the night at the foot of his bed. Rather than understanding this experience as a dream, mother interpreted it to mean that Carlos's astral body—Carlos was my brother's godfather—had kept watch over the child to make sure that he recovered from an illness.

Whenever mother went to Havana, she visited great-aunt Mina in order to have a spiritual consultation. Mina kept a Ouija board on which she asked questions, and, based on its answers, she prescribed remedies for various illnesses and problems. I always wondered whether the board actually moved by itself, as it was supposed to do, or whether it was faked while being moved by Mina. But how could one find that out?

One time when mother and Mina were busy in another room, I got up my courage and tried to use the Ouija board by asking questions of it, but it did not move for me. Maybe I was not patient enough to wait for the answers, or maybe my unbelief made it reluctant to communicate with me. After all, faith is a requisite of miracles, as Paracelsus demonstrates in Borges' famous tale.

I was forever enthralled with stories of ghosts, spirits and the supernatural, but after I turned thirteen, I no longer gave credence to them. Despite my disbelief, I experienced a series of events that bothered me. These events occurred shortly before father's death. Mother had become deeply religious after Ignacito's accident. She had abandoned any belief in the occult. She had become an Evangelical Christian and believed only in the Bible. Moreover, I had not heard her mention anything that had to do with the occult for years. Yet, three weeks before father's death, she woke-up one morning, quite agitated, and told Nena and me that we needed to pray because something terrible was threatening our family. She had a dream about the three of us being in the middle of a vast prairie, in a wooden house, when a terrible storm was approaching. The sky had turned black, the wind had started blowing furiously, and the rain hit the roof of the house mercilessly. She felt we were in imminent danger for our lives—significantly, father was not with us.

I did not put much stock in mother's dream because it reminded me of the fairy tale of the three little pigs and the big bad wolf. But I did find it strange that she had it, and had interpreted it as she did, considering that she had stopped believing in these sorts of things. The following week, she had another dream. This time we were in a forest and a very large creature—she could not determine exactly what it was—was perched on a branch of a tree, menacingly stalking the three of us. Again, father was missing. At the moment at which the creature was about to pounce, she awoke. The following morning, she was quite distressed and asked us to pray. This time I began to worry, not because I felt anything would happen to us, but because I was wondering about mother's state of mind.

A week later, she had another dream. We were in a boat in the middle of the ocean, at night. The waves were large and threatening and the boat was flimsy. Our situation was precarious and we did not know what to do. When a wave of large proportions was about to overturn the boat, mother awoke. This time she did not wait until morning to tell us about her dream. She was so agitated that she woke us up in the middle of the night and asked us to kneel and pray with her. I was seriously concerned about her behavior and wondered, with my sister, whether we should alert father.

But a week went by, she did not have another bad dream and nothing had happened, so we relaxed. Mother felt that perhaps the dreams meant nothing and I thought she might have overcome whatever had worried her and had been their source. However, a few days later father was dead of a heart attack. The storm had hit, the animal had pounced, and the boat had overturned. We were fighting for our lives.

The relation of father's family with the Catholic Church was ambiguous to say the least. After all, the Dubiés blamed the Jesuits for the collapse of their fortune, but there were also other reasons for their attitude. They were well educated and liked to read and they were interested in everything intellectual. Once I started growing up, one of my favorite pastimes was to challenge father's knowledge, asking him questions about authors I had just heard of or had recently read. To my chagrin, however, I was never able to find an author or a book that father did not know about, which I interpreted as proof of his vast erudition, although rather it was probably proof of my gross ignorance. Regardless of which, it was quite frustrating, and the rest of his family was just like him.

At the same time, many of the Dubiés, like great-grand-aunt Mina, believed in *Espiritismo* (spiritism), and some of the Gracias were not far behind. Uncle Julio and aunt Rosario were deep into it in spite of all their intellectual pretension. Uncle Carlos was different in that he did not have a strong belief in spiritualism, but he was a firm believer in Hinduism mixed with Buddhism. And my parents shared an interest in Eastern philosophies and religions. Prior to mother's conversion to Evangelical Christianity, as a typical Cuban Catholic she integrated into her beliefs all sorts of *Spiritist* views, although she was never comfortable with hard core spiritualism, being quite afraid of it. After her conversion she rejected all of it as the work of the devil.

No one in the family, however, was a devotee of *Santería*. This and spiritism are different, although often they combine in various ways. *Spiritism* has to do with a belief that in addition to the physical world we perceive, there is a world in which spirits abound. Most of these are spirits of dead people that still roam the Earth for a variety of reasons. They are not called ghosts. Ghosts are scary, but spirits are remnants of people who once were part of the living. Some of them are evil, but most of them are benign, although they might be disturbed in that they have not achieved proper rest. They still have something left to do in this world and this is why they stick around. Access to them is possible through people who have special gifts to communicate with them, the mediums who establish bridges between the living and the dead.

Santería is the belief in Catholic saints generally identified with African deities. When Africans came to Cuba as slaves, they brought with them the religions they practiced in Africa and it was just a matter of time for them to see similarities between Catholic saints and their own African pantheon. Together with their deities, they brought rituals and magic. Given the shadowy and often unstructured world of these beliefs, it was easy for *Santería* and *Spiritism* to mix.

There seems to have been a social class difference in Cuba with respect to these beliefs. The lower classes, particularly blacks, tended to practice

Santería, but the bourgeoisie tended to practice *Spiritism.* Moreover, *Spiritism* became mixed with eastern religions and philosophy in the minds of some members of the bourgeoisie. The more educated the people, the more philosophical and eastern their beliefs were, and the less educated, the closer they became to *Santería.* But the lines between these various practices and beliefs were not often sharp.

Both of my parents, and mother even for a while after her conversion, took Hindu philosophy seriously, and read on it extensively. We had plenty of books on Hindu thought at home, and the views of popular proponents of this tradition were discussed frequently. Everyone enjoyed arguing about the fine points of doctrine. Did reincarnation really make sense? Is the suppression of desire the solution to human suffering? What is the relation of spiritual well-being and yoga? What are *prana* and *karma?*

I was introduced to these ideas when I was a child, and was reading Khrisnamurti at thirteen. This created a tension in my thinking between the teachings I received in school, which were Christian and particularly Catholic, and the books I read at home on Hindu and Buddhist philosophy. The first, as is the case with the three major Semitic faiths—Judaism, Christianity, and Islam—advocated belief in a somewhat personal god, the God of Abraham, Isaac, and Jacob and conceived happiness in terms of a life of action. To be happy is to live a life of activity. For Judaism this means the practice of the Law as presented in the Old Testament; for Christianity it involves practices that express a love of God and our human neighbors; and for Islam is a life that aims to establish a socio-political system that allows the practice of Islamic law. By contrast, the recommendations of Hindu and Buddhist sages dispense with a personal God and favor a life in which desire is suppressed, for it is desire that creates unhappiness and dissatisfaction. And what example did I have from my family?

The example of father was complicated. As a free thinker, he was not an atheist, but he did not believe much of anything that had to do with the supernatural, and he certainly did not adhere to much Catholic doctrine. This caused me a great deal of pain after I started school, because my teachers were members of Catholic orders and kept telling me that, unless father went to Mass, took the Sacraments, and followed the Church's commandments, he would go to hell. In spite of my efforts to move him to do "the right thing," father would not hear about doing any of these things, and particularly not about going to mass. His response when I asked him why he didn't do it was that he had gone to enough Masses in his youth to last him for his entire life. Of course, that was not the point and I felt considerable anguish as a result, thinking that he was damned. Occasionally I was angry with him for being so thick and not paying attention to what I said. I wanted him to make sure he would go to heaven so that I did not have to worry about his fate. And I did want to see him in Heaven, for how could I be happy there when he was burning in Hell? Once, I asked one of my teachers this question, to which he answered that happiness in Heaven consisted of the vision of God and not in fellowship with Earthly parents. Needless to say, I found the answer emotionally wanting and continued to worry about it until I decided that for things to work out, everyone would have to end up in Heaven—I had become a Universalist, but of course, that opened another Pandora's box.

I was particularly distressed when I realized that father was a Freemason and a Rosicrucian, for I was told by my teachers that these were horrible sects that committed horrendous crimes, and that anyone who had achieved the level father had in the Freemasons was excommunicated and, unless he repented, he would certainly burn in Hell for eternity. It was difficult for me to believe that father was capable of committing the crimes that my teachers said Freemasons did, and to think that he would suffer eternal damnation. I thought he was a pretty good father and, with few imperfections—mainly that occasionally he did not let me do what I wanted—he was a highly moral person. When I told father what my teachers said, he laughed and responded that in time I would understand how rotten and ignorant most members of the clergy were. At one point, father added that I should look into the history of the papacy, for no one in his right mind could believe that the Pope was the Vicar of Christ on Earth when a large number of popes had been scoundrels of the worst kind. Even though at the time I did not know about Alexander VI and Leo X, his remarks gave me pause, and when I eventually got to read about the Renaissance Popes, what I read supported father's ideas and undermined the stories and views of my teachers.

Grandmother Dubié was more of a believer than father, but her beliefs were not ordinary, and she was not particularly partial to spiritism. She considered herself a Catholic, in a French sort of way. She would say the rosary every day, but she was not interested in going to church or in keeping up other religious observances. In fact, she said she was fed up with the saints and the priests and would pay attention only to Jesus. (Maybe she was a secret Huguenot!) When I asked her why she did not like the saints and the priests, her answer was that the saints had never answered her prayers and the priests were interested only in her money. So, she had given them up.

After I grew up, I understood that most members of the Gracia-Dubié family were interested in the spiritual side of things, but that they had a critical eye when it came to institutionalized religion and dogma. They never had anything like blind faith. I do not know whether they had ever heard of Kierkegaard—I suppose father had—but I think if they had, they would have been horrified that someone could reject reason so readily. I am sure they would have resoundingly rejected his Protestant version of fideism. Their religious or spiritual beliefs were matters they had worked out for themselves, taking what appeared to them to be good and rejecting what appeared to be bad. I fit right in, for it had not been easy for me to accept ideas or doctrines simply on the basis of authority. If they did not make sense, I could not accept them.

This made me a kind of rationalist, but not in a strict and unbending way. Rationalists can be as dogmatic as Fideists, for whom reason is either eliminated altogether or relegated to a subservient role in faith. It has always been difficult for me to understand how humans, who as such must depend on reason for most of what they do, can reject it so easily when it comes to what might be the most important matters for them. How can we accept something that contradicts reason, when reason, understood broadly, is one of the most important tools, perhaps the most important, that we share with other humans?

Religion began to have some impact on my life after I started school in first grade, but still it was a rather secondary concern for me. I did what was required as explained by my religious teachers. I attended Mass, I went to confession and took Holy Communion weekly, I had small daily devotional activities, and I paid attention to religious instruction in school. This was in some ways a reflection of the religious attitude in my family. Father thought poorly of the Catholic clergy, which was the only clergy with which our family had any contact. Mother was an indifferent Catholic, poorly trained in doctrine, with the usual dose of spiritualism. After my sister started high school in the establishment run by Teresian nuns, she became more devout, and this filtered down to me. But it was not until fifth grade that I began to take religion seriously. In part this was the result of my brother's accident and death and the search for meaning and consolation experienced by mother. Her conversion to a biblically centered form of Christianity was probably a decisive factor, together with the growing emphasis on religious practices and teaching at school.

In fifth grade, Catholic schools began to make a serious effort to recruit students for religious vocations. A whole week of the year was devoted to the value of the religious life and to encourage students to make a decision to join the orders that managed the schools. There was also a missionary week in which the role of the Church in Africa, Asia, and some parts of Latin America was explored and money was collected to help in the effort to Christianize the heathen and to convert members of other religions. The heroic deeds of saints and martyrs were constantly repeated and the ideals that had inspired them were exalted.

All these efforts slowly had an effect on me so that I began to look upon religious practices as essential for the good life. The emphasis on sin and the depravity, worthlessness, and ingratitude of humans toward God, and of His mercy and love for us, prompted me to increase my devotions. Eventually, I developed an elaborate system of daily practices, beginning in the morning and closing in the evening. I would go to my room, close the door and spend at least an hour saying the rosary and various prayers, meditating on how bad

I was, on my shortcomings as a Christian, and the sorrow I was causing Jesus Christ.

In school we were encouraged to castigate our flesh, offering our pain to God in order to ameliorate the suffering our sins caused Him. We were told stories of holy people who had lashed their bodies with ropes with nuts on them so that they would hurt the flesh more deeply. We were given examples of how children who loved God put pebbles in their shoes to feel pain that they offered to God as reparation for human sins. I did this and many other things that I thought earned me pleasure in the eyes of God, although I never had the vocation of a martyr and I did not like to suffer. Pain did not agree with me, and I never engaged in any of the more extreme practices that other kids my age did. At the time, I thought I was being selfish and cowardly, now I think I was being sensible and rational.

It was at this time that I learned about indulgences. I had a prayer book that gave an account of the number of indulgences one could earn by doing certain things, such as taking Holy Communion, saying certain prayers, giving alms to the poor, and so on. The book explained that for each of these one reduced one's time in Purgatory by a certain number of days. Purgatory was a place where those who were going to Heaven, but were not yet clean enough to enter it, spent time being purified further and paying some of the debts they had incurred through sin. The doctrine is that even when your sins are forgiven through Confession, they have defiled you and you need, as it were, a reconstitution, a building up, to be able to join Jesus in Heaven. It is as if through confession you were given entrance to a marvelous party, but you were still dressed in rags and you had to do a little work to earn a proper attire. Or maybe the example of a disease from which you were cured but which had left you weak, required further action to make you strong enough again.

This was the year in which students were confirmed. Confirmation for Catholics is a sacrament carried out in a ceremony conducted by a bishop. In it one is supposed to receive the Holy Spirit and its special gifts, just as it happened with Christ's Apostles and Disciples on Pentecost. The moment is solemn. The bishop sits on his *cathedra* just below the altar and holds the staff, a symbol of his pastoral authority. He is dressed in traditional solemn garbs and a pointed hat. When the candidates approach him, he stands, waiting until they reach him. Then he lays his hands over each candidate, anoints their foreheads with previously blessed oil, and finally lightly slaps their cheeks to remind them of the difficulties they face in spreading the Gospel. I was impressed and moved by the ceremony and felt spiritually stronger after it. Perhaps it was true that the Holy Spirit had confirmed my faith and as a result I had become ready to let God work through me.

Apart from daily Mass and prayers at school, there were other activities throughout the year and celebrations on feast days that were part of the

Christian calendar and in which I participated. In Ciego de Ávila we lived less than a block away from the parish church so it was easy for me to attend religious celebrations that took place in it. I met with my school mates on Sundays and feast days, particularly during Holy Week and feasts celebrating the Virgin Mary. The year was full of religious events. Sometimes these involved processions in which the statues of Christ, the Virgin Mary, and various saints would be taken out of the church and carried through the streets of the town which had been decorated to celebrate the occasion.

I belonged to the school band, and the band always participated in these processions. I played the snare drum, but also the cymbals and the triangle when there was a need. It was fun to practice for weeks after school for these occasions. It was even greater fun to go on parades and processions, playing and enjoying the applause of the people. The streets were filled with spectators, some devotedly praying to the saints, and others just enjoying the crowd and the festivities. Food vendors did good business selling *fritas,* the Cuban version of the hamburger. I loved *fritas* but seldom had the opportunity to eat them because mother was opposed to eating street food, and particularly these hamburgers which were made with ground beef, probably contaminated, in her view, and too strongly spiced. The processions were a welcome opportunity for me to eat them because mother was not present and the band stopped periodically for a rest, which were good times to buy *fritas* from the vendors.

The year in fifth grade was filled with religious thoughts and practices, although I did find time to play with my friends and do my school work. This was also the year in which I finally broke through in class and became one of the two best students. I became diligent and highly organized and my grades proved it. At the end of the year I had won so many medals that it was difficult to pin them all on my chest—there were medals for application, excellence, special activities, the band, and various disciplines.

It was a momentous year for me in many ways, and the emphasis on faith and pious practices I think contributed to make me develop a strict discipline that was self-imposed, and which was further developed in later years and has been a cornerstone of my life ever since. Why was I able to do it? Perhaps it was just a matter of genes. I had inherited my father's penchant for order—remember his philosophy of underwear? Or maybe it was the shock of my brother's early death. Or perhaps it was something else. I am not sure why it happened, but it did, and it has made my life much easier.

One other important thing occurred to me in the fifth year: I became a voracious reader. It began when I became addicted to comic books. For a while, all I thought about, apart from religious issues and school, were comic books, and all I did with my money was to buy comic books. The piles of these grew and grew to the point that mother was alarmed. She was also alarmed because, instead of playing or doing other things kids my age do, I just wanted to read comic books. Even when I went to my exercise classes for a presumed case of scoliosis, I managed to read comic books because I fortuitously found horror comic books at the gym, and I spent time reading them while I waited for the trainer.

Then something even more important happened that completed the reading cycle that started with comic books. I got the mumps and had to stay confined to my bedroom for two weeks. I felt not only sick but also quite bored. I could not even read because of headaches, and my eyes were sensitive to light. So, Nena started reading to me classic stories for children. I had always loved hearing the stories, particularly as told by mother and grandmother Dubié, but I had never liked being read to. I still remember that mother had developed a saga about animals that never ended. Every day while I was small, I curled up on her lap and she would continue the yarn, adding this time the story of a lion that was lame, another time that of a monkey that was too clever for its own good, and so on. There were cows, birds, and even fish in struggles that simulated those of humans, and the stories always contained a moral applicable to human conduct. Grandmother's stories were modifications of the well-known adventures of Sinbad the Sailor, the Knights of the Round Table, and other personages from famous books, including tales from the *One Thousand and One Nights*.

At different times during my illness, I developed a taste not so much for being read to, but for the type of stories my sister had chosen to read. Toward the end of my illness I started reading the stories myself, and this impulse continued afterwards. After I was well, I abandoned comic books for classic adventure stories, such as *Beauty and the Beast, Ivanhoe, Scaramouche, Robinson Crusoe*, and *Gulliver's Travels*, but eventually moved to literary fiction. On reaching thirteen I had become a seasoned reader. I discovered novels like *Gone with the Wind* and the books by authors such as Pearl Buck and Alexander Dumas that satisfied my fancy. This transformation was probably one of the most important events in my life, and perhaps the most important intellectual event. From that moment on I never stopped reading. In later years, even at times in which I was extremely busy, preoccupied with problems, or sad because of tragic events in my family, I kept the habit of reading at least a few pages every night. This custom has been an extraordinary source of emotional stability and pleasure in my life.

Chapter Fifty-Five

Building Up the Spirit

My spiritual development continued and got a boost from retreats in which I began to participate yearly starting in the first year of high school (the equivalent of seventh grade in the U.S.). St. Ignatius of Loyola designed a month-long set of spiritual exercises for members of the religious order he founded, the Jesuits. It was a way of keeping them aware of the ultimate end of human life, the misery of human existence when separate from God, and the need to feed a militant faith. They were properly called spiritual exercises because they exercised the spirit. They were intended to fortify it, just as bodily exercises strengthen the body. The idea was to keep Jesuits in good spiritual shape, with virtuous habits and a clean mind, just as athletes are kept in top physical shape, with well-toned muscles and healthy bodies through vigorous use of muscles and limbs.

The exercises have always been the backbone of the Jesuits and have helped make their Order an extraordinarily successful institution for the past five-hundred years. The idea that something like it should be made available for ordinary folks made sense, although it could not be expected that they would spend the full four weeks that Jesuits spent on them every year. This is how the toned-down version of the exercises became a common element of Catholic life.

The exercises for lay people were particularly popular in Cuba among young men who attended Jesuit schools, although other schools also encouraged participation in them. They lasted three days. A small group of young men were housed in a dormitory, in separate rooms, and were subjected to a slim version of the procedures designed for members of the Order. The main feature of the exercises was silence. No verbal communication was allowed among participants. They could only communicate verbally with the director of the exercises.

The director conducted a series of meditations on the life of Christ, particularly His suffering, the meaning of the faith, and ultimately the last things, that is, death, judgment, Hell, and Heaven. There was plenty of fire and brimstone in the meditations, but there were also prayers that St. Ignatius had composed. Participants attended Mass daily and had time to themselves, which they were encouraged to use to meditate on the words of the director. Daily Confession and Communion were also encouraged. The impact these combined activities had on the participants was often profound and significant. Many religious vocations developed as a result, and practically everyone who participated left with a renewed faith and the intention to live a better Christian life.

For teenagers like me, the most significant part of the exercises was the silence. At this age we are used to be in constant communication with others, but all of a sudden such communication stopped. We were alone, by ourselves. There was no external noise, no interruptions, no support or opposition. We became speakers and listeners simultaneously. Dialogues became soliloquies. Our thoughts wandered and meandered. Memories came and went. And the ideas put into our heads by the director began to lead us into unexpected directions. We experienced a kind of emptying out, "a dark night of the soul," which in turn made room for the thoughts planted in our minds by an experienced trainer. The ground had been prepared in school, by classes on religion and doctrine, and by repeated prayers and attendance to chapel. Now, alone, those ideas came back and grew roots. In the silent corridors, we moved, looking at each other curiously, wondering what the others were thinking, passing each other like ghosts. The desire to speak and share, the curiosity to find out where the others were, increased by the hour. After the first day it began to reach a critical point that exploded at the end of the second day, reaching a climax that led to a kind of spiritual breakdown. This was a spiritual earthquake and the beginning of a recovery.

The first time I attended the exercises I experienced a spiritual transformation unlike any other I had experienced before. The temptation to devote my life to the worthy cause of spreading the Gospel and becoming a Jesuit was strong, although I never seriously considered a religious life for any length of time. I read too much and I had too many doubts about the institution of the Church to jump into a life of service and the pursuit of a cause that I was willing to subject to a rigorous process of critical examination. The challenge of sacrificing oneself for others, and perhaps for God, was very tempting at an age full of idealism and the emotional romanticism that leads to embracing causes. Teenagers are ripe for a process of sublimation in which the life of hardship and sacrifice becomes a way of channeling the exploding energy that characterizes them. But I could never bring myself to take any step in the direction of a cloistered life in the Church. Still, every year that I attended the exercises, they renewed my sense of the beauty and value of Christianity, and to this day I cannot but admire the life of the Jesuit in spite of the many mistakes they have made. The complete commitment to the Order, the painful experience of the denial of self-will required by uncompromising obedience, and the militant spirit that permeates the community functioned like a candle that attracts a moth to the light that will kill the old self and be the beginning of the rebirth of the new.

Among the participants in the exercises developed a kind of competition to become the most affected by, and devoted to, the experiences to which we were being subjected. Of course, there were some who missed the whole point of the exercises and talked and made fun of what was happening. But these were fools, and they were few in number. They did not understand the purpose of what we were called to do, and missed the high that those of us who embraced the spirit of the thing and worked hard to reach its denouement. What a wasted time for them! What a missed opportunity to delve into another dimension of human experience! But perhaps they should not be blamed; perhaps they were too afraid to dig deep into themselves, used as they were to the *mundanal ruido* of which Fray Luis de León spoke so eloquently, the worldly noise that envelops us in ordinary life. I can't help but think of the mystical rapture depicted by the Bernini sculpture of St. Theresa of Ávila above the major altar of St. Peter's Basilica in the Vatican, and how it expresses well the abandon of the spirit into the oblivion of mystical passion, something close to what some of us felt.

I did the exercises every year for the five years I was in high school, and every year I felt renewed and reborn in unexpected ways. The confrontation with the last rites, with death in particular, cleaned my mind of much unnecessary rubbish that cluttered it, and kept me balanced, aware of how fragile human life is, how petty human beings are, and how short our existence lasts. The exercises were a wonderful reawakening, whether one actually believed or not in the Christian faith, into the reality that confronts us, the darkness in which we live, and the possibility of some light. Not that I became more devout, or that my faith was strengthened, or my doubts about the Christian faith were assuaged. The experience was much deeper. It went beyond the expected, the ordinary. It was like being drunk with the spirit while simultaneously experiencing an intellectual illumination that made me see clearly. I felt like Funes, the protagonist of Borges' story, and like him the results were not completely beneficent in that the experience clouded some other aspects of my life.

The Jesuit exercises originated in Spain, and in Spain also originated a different sort of retreat that was developed to take the place of, or perhaps complement, the exercises. Some thought that the Jesuit experience was too stark and too negative; their focus was the dark side of life and its inevitable end. Instead, they believed that faith should be a matter of rejoicing, of opening new vistas and enjoying what is good rather than dwelling on what is bad, and perhaps even more important, sharing the good news. Why not sing rather than meditate on death? Why not laugh rather than cry? Why not spread the Gospel rather than look into the darkest corners of our souls? Christianity is supposed to be a joyful faith intended to bring salvation and mirth rather than pain and misery, and its aim is to communicate the message of salvation to others. This is how the so-called *Cursillos de Cristiandad* (literally "brief courses on Christianity) were developed in the forties, also in Spain, as a counterbalance to Loyola's exercises.

The *Cursillos* were similar to the spiritual exercises in duration but their intent and method were different. The goal was to create leaders of the faithful so they could bring into the fold wayward Christians who had lost the zeal for the faith. Unlike in the Ignatian Exercises, participants talked to each other and shared their love for the faith and for Christ. This was an occasion for rejoicing and learning about the beauty of Christianity. It was a call to go forth in the Evangelization of the world, in a joyful sharing of the love of Christ.

I did the *Cursillos* once, but that was enough for me. I did not like them. I felt them to be superficial, false, forced. One had to laugh and be joyful when one did not feel like it. They asked those who participated in them to put on a mask of mirth with the hope that the pretense would turn the mask into a reality. But I found that difficult. The song *De colores,* which marks the *cursillistas,* got stuck in my throat. I missed the misery I experienced with the Jesuit exercises. I felt more at home with the meditations on death, at least when I wanted to get to the bottom of existence. I've never been good at faking, a reason I could never be an actor. And I've never been good at ignoring the predicaments that surround humans. Yes, I can laugh and I love to have a good time, but when all is said and done, I want to see things as they really are, and they are very grim, indeed. For this reason, I like my religion sober and meditative, with a bit of anxiety and pain, just as I like my art crunchy, as a friend of mine describes it.

Chapter Fifty-Six

First Cracks of the Faith

In fifth grade I reached the upper limits of an unexamined faith. I generally believed what my religious teachers told me about God and the world. I did not question what they said but accepted it at face value. I believed the stories they told me were true and I spent my time feeling guilty and trying to make up for the pain that my behavior caused God. But this period of my life soon came to an end. In September, we moved to Havana, where I started attending the Marist School in La Víbora.

Nothing really changed as far as the school or my teachers were concerned. The teachers continued their work of indoctrination, but the change of location, the trauma of the move and reasons for it, and the need to make new friends and adapt to the new situation created havoc in my life. My grades tanked—I went from being the first or second in the class to becoming one in the middle of the pack. I detested my classmates, and perhaps more important of all, I had started reading voraciously the previous year, and now, reading became my escape and salvation. Reading books also introduced me to thoughts and ideas I did not know existed. What I read was different from what my teachers said, and those incredible stories of bleeding, bread, and martyrdom we had been fed in primary school now found a counterweight.

I began to critically examine my views and slowly dropped many of the practices and beliefs that had been central to my life. I did not question the truth of Christianity and I did not question the good will of my teachers. But the first cracks in the edifice they had built and in which I had lived, oblivious to anything else, began to appear. In school I was introduced to ancient history, which I found fascinating. These were stories of a different kind. Yes, there was gore as well, and heroic acts, but the heroism was not for beliefs that challenged our reason, but for honor and virtue. There was a difference, and even though I was still immature, I felt it and began to appreciate it.

I experienced a crisis in the second year of high school. I had again regained my place at the head of the class, with a straight-A record in the first year. And I continued reading every book I found either in father's library, aunt Rosario's library, or those recommended by anyone. Some of the books were suggested by my teachers, some I saw advertised, and some were offered by classmates. I bought a large number of books as well. Anything illicit was welcome. I do not mean illicit because it was pornography. In fact, there was plenty of pornography to be had in Cuba, but that was not what I read. I never spent a penny on that. Most of the books in question had been placed on the Catholic Church's infamous Index Librorum Prohibitorum. The Index of Forbidden Books, for those who do not know, was a list of books the Catholic hierarchy deemed through canon law to be dangerous, and should not be read except with the permission of the clergy, the so-called *imprimatur*. Practically every important book in Western culture was in the Index, and so it was inevitable that someone who liked to read would read forbidden books. I have found it incomprehensible why some books, such as *Les Miserables*, was placed on the Index. But I also read beyond the Index.

Among the books I read that made important impressions on me were *The Twenty-Fifth Hour* by Constantin Virgil Gheorghiu, the tale of a man who suffers an endless list of mishaps during World War II while he is mistakenly thought to be Jewish because he was circumcised. Another was *The Skin* by Curzio Malaparte, a story of the American invasion of Italy. I still recall the images I formed in my mind reading this book — the assertion that black American soldiers patronized Italian prostitutes but asked that they wear blonde hair pieces on their genitals. Even more important was Françoise Sagan's *Bonjour Tristeze*, which had become a kind of existentialist manifesto for young people. The *ennui* described in that book matched well my adolescent moods.

There are too many books to list. I read everything I got my hands on, including biographies of kings, queens, popes, heroes, and artists. Among my favorite biographies were those of Marie Antoinette and Michelangelo. The stories of the popes were particularly shocking. I remembered what father had said about the leaders of the Catholic hierarchy, but I had not quite believed it. Yet, it was true. The Renaissance Vatican was a moral cesspool, one of the reasons why the Reformation was so successful (although it also was a glorious atelier). Not that it was the only, or even the primary, reason for its success, of course. Politics and power had as much to do with it as anything else. Luther was no innocent Cinderella. But the state of the Papacy certainly gave Reformers a reason for rejecting the Catholic Church's legitimacy.

All of this came to a head at thirteen, when I decided that the Catholic Church was a sham. The reason I reached this conclusion was not just that so many of the highest leaders of the Catholic hierarchy had been corrupt, but more importantly, that the doctrine did not make any sense. The idea of a God who inflicts the kind of punishment on his so-called children, whom He is supposed to love so much as to give up the life of His only Son for them, was just unbelievable. What father would behave in such a way toward his children for any infraction, even an egregious one? What kind of a father, or a god, was this?

Moreover, the idea that He would send Himself in the garb of Jesus to be crucified and die for our sins was absurd. First of all, how could Jesus die since He was God and God is supposed to be immortal? The idea that the Virgin did not die and was lifted in body to heaven was equally nonsensical. How can a body be taken to heaven when heaven is not a physical place? The more I thought, the more Catholic doctrine appeared to be nonsense to me. Of course, if I had been a follower of Tertullian, for whom the measure of faith is absurdity, this would have had the effect of strengthening my faith as it does in fact with many believers. But I have never been a follower of Tertullian; indeed, Tertullian is not one of my favorite writers or thinkers. I believe that if faith is to be taken seriously, it has to at least be consistent with reason, and better still to make sense. As St. Thomas Aquinas argued, faith need not be proven by reason, but faith should be compatible with reason.

But would giving up belief in the Catholic doctrines that appeared to me to be nonsense require that I give up all sense of spirituality? The choice was difficult because when I went to church I was often deeply moved. The procession of the Host on Holy Thursday, the singing of St. Thomas Aquinas' magnificent hymn, the *Pange Lingua*, together with the incense and the ritual, produced in me experiences that were deep and seemed genuine. Did this mean that all of this was a fake? And what of the holy people I knew, men and women who had selflessly devoted their lives to Christ and to the welfare of others? Were they complete fakes too, or were they completely stupid? How could I reject the legitimacy of St. John of the Cross' *Spiritual Canticle* or of Augustine's *Confessions?* At this time, I had also begun reading the work of Eastern sages, whose wisdom I felt deeply and complicated my situation.

The cracks that had begun in fifth grade kept growing, but I still went to church and engaged in religious activities. Rationally I had become an agnostic: I could not believe what the Church taught. Nor could I accept the views that mother tried to press upon me, the Evangelical and Protestant versions of Christianity she had adopted. I found these aberrant, even more unacceptable than Catholic doctrine, in part because of their tendency to irrationality. Still, I did not stop living as if I were a believer, even though I had not found a solution to bring together my doubts and my practices.

As a student of the Marist school I continued to live as if I believed everything the Church taught. In fact, I joined a Catholic Action group and was very active in it, although I tended to concentrate on areas of social assistance, such as helping the poor, rather than on pious acts. For a couple of years, I was in charge of looking after an old, almost blind, black woman who lived alone. I bought her groceries and visited her frequently. She was a fine person, gentle and kind, and the little room where she lived was kept in perfect order and cleanliness. I also went to religious meetings and talks at which I met a fabulous priest by the name of Durán, who was the epitome of devotion and holiness. He was a Spaniard who had settled in Cuba as a member of one of those orders that have both priests and lay members living and working together in the world. To a great extent he was the reason I kept the trappings of Catholicity. He was the real thing. We had many talks, but nothing was ultimately resolved. He tried very hard to get me to commit to his Order, but I could never do that. My temperament is neither that of the activist nor of the religious believer, and the tension between doctrine and practice was at the time unresolved. I would have periods in which I felt a strong sense of spirituality, particularly when I did the Jesuit Spiritual Exercises, but those were always followed by periods in which skepticism reasserted itself.

Chapter Fifty-Seven

Brother Balloon

Apart from faith, there were other forces, experiences, and people who challenged me. One of the people was head teacher in the first year of high school. He had been dubbed *"El Globo"* by students. He had a round face and head and when he was annoyed his face would become red, like an overinflated balloon at the point of explosion. It did not take much time for students to find the appropriate name for him.

El Globo was a frustrated man. He had aspirations of high culture in an environment that was the opposite. Some students thought he was gay because he was always very courteous and his manners were delicate and, in some ways, effeminate. His great love was literature, particularly Cuban literature, in which he eventually received a doctorate. Unfortunately for him, this was just the kind of thing that most students detested. Imagine reading poetry to a bunch of brats in seventh grade! His frustration was not primarily with students, but with his colleagues. The brothers that came to teach in Cuba were generally Spanish young men, almost boys, who had been enlisted in their villages by zealous recruiters who inspired them with a life of service and the security of a monastery. Many could not resist. Most of them were ignorant, crude country folks that *El Globo* found intolerable. What could one say to them? Their rough Christianity grieved him, and their crass sense of humor bruised his sensitive ego.

El Globo was a good man and an excellent teacher, but like so many others who enter a religious life, he had been sold a bag of goods and he found too late that what he had been given was quite different from what he had expected. His life was not happy, and he complained privately, and sometimes openly, about his brothers and the school administration. He would tell some of his best students, among whom I was, that he felt like a caged prisoner among Troglodytes. He longed for something else, a fine life of leisure, literature, and the arts, whereas he was stuck in a place where he could not have a decent conversation with anyone. He was lonely and sad. And the fact that he was Cuban did not help, for the roughness of Spaniards hurt him. *El Globo* had been born in a middle class family and had been brought up in a liberal society in which the middle class enjoyed a relatively high level of education if compared to that of his religious brothers.

I did not particularly like him as a person—I found him artificial and at times ridiculous—but I respected him and understood that he felt trapped. Eventually, however, the upheaval of Castro's Revolution made possible for him to get out of the Order and enter a new life. He got married, had children, and even wrote a novel. I never read the novel, but I fear it must be the kind of sentimental and conventional narrative that is a chore to get through. Still, I cannot but applaud the effort. He survived the Order and the Revolution; he supported a family; and he attempted to do something he truly admired, writing a fictional account.

Chapter Fifty-Eight

"¿Y Tu Abuela, Dónde Está?"

Life in Cuba before Castro had many dimensions. One of these had to do with race and racism. For those who could pass for white in Cuba, passing was the name of the game, insofar as being considered white, as opposed to non-white, conferred on anyone great advantages. The category of non-white primarily included colored, blacks, mulattos, *chinos*, and Indians. The terms, "colored" or *"persona de color,"* were supposed to be a polite term for blacks or mulattoes. Blacks were distinguished by being very dark. Those who were dark but not very dark, a sign of some mixture with white, were called mulattoes. *Chinos* comprised a category that included everyone with East Asian ancestry, not just Chinese. And the Indians were what in the U.S. are called Native Americans. Jews were called *"Polacos"* because they most often came from Poland, and were regarded as white, although they suffered discrimination in certain clubs and associations. I am aware of having met only a couple of Jews in my entire life in Cuba. One was a close friend of my sister who attended university with her, studied with her, and often visited us. She was far from Orthodox and often ate at home with us (she loved ham). I have no idea how Indians from India were classified. In spite of all the readings my family did of Hindu sages, a conversation about their race never came up and I never met anybody whose origins were supposed to be from India, Pakistan, and other countries from that part of the world. People from the Middle East, such as Syrians and Lebanese, some of whom I met, were treated as white, although perhaps they were not allowed to climb the higher echelons of the social ladder.

In my experience, race was associated primarily with blacks and mulattos, sometimes extending to Chinese. Indeed, apart from them, I hardly had any contact with other so-called races or even nationalities. I and many of my school mates grew up in a very insular atmosphere. Other nationalities and ethnic groups were rare. Of course, all sorts of distinctions among whites existed also. The main distinctions had to do with different origins in Spain: Galicians, Basques, Castillians, Asturians, Andalusians, Catalans, and Aragónese, among others. But there was also a smattering of other origins from the rest of Europe and the Middle East.

Except for very few exclusive clubs and societies, there was no place in Cuba you could not go if you were considered to be white. Entering a good private school was easier for whites, although occasional blacks were also admitted. I don't remember a single black, and only a handful of mulattoes or light mulattoes that passed for white, from any of the four schools I attended. Indeed, at St. Thomas Military Academy I remember only one light-skinned 'mulatto'.

If you were taken for 'white', you could be a member of "the right clubs" and perhaps more important, you could marry someone white, which would solidify your social status and that of your children. Of course, if you were mulatto and were able to pass for white, you never mentioned blackness. Cuban society was quite racist, although not as racist as American society has been. Still, there were denigrating expressions used for 'blacks' and 'mulattos', and the terms '*negro*' and '*negra*' were often used contemptuously.

One of my close friends in high school was a relatively light mulatto who thought he passed, even though it was clear that he had a good dose of black ancestry. In the several years that I knew him the subject of his blackness was never broached, but it was, as the saying goes these days, the elephant in the room.

Pedro (not his real name) was short and over-weight. His skin was a light brown color, so that, in principle, he could have been a swarthy Italian, Greek, or Spaniard. Passing for white was easy for him for there were few other markers for rate in his mix. The most important among these was his hair. I never saw the hair as it was naturally, but it was clear that it was curly enough to need uncurling with a hot iron and then be set with a heavy cream that kept it straight. It was as black as it could be and hard to the touch. You never saw a hair out of place.

He lived with his mother and aunt in a two-bedroom apartment in a modest building in a middle-class part of Havana, about half an hour by bus from where we lived. His father had been white and the black strain came to him through his mother. That is why a big picture of dad was prominently displayed in the living room, but a picture of his mother's parents was nowhere to be seen. Both his mother and aunt had very curly hair, now gray, and although their skin color was not darker than his, their features more clearly revealed their black ancestry.

These were wonderful people, with whom I spent many happy hours, playing games and chitchatting. The aunt took care of the house and the mother worked in the Ministry of the Treasury in the area of estates. Indeed, she helped us get our papers through the Ministry without much difficulty after father died. She worked very hard to give her son the best she could, and he was never deprived of anything that she could reasonable afford. They always treated me with affection and seemed to enjoy having me visit them. Pedro was a fine friend, although he was an indifferent student, never getting better than average grades. This was a sore point, because I was a straight 'A' student and at the top of the class. I could see that this was the only area where Pedro's mother resented me.

Next to them lived a widow with her daughter. Ana was a couple of years older than we were and Pedro was in love with her, but she was in love with me. Pedro and I visited them very often, went to the beach together, and played cards at her home. The girl was pretty in a chunky sort of way, but I never fell for her. My crush was elsewhere, with a girl who did not love me. Those are the vicissitudes of love!

Both Pedro's family and Ana's family belonged to the Club Náutico, and I first went there as Pedro's guest. Unfortunately, I could never invite him to the Casino Español. It was not that I was reticent to be seen with a mulatto, since I spent quite a bit of time with him and we went together to all kinds of places, but I was afraid that he would not be allowed to enter the place. It would have been devastating to him and very embarrassing to me insofar as he had never acknowledged to me that he was colored. Imagine the scene, with a guard saying that he could not come into the club! Would I dare ask why? That would be impossible, and yet an explanation was in order. So what could I say? What could Pedro say? That he was not black? I had never been in a similar situation and could not fathom what would happen.

I was quite conflicted about this, often thinking that I was not trying hard enough to stand by my friend, but at the same time afraid of the consequences of doing so. I could not bear the scene where he would not be allowed to enter the club. When we went to the beach, we ended up with each of us going to our respective clubs, the Casino Español and the Club Náutico. In such cases, I swam in the Club Náutico. The fact that he never suggested crossing to the Casino indicated to me that he was also worried. So, I let things go.

While I was going to the Marist school in La Víbora, we kept a very close friendship, but when I moved to St. Thomas Military Academy it cooled off because there was little opportunity to see each other. It became cooler still after 1959, because Pedro and his family were strong supporters of the Castro regime, whereas I had decided early on that Castro's plans for the island were not what they had appeared to be before his triumph.

The attitude of Pedro and his family toward their black ancestry always puzzled me. They often talked of blacks as if they had nothing to do with them. And yet it was quite obvious to everyone that they were black ('*de color*' in Cuba). What did they really think? Did they not realize that others might consider the situation anomalous? Were they convinced that they were not black? Why did they not openly discuss the situation with me? After all, I was a close friend, and spent much time with them. Would it not have been better to openly talk about this? Did they think I would be embarrassed about it?

This is not the only case in which I have had mulatto friends who have tried to pass for white and a similar silence has prevailed in our relationship about their racial situation. Perhaps the matter was so painful to them and the fear of rejection and embarrassment so great that they ignored it altogether. I do not blame them, for being black or mulatto in Cuba was a very bad thing indeed. In fact, I should not have been puzzled by Pedro's behavior and attitude. Slavery is one of the most horrendous institutions that human beings have devised, taking from a person his or her identity as a human being and his or her power to act as he or she deems appropriate. The will of the slave is supposed to be that of the master. Your master! And the master owns you. You are nothing yourself, but only insofar as you are an instrument to be used at your master's whim.

Imagine the abuse, physical, mental, and sexual, that slaves endured. Slavery eats away your identity and replaces it with what someone else wants. Of course, the shame should be on the slave masters, for how can a human being accept the role of master of another human being? This is difficult to understand in that it takes away parts of one's humanity to accept it. When I think about the fact that in my family there were slave owners, the shame overwhelms me. But the shame of slave owners was shockingly transferred to the slaves, which perhaps explains why my friend would have nothing to do with his past, since he had been taught by his ancestor's masters that to be black was to be a slave, and to be a slave was to be nothing.

This explains the importance of the question frequently asked by Cubans: ¿Y tu abuela dónde está? And where is your grandmother? Because the question has to do with race. The reference is to families that have a grandmother who is black and is kept out of sight because the family passes for white.

Cubans are a thoroughly mixed population, and the mix is primarily of white and black, although there is a sprinkling of Amerindian and Chinese in it. The native population of Cuba largely died out as a result of the diseases the Spaniards brought with them and of their abuses when the natives were de facto enslaved to work on plantations. But not completely. The Spaniards mixed with some of the natives and produced offspring whose genes entered the mainstream and generated phenotypical features that can still be seen in some Cubans. Indeed, Fulgencio Batista, the dictator that dominated Cuban politics for many years before Castro's Revolution, clearly shows Amerindian features and a mixture of black, and perhaps even Asian. In the nineteenth century Chinese workers came to Cuba and were turned into quasi slaves. They multiplied and mixed with the non-Chinese population whether black or white. Many of the most famous Cubans are a mix of Chinese, black, and white, as is the case of Wilfredo Lam, the most famous of Cuban painters. The predominant mix, however, is between white and black, and it is quite pervasive. And understandably so when one considers that at the end of the nineteenth century there were two blacks for each white in Cuba.

In spite of this reality, the illusion of white purity and the desire to be white survives to this day among Cubans of all classes, both inside and outside Cuba. This has led to extraordinary efforts to erase whenever possible, or at least to diminish, the presence of blackness in Cuba. Perhaps nothing is more indicative of this than the evolution of representations of the Cuban black patriot, Antonio Maceo. He was a dark mulatto, but there has been a slow, but clearly detectable, evolution in his representations, from the earlier ones in which he looks quite black to more recent ones in which his features have been whitewashed to make him look progressively more white.

White-washing did not affect just representations of Cuban heroes like Maceo, but became a centerpiece of immigration policy in the early twentieth century. One million Galicians were brought to Cuba at that time to help whitewash the population. Within Cuban families, the efforts to become whiter by marrying whiter people and to cover up black roots by closeting black relatives, are chronic. As a black friend of mine once said to me, "To be white is the equivalent of having a degree in Cuba." If you are white, you already have an enormous advantage, and if you are black, well, you are in for a struggle. Can anyone be blamed, then, for wanting to be lily white?

The need to recognize the mixed character of Cubans is evident in various aspects of Cuban culture. In religion, for example, the patroness of Cuba is *La Virgen de la Caridad del Cobre.* Below her likeness is always a boat with three men: the three Juanes who are reputed to have found the image floating at sea. The Virgin herself appears to be of mixed blood, two of the men are Amerindians, and one is black.

The father of the Cuban nation, José Martí, was well aware of the problem of race in Cuba, and unambiguous about the need to eliminate any privilege associated with race. His influence and that of other similarly enlightened patriots, successfully kept segregation out of Cuban law. Contrary to the situation in the United States, where segregationist laws functioned well into the second half of the twentieth century, Cuban law has generally been colorblind. Unfortunately, custom, to this day, has not.

Before the Castro Revolution, associations were kept segregated by race. There were associations for white people and associations for colored people. The term "colored" (*de color*) was useful in that it allowed the associations for black people to include mulattoes, people who were not considered completely black or white but a mixture of the two. Still, the boundary between black/colored and white in Cuba has never been very firm. You are considered white if you look white, and you are considered colored if you look as if you have a substantial amount of black blood. *Negro* (black) is reserved for people who look as if they are not mixed with white. Whence the question, "Where is your grandmother?" Because there are many Cubans who look white but in fact have some ancestor who was black. Still, as long as they keep their black or mulatto ancestors in the closet, they can pass for white.

Matters become complicated because the criterion for one's appearance is imprecise. Many Spaniards are quite dark, yet they are considered white. And many people who have black ancestors look white and are considered to be so. Indeed, in the same family you may have children that are quite dark and children that are very white. How can it be determined who is white, who is mulatto, and who is black and consequently who should be included or excluded from an association that is supposed to have only whites in it?

In pre-Castro Cuba it was impossible. And the matter was even more difficult because power and prestige also affected the criterion of looks. Surely everyone knew that Batista was mixed, as were some senators and wealthy people in Cuba. Some associations got around this difficulty by being associated with an ethnic group. For example, the Casino Español was supposed to have only members of Spanish descent, and so was also the case with societies for Galicians, Asturians, and so on. Other associations or clubs did it by being regional. The Miramar Yacht Club had members that lived primarily in Miramar, a swank suburb of Havana where few, if any, blacks resided. Still others were associated with a certain class. This was the case with the Havana Yacht Club, which accepted only members of the highest level of Cuban society. Still, it was not easy to keep colored people out of clubs and associations unless their 'black or dark mulatto' relatives were dead and no photos of them survived.

Most clubs simply fudged the issue, like the Biltmore, who accepted Batista as a member. Money and power often trumped pedigree in Cuba. And some clubs and associations had a relaxed racial standard, like the Club Náutico.

The pervasiveness of racial mixing did not make race unimportant in Cuba. Indeed, it was enormously important, and for this very reason. Growing up I was very conscious of its importance. To be considered black was a terrible strike against you. Indeed, apart from being called gay, for a young man to be called "colored" *(de color)* or "dark" *(moreno)*, and more derogatorily "black" *(negro)* or "mulatto" was the worst insult. I came from a family of people who looked white—mother, sister, and grandmother were blonde and the family roots could be traced back directly to Spain and France, except for two great-grandmothers. The last name of one of these was of Sephardic origin: Pimienta. The other grandmother had been born in Mexico. Nonetheless, I was conscious of the divide between whites and "colored," and of a general belief that "colored" people were not considered as good as white people for reasons that were never clear.

Segregation in Cuba was not simple, and the way my family dealt with it reflected this. Jokes about blacks were common, but the physician that took care of me when I was a baby was as black as you can possibly get, and my parents trusted him completely. One of father's partners in a business venture was black, and his son, who was a light mulatto visited us frequently and was considered a very close friend of our family. More significant for me, as mentioned earlier, one of my best friends in high school was clearly a mulatto, although no one ever referred to it. Yet, there had been instances of clear segregation in the family history. Remember that when mother was in her early teens and had fallen in love with a young man who looked a little too dark, grandfather rejected him, even though mother's family at the time were as poor as mice and the fellow had a flourishing future. Racial relations in Cuba were complex and cannot be easily characterized. Everyone, whether black or white, Spanish, Asian, or Amerindian, lived immersed in a mixed society in which racial, social, and familial relations formed a web from which no one was free.

Chapter Fifty-Nine

"Mens Sana in Corpore Sano"

The obsession with health and exercise is a kind of addiction that usually involves a conversion of sorts at its origin. The similarities with religion are significant. There is always a moment at which the obsession begins, and the person involved gives priority to it above almost everything else. Rituals and activities are involved, life acquires meaning fundamentally in relation to the obsession, and the obsessed feel the need to testify about the advantages of their obsession. Some go so far as to devote their entire lives to it. There is also a sort of morality and ethics that spring from it, often accompanied by self-righteousness. And the obsessed are often willing to make extraordinary sacrifices to engage in their obsession. Indeed, failure to make those efforts creates a sense of guilt similar to that which affects many religious believers. Of course, there are differences that I do not wish to minimize, but it is surprising to me that the similarities generally go unnoticed.

Although the interest in health and exercise in my family went back to my maternal and paternal grandfathers and great-grandfathers, the first strong impetus came from my maternal grandfather. He suffered from a serious case of asthma that did not seem to have a solution. He visited every physician recommended to him for his ailment, but nothing they recommended worked. Then he read about naturalism, the view that in order to enjoy health we must return to nature. This involves a regimen of food, exercise, and other accompanying practices which grandfather implemented. Grandfather immediately saw improvement and so decided to go into it completely. He had a glass room built in his house in Vuelta Abajo so he could take sun baths without suffering the effects of the sun's damaging rays. He also had a room built with all the paraphernalia of various kinds of baths—hot, cold, and steam, which targeted the lower abdomen or the feet, and so on. The baths were supposed to be accompanied by a proper vegetarian diet, and so he became a strict vegetarian, shunning all types of meat, poultry, and fish, as well as animal products such as eggs and milk. Finally, there were various yoga exercises, some intended to keep the body elastic and functioning as it should and others to promote lung health.

Prior to the economic catastrophe that destroyed his finances, grandfather had experienced considerable relief from the physical regimen he followed and his life had changed drastically for the better. He felt healthy and energized. However, after the financial debacle and the move of the family away from Pinar del Río, his preoccupation with health took a back seat. The family continued being vegetarians, exercising, and doing what they could to maintain at least the semblance of health and normality, but grandfather's will and health had been broken. He died of a heart attack presumably caused by the excess of medication for asthma he had been taking. This left the family devastated, and with that, the extraordinary efforts to maintain a healthy lifestyle were abandoned. The family could not afford what it took.

Still, the seeds had been planted in mother, who maintained a healthy lifestyle. Father was also a fan of exercise, and took long, daily walks. He had picked up these habits at military school, and maintained them until his death. But excessive smoking and the stress of his businesses affected his heart irreversibly. His first heart attack occurred at fifty, and this led our family to change a number of habits. We began to eat even better than we had before. Most fat, except vegetable oil, were permanently banned, and mother's vegetarian streak made serious inroads into our home. New dishes were designed and new ways of cooking old dishes were devised. In time, we traveled to Havana to consult Don Aquilino, the man who had married Baby, father's cousin and daughter of Mina. After father's heart attack, he would go to Don Aquilino's establishment at least once a year for a couple of weeks. Once we moved to Havana, he frequented it every week.

The most significant change in father's life, however, was that he stopped smoking. He was used to smoking twelve cigars a day (H. Upmann was his favorite brand), and also kept a pipe and occasionally smoked cigarettes. This had prompted the heart attack, according to the cardiologist, so father stopped the vice cold. From that moment on, and for several years, his life became "clean." Not only that, he decided to get serious about exercise and yoga, and to sell the farm in Ceballos because it created too much stress for him.

From then on, health and exercise became a kind of religion in the family and all of us engaged in it. Bodies had to be straight and erect, posture was important, and good food and exercise were regarded as of the essence. In time, because we moved to Havana and father had to spend considerable time away from home to take care of the sugarcane plantation, he began to neglect his diet and exercise, and eventually started smoking again. Hotel food is notoriously unhealthy and he was slowly poisoned by it, leading to two subsequent heart attacks including the one that killed him.

The tradition of health and exercise did not die with father. Indeed, after father's death, mother's vegetarian inclination deepened and we hardly ate any meat. At the same time, I became concerned about my body, its purification and survival. My interest in physical exercise had awakened while we were living in Ciego de Ávila. This was the time when it became fashionable to diagnose everyone with scoliosis of the spine and blame every ailment, real or imagined, on it. Naturally, I fell victim to the fad. When mother took me to the pediatrician for a routine physical, he declared that I suffered from this condition and needed to have it corrected by proper exercise. So, it was arranged for me to visit a gym three times a week. This establishment belonged to a physical education teacher who had built it on the back of his house. He was himself a body builder and some of the young men who frequented the place to assiduously work on their bodies had great physiques. I was only eleven at the time, but I saw the great difference between them and everybody else. Their bodies lean, muscular, well proportioned, whereas most of the population had bodies that were too fat or too thin, perhaps disproportionate, and without any muscular definition. It was the difference between a Greek statue and most Americans today. When we moved to Havana my physical therapy ended and I did not think for a while about the body. I had too many other things in my mind. However, around thirteen I began to think seriously about food. In particular, I was intrigued by how people praised foods that I did not particularly like. What did they taste in them? Why did I not like them?

At home it was usual to respect everyone's tastes in food. Although I was often told that by not eating this or that I was missing something delicious, there was no nagging about having to eat it, a situation different from the one that had been common when my siblings were children. They were forced to eat what was served, no matter whether they liked it or not. (Nena always complained that our parents had gone soft on me, while she and Ignacito had to live on a different, harsh regimen.) Over the years I had developed many likes and dislikes, but now for the first time I began to question them. I decided that I was being stupid. If something had been praised by many, credible people the food must be good and I should make an effort to like it. I might be missing something important. This was the beginning of my food education, and the first step toward a lifelong interest in my body and its health.

The outcome of this attitude was that, instead of shying away from new and foreign foods (a typical attitude in most cultures, including Cuban culture), I began to seek them. The food at home had been healthy and either Spanish or French in style because of my family's origins, but I began to seek foods from other cultures—Chinese, Italian, Indian, and so on. I also tried to taste and like foods that I never appreciated before. I remember the example of avocados, which I detested until I was thirteen years old, and which as a result of my efforts became one of my favorite foods. Lobster, foie gras, mushrooms, oysters, artichokes, and many others followed.

At fourteen, when I looked like a wet cat, I also decided that I had neglected my body long enough, so I began to visit regularly a backyard gym that another physical education teacher had set up close to where we lived. The gym had a steady male clientele. It had a section indoors and a section outdoors, and it had the latest equipment available at the time. Working out with other guys that used the gym was an incentive. Although there were some that looked like monsters, gorillas with muscles protruding everywhere on the body, most of them had built extraordinary physiques. And the owner of the gym developed a program for me to follow appropriate for my age and goals.

I would work out three or four times a week, alternating different muscles. I was never very keen on developing a body builder's physique. It seemed to me that such bodies are rather ugly and unnatural. My aim was to develop an athletic body. And this I did by combining some body building with the Charles Atlas resistance exercises that I bought through the mail. What I liked about the Charles Atlas regimen was that it combined exercise with nutrition, and recommended what to eat and when. Part of the program involved a purification period in which one started to purify one's body by progressively drinking more milk and eating less of other foods until one was completely on a regimen of milk for a few days. I am not sure whether any of this was good or bad, but I certainly felt great doing it and my body took on the shape I wanted. Yes, now I did not feel like a wimp asking a girl out!

And of course, there was yoga, which included breathing and stretching exercises. These were a matter of course for the entire family, although Nena was never too keen on them. But I had the discipline to do them. Particularly during the summer, when I did not have school, I followed a strict routine of exercise and yoga. To this day I think this is a key to a feeling of physical well- being that is unattainable any other way.

Chapter Sixty

"De Eso No Se Habla"

I do not know whether the preoccupation with sex in Cuba had to do with the heat, the genes, or the culture, but most conversations, particularly among young men, had sexual overtones, and double-entendres were common in practically all occasions. This made for a lack of seriousness that at times was exasperating—what Cubans sometimes refer to as *relajo*. This was fun, but it was like sugar, too much of it makes you sick. To this must be added that infidelity was quite common, and pornography was readily available. You were presented with pornography at the barber's, in taxis and hotels, male locker rooms, gymnasiums, and every place where males congregated.

It is extraordinary, then, that talk about sex was taboo among members of bourgeoisie families. My parents had a healthy sexual relationship up to the time when father died at fifty-nine, and Ignacito had been sexually active from a fairly young age. But talk about sex or anything that had to do with sex, was completely off bounds.

Chapter Sixty-One

Two Years of Terror

Until 1957, Havana had been a very safe city. Yes, there were slums, poor neighborhood in which the dispossessed gathered and lived in conditions about which those of us who lived in better conditions did not want to think. Shanty towns, dirt floors, lack of sewers and running water. In Havana there was a notorious *barrio* known as *Las Yaguas,* because the shanties were built with dried palm husks. In Camagüey another was called *Las Moscas* because of the numerous flies it attracted. These were not different from Rio de Janeiro's *favelas* or Buenos Aires' *villas miserias.* They had no hygiene or medical services, no paved roads, and no security. Both petty and violent crime were endemic in such places, but outside of these circles of poverty, the situation was different, beginning with low middle class enclaves and extending all the way up to the wealthiest *repartos.* The main problem in these pockets of poverty was that they were sources of petty crime and robberies. Indeed, while Nena was at a clinic giving birth to her first child, someone broke into her apartment and took all her jewels, including diamond earrings, many gold bracelets, and a heavy gold chain with a sixteenth century Spanish doubloon. Still, although petty crime affected these areas of the city, one never felt physically threatened even in socially mixed neighborhoods.

From the time we moved to Havana, I was able to use public transportation to move about the city. I went to the movies, visited friends in areas of the city that were quite far from the place where we lived. I never had any worries about my safety, nor did my parents, who allowed me considerable freedom. The only strings put on my movements were that I had to tell mother where I was going and how long I planned to be there. Of course, being out very late at night was forbidden, but this did not mean that I had to be home before ten or eleven in the evening. There were occasions when I forgot the time I had told mother because I was in the middle of something exciting and I caused her considerable pain. At such times she chastised me for my insensitivity, but even then no one was really worried about a teenager running around the Havana by himself or with his friends.

Things began to change in 1957, when revolutionaries intensified their efforts to topple the Batista dictatorship. There were assaults to army installations, killings, and shootouts. Still, these were isolated events that did not generally affect the population at large. The aim of revolutionaries was not to kill civilians, but to destabilize the government. For ordinary people this meant taking certain precautions. One had to be careful about where one went and one had to keep one's eyes open to avoid situations that might prove dangerous.

And danger did arrive. Among the many factors that changed Havana were the frequent bombs that exploded in public places. Again, the aim of revolutionaries was not to kill civilians and I don't recall instances in which any of them were killed. They merely wanted to prove their presence and their power, showing that they could act with impunity. The reaction from the government was to increase surveillance, and to follow any leads that would take them to the activists. They showed no mercy. Mere suspicion was enough to get you abducted by the secret police. This was the source of greatest fear. You disappeared all of a sudden. The only effective way of tracking disappeared persons, or to get them liberated, was through political influence or money. Time was of the essence because the object of the secret police was to find out the identity and hiding places of those who wanted to bring down the government. And the methods of extracting such information from suspects were horrific. Tortures of all kinds were gratuitously used. Fingernails were pulled off, electric shock was applied to testicles, lighted cigarettes were put out on the flesh, and merciless beatings were de rigueur. To this were added psychological torture and sexual abuse, regardless of the prisoner's sex. Many revolutionaries were young people and so they fell prey to the sick and sadistic practices of their torturers.

A good number of those subjected to these treatments had been caught near places where bombs planted by revolutionaries had exploded, even if they were innocent of any covert action. They were just unlucky to be in the wrong place at the wrong time. Indeed, the greatest fear was not to be injured by an explosion, but to be caught close to it and become a suspect of the secret police. Inquiry and even death were blessings compared with the pain resulting from the methods of torture practiced by Batista's secret police.

No matter what measures the dictatorship implemented, bombs continued to explode. At the beginning, bombs were few and far between, but slowly their number and frequency increased. Bombs were planted in inconspicuous places, such as theater restrooms. Going to the movies was not risky, but going to a men's room in a movie theater was playing with your life. Many a time I arrived at a movie theater just a few minutes after a bomb had exploded, or left the movie theater for the same reason. Going to the movies became a gamble. Eventually it became reckless to go to any gathering. On December 7, 1957, the rumor had it that there would be one hundred bombs detonated in Havana. We all gathered inside our houses, afraid to go about. And yes, the explosions began after dark. I forgot to count and eventually went to bed, going to sleep in spite of the periodic booms that came from near or far away. How many innocent people would fall in the hand of the criminals paid by the dictatorship because of these bombs?

Havana had changed. The carefree, secure city I knew in my early teens had become a sinister trap. The playground of the Caribbean had ceased to be what it had been and had turned into a frightening and dangerous place.

Chapter Sixty-Two

A Beach House at Last

Ever since I can remember, everyone in our family, except father, wanted to have a house on the beach. It was an obsession. The summers we spent at the beach house had whet our appetite and we longed to have a place where we could go not just for the summer, but also during the year for weekends and short stays. After we moved to Havana, this desire was even stronger because we could have a place on the beach east of the city that had become relatively close after the Havana Bay tunnel was constructed.

Father loathed the idea of a beach house. His point was that for the summers we could continue to rent places. This had the advantage that we would not be wedded to any place in particular. Financially, this made sense to him, for a beach house was a dead investment insofar as such places did not rise in value, consumed considerable resources, and were used only sporadically. One would have to worry about upkeep and security, not to mention the family and friends who would want to join us or borrow the place. It was, in short, a headache that we did not need. Renting made more sense for him, financially and otherwise.

Looking back, in hindsight, I must agree that financially he was right. But we were not concerned about what made financial sense. We liked the idea of going to the same place every summer so we could have friends from year to year and establish ourselves as part of a summer community. Father remained unconvinced.

He also had a card up his sleeve after we moved to Havana. For then he had agreed that we would build a house in the city, and if so, then buying a house at the beach at the same time did not make any sense. Besides, we had become members of the Casino Español and this had excellent beach facilities right in the western part of Havana, where we could go everyday if we wished and enjoy a great beach and all the amenities the club provided.

Again, he had a point and, since he controlled the money, nothing was done about the beach house.

His death, however, changed all that. For now, his money was our money and we were not so interested in increasing it. We wanted to live in the way we wanted and we thought we deserved! And had the Revolution not brought in havoc into our lives, I think we would have managed quite well. After father died we were able to keep our finances in fine shape in spite of his absence. The sugarcane plantation continued to be quite lucrative, the apartment house produced a steady stream of income—it had thirteen apartments in it which were always rented –the revenues from the pharmacy were increasing, and even the oil stock father had bought on a whim was doing fantastically. Mother and I bought the little farm in the area of Ciego de Ávila to help us with the trips to the plantation. There was the money from life insurances that father had left for mother and me, which added to his pension, plus the additional little bits here and there. We had experienced a rough patch at the beginning because of our inexperience and the attempt by our lawyer to profit from our condition, but after a year things had fallen into place and we felt comfortable enough to begin to make plans for the future.

In particular we began to think about buying or building a beach house, and postponing the idea of buying or building a house in Havana, although at one point we considered buying a condo at the FOCSA building. This was the only skyscraper in Cuba and had attracted considerable attention. I remember when we went to see it, and how impressed mother and I were. The views were breathtaking, but it really did not make sense for us to buy anything at this point, and mother was not excited about living in what she called a birdcage. Yet, our visit to the FOCSA prompted her to refurbish our apartment with some ideas that had been implemented at the FOCSA. Instead of moving to a new apartment, we ended up with new furniture and the resolve to buy a house on the beach. The beach house made sense for it was something that Nena and her family would also enjoy.

After much thinking and research, we settled on Celimar, a small beach development not far from Havana that had been recently opened. The north shore in that area was rocky, but there was a large basin carved within the rock, with a narrow entrance to the ocean, that created a wonderful natural pool, with crystalline water and some waves but not enough to be dangerous. The developer had smoothed out the rock on one side and created a ramp where he poured sand, so that there was a small but fine beach. He had also built a nicely appointed two-story clubhouse. We thought this was the right place for us. We purchased a parcel of land that was right on the corner of the street that bordered the ocean and one of the side streets. There were only two parcels of land on the block which meant that the parcel was quite large, allowing for a good size house to be built on it.

The plans made by the architect were for a duplex. The downstairs house was to be for mother and me, and later for my own family, and the upstairs for my sister and her family. The building would be very modern with many windows and large terraces from which we could enjoy the ocean view and the sunsets. We started construction as soon as the plans were ready, but very little had been done when it was clear that the triumph of the Revolution had created uncertainties. These uncertainties became certainties within a short time, and we had to rethink our plans. Rather than a two-story duplex, a smaller, one story two-house plan was adopted. I never saw the completed structure, but mother and Nena's family used it for several years, until it became impossible to keep it up. It was a delight to swim in that pool of water and to sit and watch the sunset in the evening. There were few people around because only a few families had managed to build houses in the development, and that made it all the better.

Eventually, the neighborhood deteriorated, the streets became full of potholes, and the clubhouse started to crumble. But the main problem was vandalism. Government militias would come into the neighborhood, breaking doors and windows, filling toilets with sand, and writing insults and expletives on the walls. The government, of course, secretly encouraged this sort of thing while at the same time forcing owners to fix the properties. In addition, transportation became a problem. Cars ceased to be dependable— one never knew when a car would decide to break down.

I have never mourned the financial losses that my family incurred in Cuba resulting from the imposition of communism on the island. I have made a life for myself in the United States and Canada. In general, I do not dwell on the past. I never think about getting anything back if the failed Cuban social experiment ends, but I do think about the beach house and also the *finquita,* the small fruit farm mother and I bought near Ciego de Ávila. They were ideas, illusions at the point of realization. If things were to change in Cuba, I would visit both locations, although I am sure very little of them will have survived in any usable shape and I doubt I would be able to claim them. Still, the land will be there. After more than a half a century of neglect, abuse, and nature, it would be a miracle for anything to have endured. Maybe some of the fruit trees in the *finquita* would still give delicious fruit and I am sure that the ocean at the beach would still be as beautiful. Miracles do happen sometime.

Chapter Sixty-Three

Love and Prejudice

Father's sudden death changed the lives of every member of my family in substantial ways. Mother did no longer have the constraints that father's presence put on her tendency to embrace religious fundamentalism, so she gave way to her instincts. I no longer had father's pressure about my future, and I had to find my own way by myself. There were possibilities that became realities that would never have been even considered had he been alive. But perhaps the person that was most directly and immediately affected by father's absence was Nena.

At the time of father's death, Nena had already turned twenty-seven. Not only was she unattached, but the prospects of a serious romance that would end in marriage seemed rather remote. In plain language, it was beginning to look as if she had reached the status of an old maid. No one talked about this in our family, but it was something of which everyone was aware. Mother, of course, was not worried about it because she thought that God's hand determined the future and knew what was best for all of us. Father also had not seemed to be worried about it before he died; he was not looking forward to grandchildren and his hopes for the future clearly rested on me. He did not put any emphasis on Nena's following a career, nor was he particularly intent on getting her a husband. He knew that when he died, all of us would be well provided for, and that was his main concern. I thought occasionally about Nena's situation, but as a teenager I had too many other things in my mind to dwell on it extensively.

Three years prior to father's death and after we had moved to Havana, Nena had started taking accounting classes at the University of Havana. This profession would certainly be useful for her to help father with his various businesses. But Batista closed the University in December of 1956 to prevent student unrest. This prevented Nena from following the studies she had planned to undertake when we moved to Havana, forcing her to continue her training in a private academy. The closure of the university was one of the extraordinary scandals that occurred during Batista's dictatorship.

After father's death, the only member of our small family circle that could help with the financial issues that came up was Nena, precisely because of her accounting background and because she had nothing else pressing to do. Mother had no training in anything but managing our household, so she was useless when it came to asking the proper questions and making decisions about the challenges we faced. I was merely fourteen and had no idea about anything pertinent. The truth is that I had no interest whatever in the plantation or in managing it. I was interested in books, culture, art, and music. I had ambitions of doing something that was worthwhile, of becoming a writer, and had no intention of burying myself in the plantation, particularly when it had already done so much harm to our lives. My interest in it ended at the cash that it generated so I could pursue other goals and interests.

In short, it was Nena who had to deal with the brunt of the financial aftermath after father's death, insofar as she was of the right age, had some business background, and had no commitments that would interfere with it. This required her to meet with lawyers, tax accountants, the plantation's bailiff, uncle Carlos about the pharmacy, real estate agents to sell the properties we owned in Ciego de Ávila and in which grandmother had lived, and to uncle Julio and the management of the apartment house we owned. She had to go to meetings, some of which mother did not want to attend, and which I seldom attended because of my school and age. This meant that father's driver at the time, Eduardo Riverol, known to everyone as Lalo, spent a lot of time with Nena, driving her to various places. And the chemistry between the two of them seems to have worked well. In short, they fell in love, and Nena told us that he was going to ask mother for her hand, which he did.

Lalo was a couple of years older than Nena. He was a handsome guy with a womanizing history. He had grown without a father because he had abandoned his mother when Lalo was a child. As a result, they had struggled, but survived in spite of what looked like tremendous difficulties. Lalo and his brothers had managed to acquire trades that made possible for them to earn a good living. Lalo was smart and had become an excellent machinist. He could make any part of a machine that anyone could possibly want. He could read engineering blueprints and knew the characteristics of pertinent metals. Obviously, he could have become an engineer if he had had the advantage of a university education, but that was a path that was not open to him given his family circumstances.

Mother and I were quite aware of what Nena's marriage to Lalo would mean for her. To put it bluntly, she would be moving from a professional family, member of the Cuban bourgeoisie, to a blue-collar family, part of the working class. Would this work? Nena had inherited one sixth of father's estate, as I had (mother inherited two thirds because she had inherited half of the estate plus my deceased brother's share). This would be enough to allow Nena and Lalo to live at a level that would make up for the decrease in income resulting from her marriage. But the question was not just about money; it was also an issue of class. Lalo was not an educated man and he had been brought up as a member of the lower middle class. Besides, we were not even certain about his ancestry. However, mother looked at the marriage as a godsend. She had pretty much given up on Nena getting married and this was perhaps the last opportunity she would have to do it. Mother could care less about the issue of class, race, education, or money. Class had never been a consideration for her. The history of her family proved to her that class was an artificial creation of circumstances over which we often had very little control. Her family had gone from a well-established position in Vuelta Abajo to a very precarious financial situation. As a result the children were not as well educated as they could have been. And with respect to race, she remembered quite well that her first love had been a young man whose ancestry was also in doubt and, because of it, she had to give him up. For her, Nena's marriage was a matter of love; the real question was about the love between Lalo and Nena, and whether Lalo would make Nena happy. The only thing that worried her was that Lalo might not really be in love with Nena but that he wanted to marry her because of her inheritance. If this were the case, then Nena would be disappointed. There was also the matter of his notoriety as a womanizer. Mother had a few experiences along those lines even with father, who had an unimpeachable reputation, so the question in her mind was whether Nena was prepared to deal with this sort of philandering should it turn out that Lalo was unfaithful.

I was not as sanguine about the match as mother. I took more seriously the matter of education in particular. Could Nena be happy with a man like Lalo? She thought she could be because she was in love with him, but often the reality of a situation does not hit us until we are immersed in it. It was possible that she would regret the marriage, and what then? What about the children if any came with the marriage? Obviously, my prejudices and views about love and marriage were less romantic than mother's. But from the outset I knew my opinion would not count, and rightly so. Indeed, even mother's opinion did not, since Nena was of an age in which she could decide for herself, and she was financially independent to boot. What counted in all this was Nena's opinion and what she wanted, and obviously she wanted to marry Lalo, and Lalo wanted to marry Nena. So they got married.

No marriage is above criticism, and there is not one person I know who thinks of his or her in-laws as perfect. Both mother and I found things to criticize in Lalo over the years, and I know he found things to criticize in us. But I can honestly say that these were irrelevant insofar as Lalo seems to have made Nena happy. He was first in her affections and she was first in his. Lalo turned out to be a steady hard worker who fought fiercely for the welfare of his family. The loss of Nena's inheritance did not faze him a bit. He loved his children, and although at the time, I disagreed with some of the ways he raised them, I must say that in the long run they all have done well. In Cuba, the family had to suffer incredibly because of the way the government treated those who disagreed with it, but Lalo was savvy in ways that others could not have been, sparing them much pain, and saving them from utter catastrophe.

Nena and Lalo were married almost a year after father's death in a simple ceremony in the Catholic church of the parish within which we lived in 1958. The reception, also very simple and attended only by few family members and close friends, was at our home. The newlyweds spent their honeymoon at the beach and they moved into a second floor apartment in a building we owned. Their first issue, Eduardo, was male and born nine months after the marriage, following a tradition established by father and mother. Three other children were born at intervals of about a year—Mercedes 1960, Leonardo 1961, and Susana 1962. Altogether four children were born in Cuba and one several years later in the United States, although he had been conceived in Cuba.

I enjoyed Nena and Lalo's children tremendously when I was in Cuba, particular the first, Eduardo, of whom I have always been very fond. I remember how he loved for me to sit him on my lap while he investigated the contents of my shirt pockets. He was a handsome child with a wonderful disposition and a winning personality, features that he still preserves as a grown man. I had to take Nena to the clinic for the birth of Leonardo because Lalo had gone away to our sugarcane plantation. I remember how nervous I was to be driving, whereas she kept saying, *"No te apures."* I continued to press the accelerator even harder. I was terribly worried that the birth was going to take place in the car before we got to the clinic. For those of us who were waiting outside the delivery room, the moments were quite tense. The birth of the second child was particularly worrisome because Nena's first had been delivered by caesarean section and she had been warned by her obstetrician not to have another pregnancy right away. But she did get pregnant almost immediately, and the child, and her three subsequent babies, were born naturally.

Because we continued having serious trouble with the bailiff of the sugarcane plantation, Nena and Lalo moved to the plantation to oversee its management. This was an enormous sacrifice on their part. They already had three small children and the plantation had no appropriate place where a family could dwell. Two sets of buildings existed. One had been an original house of the sugar plantation, which at some time had been a fairly decent dwelling. It was located on a piece of land where many large cashew trees (*marañon*) had been planted. It was a two-story structure that had a sufficient number of rooms for the family, but it had been used for storing plantation equipment, so it was in a complete state of disrepair.

The other cluster of buildings was the *batey*. One building was a store, attached to which were living quarters. These had been continuously used, so they were in better shape than the original house—my brother had stayed in them while he managed the plantation before he died. Unfortunately, the worker quarters were close to it, and the workers were rough types whose language, manners, and customs were offensive to someone like Nena. Still, there was little else that could be done. As the saying goes, Nena and her family *"hicieron de tripas corazón"* (had big hearts and strong guts), and managed to live on the plantation for over a year. They left only when it became clear that the Revolutionary government was going to confiscate our plantation. It was a valiant effort on their part, which I do not think we appreciated enough at the time.

Chapter Sixty-Four

Quest for Freedom

Freedom! Perhaps the thing that humans crave the most and yet, as Rousseau suggests, we are born free but everywhere we are enslaved. Freedom to decide what we want and what to be, to mold our lives, immune from the interference of others. Freedom to live where we wish and to associate with those we appreciate. Freedom to believe or not believe. Freedom to disagree with others without risking our lives and our comfort. Freedom to join communities—racial ethnic, national, cultural, and religious—with which we share something important to us. Freedom not to join communities when pressured to do so. Freedom to devote our lives to ideals that we regard as fundamental. And, of course, freedom always subject to the condition of not interfering with the legitimate freedom of others, their rights, and their welfare.

Who has not felt this craving, indeed this need? The search for it begins when we are barely aware of who we are and continues until the end of our lives. We often feel that we would like to sever the tethers that tie us to places, times, family, friends, country, society, religion, and everything that imposes itself upon us, circumscribing us to places, ideas, beliefs, and communities. It is so seldom that we feel truly free! I felt the need for freedom when, as a two-year-old child, I would walk naked on the public square in Chambas. I felt the need for freedom when I decided to leave home, as a four-year-old child, to punish my parents for their insensitivity to my needs. But it was when I reached the teen years, after father's death, that I felt the urge for freedom more strongly.

At fifteen, I began to feel trapped in my school and at home. I needed room, a place to breathe unconstrained by all the rules and regulations imposed on me. I wanted to fly the coop and move away, getting to know other places and people and having a new beginning that would allow me to chart my own course rather than follow on the path that my family and my society had predetermined for me. In particular I was sick and tired of my school and also of living with mother. The Marist School in La Víbora was a boys' school, run by a religious order of brothers. I thought most of my teachers, Marist Brothers, were narrow-minded, uncouth, and stuck in the Middle Ages. I had already begun to read voraciously and the contrast between the world described in books and the limited horizons imposed by my teachers suffocated me. To make matters worse, after father's death the influence he had over mother had been severed and she had given free range to her religious zeal. For a young man in puberty, this fundamentalist and fanatic attitude was intolerable. Everywhere I turned I was told "NO." I had to escape!

My original idea was to leave Cuba altogether and go to Switzerland or Canada, two countries I admired, and where I had read about extraordinary institutions for young men like me. I did not think of a prep school in the United States—that was too *blasé*! Latin Americans have for a long time idealized Switzerland and Canada, countries with impressive landscapes and traditions that are different from the run-of-the-mill. Not that these impressions are realities, but it is how I thought of them. For someone who had lived under the conviction that France was the epitome of culture and sophistication thanks to my Francophile relatives, the idea that I would be able to learn French in Switzerland or French and English in Canada was an added incentive. Little did I know that outside of Quebec, Canada is pretty much English-speaking, and that Swiss French is not quite Parisian French.

It was wonderful that this dream was within my possibilities. I counted on the education insurance father had left me and with one sixth of his estate I had inherited. Of course, I was under the legal age of consent, so I needed permission from mother to do anything, but I relied on her to go along with what I wanted if I wanted it badly and my plans had a worthy goal. By the end of the third year of high school I had had enough of Catholic fundamentalism *a la española* in school and of Protestant American fundamentalism at home. So I began to implement my plan by writing to various schools in Switzerland and Canada, narrowing down my choices and eventually settling on two schools, one in Fribourg and one in Windsor. After considerable thought I decided on Canada, based on all kinds of gross misconceptions. If I had known what Windsor, Ontario, was like at the time, I would have had second thoughts. I was also under the impression that I would be able to learn French and English, and neither the Canadian embassy nor the schools dissuaded me of my mistaken assumption concerning French.

I obtained the visas, we paid the registration fee, and everything was on course for my departure. We had only to buy the plane ticket and I would be on my way to freedom and adventure. I was looking forward to being liberated from the shackles under which I felt I lived. But mother was not happy. She was a recent widow and she was lonely. She did not want me to go. She used every argument she could to persuade me against leaving and finally I gave up, but with the condition that I would change schools and go to a more interesting institution. This is how I ended up at St. Thomas Military Academy. This establishment was in the 'country', a select and secluded residential area of Havana, and advertised itself as incomparable. The reality, as usual in these cases, was quite different.

Chapter Sixty-Five

School for Toy Soldiers

Private military academies became fashionable in Havana in the fifties. They had great advantages. For one, the spoiled children of rich parents needed some control and regular schools did not do the job. Havana Military Academy was famous for being a kind of reformatory school of ungovernable kids, some of whom, it was rumored, were nothing short of ruffians. This was the reputation of the school, often spread by rival military academies, although since I never went there, I cannot vouch for the accuracy of the judgment. The thought was that military schools would get pupils into shape, teach them some much needed discipline, and absolve their parents of the responsibility of educating them and the blame for having made a mess of raising them. This school was reputed to have taken its job a little too seriously and the company was rough.

An alternative was Loyola Military Academy. The name signaled something different, a bit more civilized and perhaps religious—the facade of religion was always very important for Cuban society and the name of St. Ignatius of Loyola, founder of the Jesuits, carried a lot of punch. Here you could send children who needed some supervision and discipline but who were not on the verge of disaster. At the same time, they could enjoy the perks of a military establishment, the uniforms, and the dubious distinction of going to an expensive school, because these academies were very expensive, vastly more expensive than regular schools. Just the uniforms and gadgets, let alone the tuition, cost 'an arm and a leg' and were beyond anything that middle class families could afford.

But even Loyola lacked the reputation of intellectual excellence and the reputation of having a special connection to the United States. The school that had all this and was the favorite of parents who wanted to have their children to learn English and become as Americanized as possible, was the

Ruston Academy. This was a very fine school indeed. Those who attended it did better than any other students in Cuban schools to learn the ropes of becoming American. The school was modeled after American schools. But the Ruston was not a military academy and it lacked the panache of uniforms and the kind of discipline needed for spoiled children. A school that combined the benefits of a military establishment and a truly academic environment was needed, which was the raison d'etre of St. Thomas Military Academy. It was the dream of its founder, a wealthy man with fine educational ideals and aspirations who ironically had 'Castro' as his last name, although he was not related to the revolutionary.

St. Thomas Military Academy was founded just before the Revolution triumphed. Its first high school graduating class was mine, and the year was 1960. The brochure painted an idyllic place and in many ways it was, although in other ways it fell quite short of most of what it promised. This was by far the most expensive school in Cuba. Its tuition alone was higher than the annual salary of a well-established white collar worker. And the cost of the paraphernalia that went along with the tuition was enough to put it out of reach for most Cubans. It was, then, the perfect situation for those who wanted to be apart, above the masses that they thought made up the Cuban populace. The idea was to create an elite school for the privileged that would allow them to occupy the places they thought so rightfully belonged to them because of their pedigree or their money—and mainly because of their money.

The enticements were extraordinary. The school promised intensive English and French classes, special tutoring, training in proper table manners (which were of course, not European, but American), parties and dances that would educate students to behave adequately in society, discipline, sports of all kinds including fencing and tennis; in short, anything that parents would want for their children. No less important was an impressive list of faculty, specialists in various fields that had posts at various public and private universities and well-known high schools in Havana. Students were exposed to field trips of interest and the classes promised to go well beyond the ordinary, with first-hand work in labs. Added to this was religion classes taught by monks from the famous Iglesia de Jesús de Miramar located on the fashioned Quinta Avenida. The promise of a first-rate education sounded convincing.

The brochures did their work, and so I was enticed to leave the dreary world of the Marist Brothers in which I had received all of my previous education except for the year I had attended the Escuelas Pías in Guanabacoa. I was tired of the insularity, the religious conservatism, and the intellectual dearth. There was nothing in the place but religion and sports, and both the students and teachers were prejudiced against anything they did not know. And about girls, well, where could one meet any? Where could one go to a party or a dance? Yes, there were the clubs for those who belonged to them, but these were not part of daily life and it was the daily life that I found constraining. I read widely, and this made me long for a world different from the one in which I lived. St. Thomas Military Academy promised to be this world, opening doors to new experiences which heretofore had been closed to me. The brochure made it look like the perfect school in Cuba. Of course, it was not the same as the schools I had investigated in Switzerland and Canada. I would still be trapped in Cuba. But it looked at least like a good preparation for the adventures I dreamed of undertaking at some point in my future life. Besides, father had been a cadet at the national military academy and he always had talked fondly of his experience. Maybe I would learn to appreciate numbering my underwear!

The visit mother and I made to the school proved quite satisfactory. Partly it was the grounds and the facilities that convinced us that this was the right place. The school was located on a former mansion of generous proportions in the 'country'. Apart from the main building, there was a large parking garage plus servant quarters. The buildings had been remodeled to accommodate the needs of a school, but most details from past glory remained, the marble floors, the stucco moldings, the mahogany paneling, the elaborate frames, the fireplaces, and the chandeliers. The first floor of the mansion was occupied by the administrative departments, a couple of classrooms, the library, and the offices of faculty and the military men responsible for military training. The second floor was devoted to classroom space. The garages had become the lab, and the upper floor became the dormitory for the small number of the students who were boarders. In addition to these buildings, a building under construction that contained the dining room and the gym, was to be completed by the opening day of classes. A large, Olympic-size swimming pool was planned for the following year.

I remember the excitement and preparations before the first day of classes. The uniforms were to be bought at El Encanto, Havana's most chic clothing store. Who would not want to be dressed like that? The anticipation, and fear, of that day in which I would begin a new life! The gala uniform was extraordinary, with a superb hat, brass buttons, gilded epaulets, and tails. Looking in the mirror at El Encanto, I saw a British royal guard! Even the daily uniforms were superb, and so were the uniforms for the sports teams.

Contrary to my naive expectations, the reality was nothing like what the brochures promised. No one spoke English and the English classes were no different from the ones I had at my previous school, which taught me nothing, as I was going to find out when I arrived in the United States two years later. About French? I do not think there was one person on the premises who knew any French, indeed not even the French teacher. French was one of the two fields in which I failed to get an 'A' in my final year—in fact I failed the mid-year exam and had to take a make-up exam. The sports were no different from those played in other schools, with plenty of baseball, in which I was a dud—I ended up with a huge black eye because I did not see a ball coming my way. The fencing classes were a joke, since the teacher was a slob who knew as much fencing as we did, meaning none. And the pool we were supposed to get never materialized. So, there went the swimming.

The teaching was quite mediocre precisely because some of the teachers were university professors and had no idea of what they needed to do to teach high school students. It was nothing like the competent physics classes of Brother Rafael, or the psychology classes of El Globo. For the first time in my life I felt I was not learning in some classes. The only thing that worked fairly well were the parties and dances; they constituted good training for a young male, and I enjoyed most of them. Of course, it was painful sometimes to behave properly while being a teenager, but on the whole I would give the experience a B+. Moreover, the school atmosphere was different from the one in which I had been immersed before, and the nice uniforms impressed the young ladies. Then the Revolution came and nothing mattered anymore because everything changed and I ended up leaving Cuba anyway.

The first day of classes came and went, and so did others. I soon came to accept that the reality was much less than the promise. In many ways, the school was a sham. And yet, the two years I spent at St. Thomas Military Academy were superb years. The school was very small, less that one hundred fifty students overall, and my class had only seven students. On the whole, our class got along well and we enjoyed the military atmosphere. I would be lying if I said that I did not like it. Indeed, I loved it so much that for a brief moment I, like some others of my classmates, considered a military career. The parades, the regulations, the discipline, there was something in it that appealed to young males. It accorded with our testosterone, I imagine. And then there were the dances, the social events, and a general atmosphere of fun. Many of the students were members of powerful elites in Cuba. Sons of senators, high administration officials in the government, important bureaucrats, members of established families, and children of famous professionals and celebrities. One of the students was the grandchild of the man who controlled a major lottery operation in Cuba, *La Bolita.*

There was a certain homogeneity in the student body that was comforting, even though I would find it disturbing today. This was not Cuba, of course. Cuba consisted of sugarcane workers, low middle class shopkeepers, middle class white collar employees, blacks, mulattoes, and a good number of poor people. But we did not see them at school. They did not exist in our ivory tower of privilege. We occupied ourselves with marches and displays, and knew and thought nothing of the reality of hunger, depravation, oppression, and racial discrimination. Yes, we were being educated, but educated to be proper members of the groups to which we belonged, not educated to understand the complex Cuban society or the world in which we would have to live.

At the dining room we were taught proper etiquette. Money does not mean sophistication automatically, and some of the students did not know how to behave politely at the dinner table. And those of us who knew, had learned to eat in a European fashion, so we had to learn the American way. It was very important to know how to hold your fork and where to put your knife, more important than knowing the proportion of the population that went hungry or was malnourished. But it was pleasant, and fun, and I thoroughly enjoyed it.

I sometimes wonder what my life would have been like if the Revolution had not changed everything. Would I have continued to sail through a calm sea of insensitive privilege? Was St. Thomas Military Academy an anticipation of that future? Or would I, at some time, experience a rude awakening?

Chapter Sixty-Six

A Teacher Who Could Not Teach

One of the problems with St. Thomas Military Academy was the occasional teaching disaster. One of these was Papo. He was the chemistry teacher in the fourth year of high school at St. Thomas. Poor man, he had to suffer indignities from his students that no teacher should ever have to suffer. He had to deal with a rowdy, uninterested group of trouble makers, spoiled rich kids with nothing to do but have fun at his expense. Not that we were completely callous, but Papo was the kind of weak and pompous little man—and I do not mean little in physical size—who may have meant well, but did not inspire respect or loyalty. Even some of us who felt sorry for him did not stand up for him.

Everything about him was round—his head, his face, his abdomen, his nose. A short man without angles, plump, manicured (standard among Cubans who wanted to make sure they were not confused with working class people), round hands and silly mannerisms. He cut his hair short and the sparse stubs stood out like the spikes of an urchin. His ears were small, thick appendices on each side of his head. The overall impression he gave was of a well fed piglet ready for slaughter, and slaughter he got every day for the duration of the school year. And then his voice, oh his voice! It did not help him at all. It was too high and squeaky, having a tone appropriately like that of the scream of a pig being dragged to slaughter. No matter what school administrators did, no matter how many heart-to-heart talks Papo had with us, no matter how often we were punished, no matter how many incentives and bribes he offered us, nothing stopped the mischief.

The situation was made worse, even pathetic, because he could not resign. He needed the money! In some ironic way, he was as trapped in his job as a sugarcane cutter was. He was a professor at the University of Havana, but professor salaries were not generous. They had to take other jobs, such as teaching in high schools, to make ends meet, unless they were independently wealthy or they were willing to put up with inconveniences. Papo was no exception.

The problem began right away, on the first day of classes. We met in a room on the second floor that overlooked the road through which one entered the school, one of the upper bedrooms in the mansion that served as the main building. Behind the room was a bathroom, which was going to be a source of constant frustration and pain for Papo. The moment he entered the classroom and opened his mouth, he was doomed. His demeanor, the high-pitched squeaky voice, and the self-importance that permeated his opening speech was enough to make us laugh. The man was ridiculous. And, of course, chemistry proved to be a dull and uninteresting subject for all of us. None of us liked it. I was the best student in the class; indeed, I was the best student in the school, with a straight A record in my previous school, which was much tougher than this one, and yet through him I learned to detest chemistry. Chemistry! Which had always been the bread and butter of my family. But perhaps Papo was not to blame since I don't believe he was ever able to teach an entire class period.

Diversions were many. But if there were no obvious ones on any particular day, we could count on some being created. A favorite one was to go to the bathroom at the back of the room. This took a request for permission from Papo, but of course the request was always made in a way that it was clear both that the need was phony but that it could not be turned down. Then the student would go there and start making noises that could be clearly heard in the classroom, producing laughter in all of us. At other times two students would want to go to the bathroom together, and this was an occasion for faking noises as if they were having sex with each other. At other times some pupils got into a discussion and argument and when Papo tried to mediate they accused him of being uncourteous, arbitrary, and abusive. Threats would come out about his handling of us, poor delicate victims. The man was desperate. There were also endless tricks played on him. Stink bombs, dye or glue on his chair, fresh paint on his desk, and sticking signs on his back that said the most outrageous things in the foulest language.

Of course, he tried to fight back without jeopardizing his position at school. He wanted to keep things under wraps, and we knew it, so in effect, without uttering a word, the class blackmailed him mercilessly. There was something very cruel in what was happening, but even those of us who did not sympathize with many of the indignities that were inflicted on him, kept quiet and let him manage it. In part this was because of peer pressure, and in part because we thought that it was his responsibility to keep order and make sure we would pass our courses. But there was a third reason, perhaps the most important: he was not only weak, we perceived him as duplicitous in character and incompetent as a teacher. For the first time in my life I was afraid I would fail a course, and indeed, I failed it and had to retake it after getting some tutoring. This was the first and only subject I had ever failed in school, and only the second academic subject in which I had received less than an 'A', which was French. My performance in chemistry was a great disgrace for me, because father, grandfather, a great-grandfather, an uncle, and my only cousin on father's side, had doctorates in chemistry. A small consolation was that father did not have to witness my humiliation.

I don't know what became of Papo after the Revolution took over St. Thomas Military Academy. I assume he left Cuba, although he was too old to make a new life in the United States. It is also possible that he joined the Revolution with zest. I would not blame him if he did. After having been abused by a bunch of spoiled, rich kids for two years even a saint would have wanted revenge against the Cuban establishment. I can picture Papo shouting a favorite Revolutionary slogan: *"Al paredón"* (to the wall; to be shot) while thinking of us.

Chapter Sixty-Seven

"I've Got Wheels!"

My life at St. Thomas Military Academy was greatly helped because I had a car. What is the greatest dream of a teenager? Surely it is having a car—the dream of every young man. Imagine what a car means at this age. First of all, it does great things for your ego, since it makes you stand out. Indeed, in Cuba in the late 1950s the number of teenagers who had cars of their own was very small. Teenagers had to depend on the willingness of their parents to lend them their cars, and the parents did so only on very special circumstances because cars were expensive and they did not want their children to crash them.

Having a car at your disposal twenty-four hours a day, and one you controlled completely, was something extraordinary. A car gives you enormous mobility and freedom. It makes you the center of attention, and you become automatically included in everybody's plans. And girls? Well, not only does it make you the particular object of their attention, but it creates a venue for rendezvous, furtive kisses, and various levels of love making. Oh, what a life a car creates for a young man!

For a teenager like me to have his own car in the Cuba of the fifties was heavenly, almost as good as having had my own horse when I was six. None of my had cars of their own. They were allowed to drive family cars, which they borrowed for parties and other special occasions, but I was the only one in my class, and probably one of very few in the school, that had his own car.

The year before the triumph of the Revolution, 1958, the Cuban government extended the privilege of driving to sixteen-year-olds and made it possible for me to own a car. I thought a lot about the car I wanted to buy. Contrary to the standard view of my classmates and young people in general, I dismissed the idea of buying an American car. The favorites at the time were cars with enormous tails. But I wanted a real car, something small that I could use for a variety of purposes, and I wanted it to be a European car. I didn't want a car that was all show and no substance. I didn't want a car that said I was a playboy because neither was I one nor did I want to be one. And besides, there was something in bad taste about driving an American, rather than a European, car. So, I chose a Simca Aronde. I also seriously considered a Renault Dauphine because I liked that it was French, it was small, and it had interesting lines. It was nothing like the flashy American convertibles that were popular at the time. I went to buy the Simca Aronde with a friend, who did not know how to drive himself. I paid with a check, got into the car, and drove away. Imagine a sixteen-year-old doing this, without an adult!

But something seemed wrong! The car felt heavy and unwieldy when I picked it up. I did manage to get out of the parking lot and drive some blocks, but I began to wonder whether I had gotten a lemon. What could be wrong? I kept driving while my friend frantically looked at the manual to see what could be wrong. The car just did not respond. I pressed the accelerator to the floor and the most I could get it to go was at a snail pace. After a while we started smelling something burning. What could it be? Alarmed I stopped in a gas station and asked the attendant to give me a hand. He looked at me as if saying—what an idiot this kid is! He got into the car and lowered the emergency brake!

Oh, what a relief! There was nothing really wrong! But of course, after driving the car with the emergency brakes on for several miles, there *was* something wrong. I had worn down the brakes almost completely, and the brakes did not respond well. In my ignorance, I again thought that I might have destroyed something irreparable in the car, but when I got home I asked my brother-in-law about it and he told me that this was a simple thing: the car needed new brakes. I'm sure he also thought, and with reason, that I was an idiot, but he was a prudent man and said nothing.

After getting my own car, I felt as I had when Ignacito gave me the mare, *la Yegüita*. From then on, as I had done with my horse when I was six, I lived in the car. The mobility that it gave me was fantastic. I could drive around visiting my friends. I drove to the club whenever I wanted. We drove on excursions, and, most pleasantly, instead of going to school on a bus, I drove there in a few minutes. It was a wonderful experience. I remember piling up ten friends in a car that could barely hold five people, and driving in the middle of the night with open windows, shouting and making a racket on Quinta, stopping at a green light and starting when it turned red, in front of the church of San Antonio. I became indispensable to everyone. Of course, the envious types in school made fun of me because I was not driving a ducktail Cadillac. But I gave them the finger, and when push came to shove, they gladly joined me in my car to go places. I had bought a car that was mine, not borrowed from someone else.

Not everything was fun, however. When the Revolutionary government took over, they cancelled driver licenses to anyone under eighteen. The reason was that they did not want to encourage mobility among young punks they considered to be anti-Revolutionary. Only well-off kids could afford to have cars, and the Revolution would have nothing to do with us. Under the circumstances, I had no alternative but to ignore the law and continue driving, being careful not to violate transit regulations. But as a precaution I did stop loading ten teenagers in the car at three o'clock in the morning. What else could I do? I took my chances. But there were a couple of close calls.

One time I drove mother and grandmother to our place at the beach in Celimar, and had stopped behind a bus at an intersection when we were coming back. All of a sudden, bang! An ancient *fotingo* slammed into us from behind, pushing my car into the bus in front of us, like a piece of bologna between two slices of hard bread. Grandmother hit her nose (remember, no seat belts at the time) and began to bleed. I told mother, "Put a handkerchief on *abuelita* and let me deal with this." I got out of the car and looked at the damage, front and back. It was substantial but there was no apparent damage to the motor. Nothing was leaking and the motor kept running. My first priority was to avoid involving the police, because if they got wind of it, they would make me responsible for all the damages—even though I had not been responsible for the accident—because I was driving without a license. Sure, the guilty party was the other guy, and he knew it, but he had a license to drive and was over age. Besides, the officers of the law would not be sympathetic to me with a shiny, new, imported automobile, even if now it looked more like an accordion. They would take the side of the poor guy trying to earn a living by driving an old clunker, even if, contrary to regulations, it had no brakes. They would regard me as the irresponsible kid who deserved what he got. Can you blame them?

I had to think fast to get out of this potentially serious situation. I told the guy that clearly he was responsible for the accident and would have to pay for the damages. His face became desperate. So I figured he was ready to negotiate. Trying to sound collected and substantial, my insides were fluttering with fear and I felt that at any moment I would pee my pants. I added that I had insurance that would pay for my damages, so, if he agreed to pay for his, we could go our separate ways and forget that this ever happened. Fortunately for me, the poor guy did not smell the rotten fish I was trying to sell him and readily agreed. He was exultant and probably thought that I was a fool. A dumbbell, no doubt. But in fact it was he who was missing an opportunity to make a fast buck. If he had been savvy he could have made a nice little profit from the incident, for I would have paid anything to get out of the jam! But he was probably a poor man, used to being pushed around, and when he saw a kid driving a new imported car probably figured my father could make life difficult for him even after the Revolution. Class and its trappings are superb for those at the top, and often a self-imposed trap for those at the bottom. "That was Cuba, *chaguito!*"

When we got home I called our insurance agent, a guy who had handled all our insurance over the years. I fudged the events, of course—I had already a predisposition for casuistry—and although he was suspicious, he did not question me. The insurance paid and everything was fine. Fortunately, I did not have to wait too long to turn eighteen and obtain a new driver's license.

Chapter Sixty-Eight

Playground of the Caribbean

With a new car, I was ready to take advantage of the playground of the Caribbean. Havana offered a rich and varied night life in the fifties. I do not think that there was anything like it anywhere in the world at the time, except for a few places in Europe. The city had everything one could want, from the most sophisticated, high-brow productions of classical music to the lowest forms of entertainment, and every level in between. Alicia Alonso and her ballet were at the peak of popularity and success. The symphony played fashionable music and Cuba counted with composers of the caliber of Ernesto Lecuona and Alejandro García Caturla, who had integrated Spanish and African rhythms in pieces that have become classics. Popular music, with its intoxicating rhythms and use of African and Spanish motifs, was flourishing. Small experimental theaters put on the latest shows from Europe and the United States, and there was a fantastically rich season of *zarzuelas* every year. Havana was also a city of sin. Gambling, prohibited in most cities in the United States, was a mainstay of the town, and if what one wanted veered toward prurient interests, there was available anything that would capture human attention. Havana was like a paradise of pleasure, from the most exquisite to the most vulgar and so tourists, as well as *habaneros*, rushed to them in order to satiate their passions with whatever was au courant.

For a young man in Havana the first step in the right direction was to learn how to dance, because Cuba has always been, more than anything else, about music. This was a time of creativity. I remember when the Cha Cha Cha was invented and how we were all trying to learn the steps. I was nine at the time. And there were the traditional dances: the elegant *Dansón*, the wild *conga* and *rumba*, the intoxicating *guaracha*, and the mad *mambo*. To be Cuban is to love music and a Cuban who does not dance is a contradiction that deserves to be nationalized.

However, it was not easy to learn how to dance. How do you learn if you go to schools for boys where the opportunities to dance are nil? Taking dance classes was frowned upon as a kind of sissy thing. Remember, one had to be careful not to be identified as gay. There were opportunities to dance at clubs, but you did not want to make a fool of yourself in front of all your friends. So, if you went to a party where there was dancing and you did not know how to do it, you had to give some excuse in order to abstain from dancing.

I solved this predicament by asking cousin Marta to teach me some of the basic steps after I turned fifteen, the age at which one would expect to attend parties and when I had my first invitation to a dance. We met a few times and she helped me sufficiently so that I was able to perform reasonably well at my first party at the club. Then, it was a matter of continuing to go to parties and practice, until eventually I let myself go. Dancing manuals that taught the basic steps were also useful. And I learned many steps by watching others who knew what I needed to learn either at parties or even at the theater. I remember well that I learned the steps of the waltz from a production of the Merry Widow. The music was enchanting, so after the show I went home, put a record of Viennese waltzes on the record player, and practiced the steps. Waltz was an indispensable dance to know because a waltz was a piece de rigueur at parties that celebrated the fifteenth birthdays of girls, and at least one waltz was always played every night in nightclubs.

For young men and women, the night life in Havana in the late fifties was all about partying at night clubs, what we called at the time cabarets. Havana was veritably the playground of the Caribbean. Places like Cancún, San Juan, and Cartagena, did not exist on the tourist map, and Miami was a dying place except for a few hotels at the beach like the Fountain Bleu and the Alexander. Havana, on the contrary, had everything the world, and particularly Americans, wanted: music, women, men, gambling, drugs, and perversion. Cabarets sprang up to fill some of these demands. The most famous were Tropicana and Sans Souci, where almost nude women paraded on stage in elaborate, but minimally covering, costumes. Many other cabarets were associated with large hotels such as the Hotel Nacional, Havana Hilton, Riviera, and the Capri. My favorite was the Casino Parisien at the Hotel Nacional, where I spent many wonderful nights dancing, dining, and listening to music.

The routine for a young man with some means was to take out young ladies to one of these cabarets for dinner and dancing on weekends. Two or three couples would get together and spend the night out, until the wee hours of the morning, when hungry and tired, they would drift to Chinatown to have some soup before crashing in their homes. Some nights would last longer, and it was frequent to end up having breakfast somewhere by a beach or watching the sunrise at the Malecón. The young women would dress in fashionable dresses and the young men would pick them up, sometimes bringing corsages that the women placed on their wrists, imitating the American custom. At reputable parties there would always be at least one chaperone, one of the mothers of the young ladies who supervised the proceedings so that nothing untoward happened. Sometimes, a couple of parents would come along, removing the problem of having an older woman sitting by herself, bored to death, in some corner of the room. At other times a couple of the matrons would come, and so they would gossip all night long, while the youths did what they do.

Chapter Sixty-Nine

Chaperones

The chaperone was a well-established institution in Cuba. Its aim was to preserve the virginity of young women so that the men they married had the satisfaction of "being the first to penetrate their virginal holy of holies." A chaperone was usually a mature woman, belonging to the family of the young woman, who ensured that the young damsel was never alone with the young man. Her charge was to prevent from happening what could happen when the couple were alone, if the presumably hot-blooded Cuban male could not control his urges and the young lady did not put up a strong enough defense. Like all institutions, the chaperone had its successes and failures. The purity of the proceedings was not always preserved. Some couples disappeared for a while with the help of other couples, and some got completely lost. In such cases the old ladies tried to make the best of it by putting the best face on difficult situations. As *Abuelita Belé* ironically used to say, "it is difficult to understand how young girls keep getting pregnant when they are supposed to be always and effectively chaperoned. Maybe," she speculated, "it is a miracle." The custom in grandmother's time had been to have the couple in the living room with a table between them and a chaperone sitting in the *saleta*, from where she could keep an eye on them, sometimes appearing to dose off so that the young man could steal an occasional kiss from the object of his desire. Yet, the couples found ways to circumvent chaperone vigilance and the young women occasionally became pregnant.

The institution applied primarily to young ladies from the Cuban bourgeoisie—both poor and immensely wealthy families were often beyond this institution. The poor and the aristocracy have always disregarded with impunity the regulations that apply to the bourgeoisie in most societies, as it was the case in Cuba. It was at this bourgeois level that marriage was an important family affair, entangled with issues of family name, family honor, and perhaps most important of all, family money. Losing virginity was bad enough for a young lady who had aspirations to marry well, but having an illegitimate child was a catastrophe not easily overcome. It was particularly serious because abortion was out of the question for many bourgeois families due to their strong, conservative Catholic roots, although often fear trumped religious commitment and abortion was undertaken. Abortion was illegal in Cuba, but everyone knew of physicians who performed abortions for a fee, and they certainly made an excellent living. The alternative to have the out-of-wedlock baby and give it for adoption required that the young woman disappear for a while. A trip to the United States or Europe was the favorite excuse, although often the pregnant young lady did not go anywhere but stayed in Cuba, in the country, out of sight.

The system of chaperones was cumbersome and archaic, a remnant of a different age in a society that had not adapted to new realities. In the mid-1950s, when I started dating young women, it was very difficult to arrange going to parties and doing things together, because we always had to have the chaperone accompanying us. It was particularly difficult when the young man did not have a car, for how was the couple to go anywhere? This is why most of the dating and courting was done at the clubs, where it was also not difficult for the chaperones to keep an eye on the young people, and for the young people to sneak somewhere for a few minutes of frantic making out. Clubs had parties and activities of various sorts, which solved the chaperoning problem.

At St. Thomas Military Academy, the parties we had at school posed the problem of transportation. In some cases, the driver of the chaperone drove the young couple to the party and waited for them. At other times it was someone from the family of the young man who took everyone to the party. In every party, there were plenty of chaperones sitting around, bored stiff or gossiping. "Doesn't the daughter of so and so look beautiful? Too bad what I heard recently. . . ." And another: "They make a wonderful couple, but I don't think they will marry, because her father lost most of his fortune recently and the young man is poor as a mouse."

For those of us who had cars, life was much easier. Various options were available. We could drive the young woman and the chaperone to the party in our cars. Or we could drive in one car and the chaperone would drive her own car. When it came to a cabaret, sometimes the parents of the young woman were interested in a night out. Or they, together with some friends, went to the night club where the young couple and another young couple would be going. They would sit at tables distant from the couples under surveillance, but still visible, so control, or the appearance of control, could be maintained.

Indeed, the chaperone system was not meant so much to prevent the young people from doing what they wanted to do, but to present a picture in "good society" about the young woman and her parents. It was all a show that helped to keep their good name and make possible a good match. Indeed, it is not clear how many young ladies were virgins when they got married. Still, if appearances were kept, who cared? I am sure most young men cared very little about the presupposed virginity of the young ladies, particularly if they were in love with them, they brought some connection or money to the marriage, and they were accessible to them before they married. Chaperones were more a front than a reality, a social convention that had lost its original significance and much of its power.

Once the high school years were over, things became more relaxed, although still somewhat controlled. Most common were situations in which groups of young people, individually or in couples, got together and went places. These situations did not lend themselves to sex, since the women were usually friends with each other and kept a watch on their virtue, reminding themselves of the problems that could result from a mistake. Of course, things happened. My sister told me that once she went out with a very close friend for what she thought was an innocent double date, and in the middle of the date, the friend with her date disappeared for two hours. Obviously, the couple was not playing tennis. Nena never went out on a double date with that friend again; she was furious about what this woman did without consulting her.

Chapter Seventy

Puppy Love

"Love is a many splendored thing" isn't it? I've had a predisposition to fall in love from the time I was a small kid. My first love was a girl that towered over me. Milagros was her name, and she lived in Chambas, in a house that was, like ours, on the *parque* (main square). I adored her, and our relationship was immortalized in a photo in which I am straining up on my tippy toes to give her a little kiss, because she was taller than me. Milagros, or Milagrito as everyone called her, was a well behaved, lovely girl, the one that one delights in looking at. Her sister Idánia, on the other hand, was very different; she liked to torture me. In part, this was because her father liked to play with me and she was jealous and, in part, I flattered myself, because she loved me and was jealous of her sister. (Obviously, this was a complicated love affair.) She had green eyes and blondish hair. The truth of the matter was that I was in love with the idea of Milagrito, but the girl I really liked was Idánia. Don't they say that love and hate are very close? Well, this seems to be a case in point. I was torn between these two girls, loving the idea of one and the reality of the other, and suffering for both.

After we left Chambas, I quickly forgot Milagrito and Idánia and made Nena's friends from high school the objects of my affection. When I was four, Nena was sixteen. Her friends would visit us at various times of the year at Ceballos, and during the summer, sometimes for long periods. I never failed to fall in love with some of them. But I had standards: the objects of my passion had to be beautiful and nice. It was a mutual relationship, or so I thought. And of course, it was not difficult for them to like me. I was a cute kid, and well behaved with strangers—I was a terror with members of my family (as readers who have put up with the narrative to this point should have gathered)—but they should be held responsible for that behavior insofar as they let me do most of what I wanted. With visitors, however, I was always a model of proper behavior, and naturally was recompensed for it.

Not that everything was nice and pleasant. I suffered great bouts of jealousy when Nena and her friends got together with males of their same age and paid more attention to them than to me. It was excruciatingly painful to see how they put on airs and acted coquettishly with them. It was disgusting! I brooded and sulked, and tried to sabotage their meetings, showing up when they wanted to be alone, and watching every move they made so I could casually report it to mother. The girls took this in stride and used it to keep the guys at bay, but some of the guys, who initially liked me, began to detest me with a vengeance. They surely could not kiss and make out with the girls while I was watching. Not that the boys cared that I saw them doing it. What they did not want was that I inform mother of what was going on. Still, I had my uses, for it was better to be chaperoned by a kid, which happened frequently once I grew older, than to be chaperoned by a mother or an aunt of the girls.

An important aspect of my 'love life' at this time was that I only loved "older women." I had no use for girls of my own age. In fact, I hated them. I found them to be prissy, bossy, and to be constantly running around to grown-ups tattle telling about things I and other boys did. What a nuisance they were! And yet, there was some attraction involved. I liked to play with them, occasionally, but it was hard to understand and put up with their rules of conduct, which I never understood. Why couldn't a girl be more like a boy? A girl was a poor substitute for a boy, but if there were no boys around, one had to put up with them. Grown up girls, however, were lovely. They knew how to treat an aspiring young Adonis like myself.

Love evolves with time, and so it did with me. My emotional crushes on Nena's friends eventually disappeared. They ceased to respond to me as I got older. I was no longer a cute kid, and became an awkward teenager. At thirteen, or even before, at twelve, I had grown too fast. My arms and legs were too long and my face was covered with pimples, I did not know what to do with myself or my body, and I had become too shy to respond when females addressed me. I look at photographs from that period and ask myself, what happened to the cute kid, and how long did it take to become the attractive young man that, as I flattered myself, I became? At the same time, Nena's friends had ceased to be teenagers themselves and had become obsessed with catching themselves husbands, which as years passed became desperation. When they reached their early twenties, panic set in and all their energy was concentrated on getting a man, *un buen partido,* as their mothers called it. They surely did not have time for an awkward and unattractive teenager.

These were very difficult years for my "love life," which were made worse by the fact that I attended a boy's school. I lived immersed in a masculine society. Not that I minded. I liked to play with boys and established good friendships with some of them, but I had become curious about girls and longed to get to know them better. Unfortunately, in a boy's school there were no opportunities to do so. Indeed, until I moved to St. Thomas Military Academy, I never got to know any girls except occasionally. Yes, at the club I met one or another here and there, but the girls stayed with girls and the boys stayed with boys. Mixing did not often happen.

This was one of the main reasons I wanted to move out of the Marist school. Of course, public schools were co-ed, but public schools were out of the question. In bourgeois Cuba, very few "respectable" families sent their children to a public school. It certainly never entered the mind of anyone in my family and so I never considered it myself. I did know, and envied, some boys who went to public schools and mixed with girls, but at the Marist School I had no opportunity to do so. St. Thomas Military Academy was much better at intermingling boys with girls, although the school was by no means ideal since it was, after all, a military academy for boys. A co-ed school, like the Ruston Academy would have been different in this respect, but having gone to boy's schools all my life, neither I nor mother raised that possibility. In any case, St. Thomas Military Academy organized parties, dances, and other activities to which girls were invited. For most of these events, boys had to invite girls, and if you had never gone to a school where there were girls, how in the world could you be expected to know any girls to invite? We were all stuck in this respect and had to scramble to find partners, but even under these conditions the situation was better than at the Marist School.

I dated many girls while at St. Thomas Military Academy. Some were thin, others chunky, some were blond and others brunette, some were pleasant and others unpleasant, some were beautiful while others were not, although usually those less favored by nature were the most interesting. Of all of them, there was one in particular, as it usually happens, for whom I fell completely in love. I took her out regularly. We went dancing and dining. I took her to the club and I talked to her on the phone every day for hours. I now cannot imagine what we talked about. She was a dark beauty. I have dated many blondes in my life, but have never fallen for one. It is always the dark ones that attract me. With this girl I did everything I could to make her love me, but I failed miserably. I took her to the most expensive cabarets and restaurants in Havana and spent a fortune (by my standards) on flowers and chocolates, which were the only gifts from me that she would accept. My life became tragic. I could not live without seeing and talking to her, but she would keep me at a distance. She would not even allow me to kiss her. Finally, after months of pain and disillusionment, I gave her an ultimatum. Either our relationship—if it could be called that—became more than friendship or I would stop dating her. She responded with the usual. That she liked me very much, but that she did not love me except as a friend and that in any case she was not ready to become serious.

This conversation had taken place on the balcony of the apartment where she lived. From it one had a lovely view of the entrance to the University of Havana, with that marvelous staircase, but I hardly paid attention to it. After her response, I told her that we should then part, and I left. I never dated her again or called her. It took me several weeks to get over the pain, but I did. The next time I saw her was at a Ruston Academy prom. I had been invited by a magnificent blonde. She is probably one of the most beautiful women I have known. So, I felt quite confident and I made a point of saying hello to my nemesis. While we were dancing, I lead my partner close to her and her partner and nodded as we passed, making sure she got a good look at my partner. She smiled and waved pleasantly, but I hoped that I had made her feel some regret, for objectively she was nothing like the girl with whom I was. Oh, how I would have liked for her partner to be insignificant! He was just the opposite, a hunk who looked older. Perhaps he was a real marriageable prospect, which I certainly was not. Still I hoped I had made her feel some regret. That is how pitiful puppy love can be. I did not seek another encounter and never saw her again. Perhaps she stayed in Cuba, considering that her family were sympathetic to the Revolution, or like so many others, eventually became disenchanted and left the island.

While attending university in my last year in Cuba, I made friends with a group of students, composed of four women and three men. We went everywhere together and had the time of our lives. Among them, again, there was a dark beauty, petite, and with a lot of *salero,* for whom I also fell. But she did not return my advances, she had a serious fiancé outside the university. But I was not the only frustrated lover, for the girl in the group that wanted me was not an object of my feelings. Clearly, my romantic life in Cuba was unsatisfactory, and at the end of my last year there I began to think that I would never be loved as I loved. Obviously, I was very young and inexperienced!

Chapter Seventy-One

Graduation and a Prom of Sorts

The two years I spent at St. Thomas Military Academy went very fast. In part, it was because I was enjoying myself in ways that were impossible at the Marist school. Also, it was because Cuba was in turmoil, experiencing a Revolution and its aftermath. The news brought something unexpected every day, and so life seemed to move at a very fast pace.

Graduation time came around before any of us had given it much thought. My class was the first that would graduate from St. Thomas and so we wanted to do something that was precedent setting. Of course, in a military school there is plenty of fanfare that can be easily whipped up, and since we had the blessing of the founder and owner of the school, we did.

Graduation celebrations began with plenty of marches and displays, as well as the usual ceremonies, such as granting prizes and medals, and recognizing special achievements. Those were followed by the high school diplomas, *Bachiller en Ciencias, Bachiller en Letras*, and in my case *Bachiller en Ciencias y Letras*. Each member of the graduating class walked with his parents, and in my case mother, to receive our diplomas. There were speeches by various people, which were not memorable since I don't remember any, and finally a reception well stocked with fancy culinary delights.

Those of us who were graduating were dressed in formal uniforms with wonderful gold epaulets and swords used by Cuban army officers. Mother was her usual elegant self in a fashionable black raw-silk dress. Other mothers were also dressed to the hilt. Many students had left school already because their parents had anticipated what was coming to Cuba and had emigrated to the United States and other places. Sadly, in spite of the celebrations and the wonderful display of food, uniforms, and 'beautiful people', there was an aura of doom that we all worked very hard to keep on check. We did not talk about the present or the future, but rather reminisced about the two years that we had spent together. Very few of us knew how long we would stay in Cuba or what the future was to bring. It was an uncertain time of change that went beyond ordinary happenings and, although we did not show it, there was an implicit fear attached to the sense of doom. But we did the best we could and the memory of those moments, the last time that we, the graduating class, were together, encapsulated who we were and what we had been to each other.

A more difficult question for us had been what to do for the graduation party. When it came up, we were a bit at a loss. Other prominent schools had proms *a la Americana*. Perhaps the most typical were at the Ruston Academy, two of which I attended. But the same thing did not make sense for us. The graduating classes at Ruston were fairly large in comparison with our class. We were just seven graduating students, and the idea of a prom was absurd for a class of that size. Proms were known in Cuba, particularly in schools that had ties to the United States or tried to emulate American customs, but St. Thomas was too small to justify this kind of celebration.

At some point the idea of going to a cabaret came up, and I suggested my favorite spot mentioned earlier, the Casino Parisien. This nightclub always had a nice show, good music and dancing, and excellent food. We looked into our war chest and found we had a very substantial sum. The question was whether we could spend it all. I needed to consult with someone knowledgeable, and there was no one better than my cousin Marta, who knew the rounds well, and was my *consejera*, to discuss what to order from the menu and the list of drinks and wines. It was a very instructive session because until that time I had not paid any great attention to such details. When I went to cabarets with dates, my date and I picked whatever we liked. But this was to be a special occasion, with a meal of several courses accompanied by different wines.

Of course, there should not be a prearranged selection common to everyone. We would all choose from the menu *a la carta*. But she advised what were the most appropriate dishes for the occasion. In any case, my date would normally ask me to order for her, so I needed to have something particular in mind. We settled on *caviar con blinis* for appetizer, *sopa de champignones* for first course, *filete mignon con papas a la portuguesa* and *palmitos con salsa golf* for the main entree, *ensalada verde* to clean our palates, baked Alaska or *platanitos flambé* for dessert, and a plate of French cheeses for the grand finale. Most likely, she thought, I would be the only one at the table asking for caviar and blinis, but that was fine as long as my date and I liked them. I should ask my date if she did, and if she said no, then I should order something ordinary, such as *cocktail de camarones*. The caviar with blinis would certainly make me stand out, even if we ended up not ordering it, which was the idea of the whole thing, right?

She suggested that I discuss the wines with the sommelier; he would know what best to order with each dish. However, I should be prepared to mention some alternatives to him, and these were the ones she mentioned: vodka for the appetizer, a Riesling for the soup, a robust Marques del Riscal for the main course, Dom Perignon for dessert, and Lacrima Cristi or a twenty-year-old port for the cheese. For coffee, a Spanish *Carajillo* (strong coffee with Spanish cognac in it). Cocktails would precede the dinner, of course, and postcede it insofar as we were planning to make a full night of the celebration. She wanted to know: Did I know the rigmarole concerning the tasting of the wine, inspecting the cork and smelling the aroma? Yes, I did, from observing my father do it when he drank wine, and I had practiced on my other dates.

The night went quickly. Dinner was at ten and we went to see the sunrise at the Malecón. We spent every penny we had. I felt very debonair; it was a night to remember. My only regret was that I was not accompanied by the girl I still loved. I wonder what Lenin would have thought of that night!

Chapter Seventy-Two

Starved for Culture

My life was not entirely devoted to the school and nightlife while at St. Thomas. I was maturing, and the extensive reading I had been doing from the time I turned thirteen had infused me with an intense desire for culture that it is difficult to appreciate. I wanted to experience all the great things that others throughout the history of the world had experienced. I wanted to know about the classics; I wanted to hear the best music that had been composed; I wanted to learn about art and dance; I wanted to travel to appreciate the beauty of architectural masterpieces, and I wanted to experience the great emotions that others had experienced before me and had led them to compose the great pieces of literature I had been reading and to paint the great works of art I had seen.

    I bought every book of which I heard and went to every art exhibition, concert, and play that I could. Yes, I enjoyed dancing to popular tunes, but I was not satisfied with that. I also bought recordings of famous pieces. I remember when I bought and listened for the first time to the Rachmaninoff Piano Concerto No. 2 in C minor, Op. 8. I could not believe that anyone could have produced such sounds. How could they be described? Words would certainly not do. Words were good, but for other purposes. The beauty of this music could only be expressed by itself. No description of the concerto could do justice to it. The concerto was its own tribute! How many times did I listen to it? I do not know, but I almost memorized every phrase of the music, every change, every peculiarity of it. To this day it is still one of my favorite pieces.

Chapter Seventy-Three

Recreating the Garden of Eden

Havana had such enticements that it would seem difficult to make room for anything else in our lives. But those of us who have lived in the countryside and love nature could not ignore them. Love and convenience joined hands in a project that became dear to mother and me, an effort to recreate the Garden of Eden, which for us had been the orchard in Ceballos. The practical rationale was the obvious fact that the periodic trips to the sugarcane plantation mother and I had to make after father's death would become easier if we had a permanent place to stay nearby. So, we decided to buy a place at a convenient location. After looking around, we bought a small farm located right on the Carretera Central, the main traffic artery in Cuba, a few miles from Ciego de Ávila, the closest town to the plantation. We put aunt Maruca and her husband Fernando in charge of it. The location made it easily accessible.

The land was about seventy-five acres and mostly uncultivated, but it had a patch of mango trees whose thousands of fruits covered the ground when in season. There were also a couple of avocado trees, the lemon trees de rigueur at every country house, a sour orange tree, and some regular orange trees. A sugarcane patch on the farm had a quota to be sold. In order to control production and not to over produce sugarcane and cause a collapse of prices, the government had instituted a quota system that controlled the amount of sugarcane that could be sent to the sugar mills by each plantation. To have a quota ensured a sale.

A windmill brought-up water from an artesian well and generated electricity. The house was very simple, small, and ugly. It was one of those structures the Batista government had erected for farmers in the countryside in order to claim public works and simultaneously move money around, most of which would stick to the hands of government officials. It was completely inappropriate for the climate, with brick walls and a zinc roof that did not become unbearably hot only because large trees cast a shade on the house. Behind the house was the old *bohío*, where the family originally had lived. It was a traditional Cuban country house, with wooden walls and a thatched roof. It was spacious and had a rustic, native charm. In contrast with the house, it was cool and pleasant.

Particularly attractive when one entered the property were lush hibiscus bushes with red flowers bordering the front gate and a gravel road lined by coconut trees leading all the way from the gate to the porch of the main house. The coconut trees made music when breezes waved their branches. To sit on the porch on a warm night, listening to the harmony that the coconut tree leaves made with the myriad of bugs that sang and scratched, was a delight. I remember well how grandmother used to sit there, in the dark, to smoke one of the cigars she rolled every day. She smoked in the dark because a lady would not smoke in public, of course, but the blood from Vuelta Abajo still ran strong through her veins.

Once the property was purchased, mother and I immediately set out to implement our plan. The land was fenced in, and, taking a cue from the avenue of coconut trees and the hibiscus on the front gate, we proceeded to plant hibiscus bushes interspersed with coconut trees all around the property. Then we went to the best nursery in Havana and bought fruit trees sufficient to cover the entire available grounds. We planted avocados, tamarinds, oranges, grapefruits, mandarins, lemons, limes, zapotes, mameyes, cashews, passion fruit, guanábanas, anoncillos, anones, papayas, plantains, guayabas, and mangos of many kinds, and other varieties of tropical fruit trees. They were sent by truck to the *finquita* (little farm), as we baptized the place, and planted according to the strictest indications from the nursery. The idea was simple: replicate on a smaller scale the farm in Ceballos where we had been happy before tragedy struck.

Having had the fruit trees planted, we turned our attention to the living quarters. We added a bedroom to the small house that had been built by the government, so that Maruca and Fernando would be comfortable in it. Next we had in mind to refurbish the *bohío*, making it a lovely rough living quarters for us when we came to spend time at the *finquita*. The bad wood would be replaced, a wood floor would be laid, and the roof would be rethatched with guano. When we were done, the place would look paradisiacal, and in a few years it would become the Eden we had intended.

The Cuban Revolution interfered with all this, preventing the refurbishing of the *bohío*, but it did not stop the plants and trees from growing. As they grew, they covered the grounds and produced bountiful harvests, which I never saw because I left Cuba in 1961, and the fruit trees required another four years after planting to reach maturity.

Eventually, aunt Maruca and Fernando had to move away from the country because of her increasing asthma attacks, which were caused by strong allergies to certain plants. Mother arranged for someone else to move into the *finquita* and manage the place. She did not have to visit our sugarcane plantation any longer, since it had been confiscated by the government, but was attached to the *finquita* and occasionally made the trip to see how things were there. Her letters to me after each trip were glowing. The fruit trees gave a yearly bounty harvest of the best fruits that grew in Cuba. The hibiscus were lush and the coconut trees grew to maturity, providing not just fruit and beauty, but an increasing serenade of strings playing as the breeze moved their branches. The farm had become a true paradise. For mother, nothing compared to the pleasure of sitting on the porch in the evening, listening to the sounds of a tropical night, the chirping of crickets, the singing of frogs, and the scavenging sounds of night predators. No artificial lights disturbed the sky, where she could see every constellation and star. During the day she walked under the fruit trees and marveled at the lushness of nature.

When mother was not able to visit, the man she had put in charge sent her crates of fruits which ameliorated the shortages that were common in Cuba after Castro's ill-conceived agricultural projects. Eventually the boxes stopped coming, her letters went unanswered, and she heard that the caretaker had let pigs and goats roam below the fruit trees. This began to affect the trees adversely. Humans had again violated God's commandments and had to live with its results, the end of paradise. Eventually the land, small as it was, was confiscated by the government and the family that lived there was confined to a small area around the house. No one cared for the fruit trees, and the orchard was frequently vandalized in a country where scarcity was the rule. The *bohío* suffered irreparable damage from lack of maintenance, and diseases infected the delicate fruits.

Chapter Seventy-Four

From Hope to Despair

After the seven years of misery passed, between 1949 and 1957, things were going relatively well for us. My sister was married and had already began to produce children; mother and I had settled on the administration of the sugarcane plantation; uncle Julio was managing the apartment house reasonably well; and members of the family were healthy. However, the fight for the political future of Cuba had intensified. The years 1957 and 1958 were filled with attacks by revolutionaries against the government, and of counter attacks by the dictatorship. Indeed, the situation in Cuba had reached a crisis point. Castro's forces had steadily gained advantages in the east of the island and the brutal response of the Batista regime had created a situation in which only those who depended on the regime, and profited in various ways from it, continued to support it. The bourgeoisie found it increasingly difficult to justify that support in a climate of corruption, brutal retaliation, and widespread fear. At the beginning of those two years, when father was still alive, he had made a bet with aunt Maruca that Fidel Castro had been killed and revolutionaries would slowly fade away. Maruca, on the contrary, held that he was still alive and that the revolutionaries would not stop until they marched into Havana and turned things around.

And turn things around they did. We felt it quite close to us in the last trip we tried to make to the sugarcane plantation before Castro's triumphal entrance into Havana in 1959. It was customary for mother and either Nena or I to go to the plantation once every fifteen days to pay workers. We took turns, because my sister Nena had a family and I was in school. It was my turn, so mother and I got ready and set out on a trip from Havana to what we called nuestra *finquita* where we stayed. We had heard that the revolutionaries had taken several towns not only in the east but in the central part of the island as well. But we felt that we needed to go—the workers needed their money—

and we could not neglect them. We understood that we should be prudent, but we were not afraid. In the first place, we were in favor of a change of government and in second place we had no connections with either one of the two groups fighting.

The trip usually took about seven hours, depending on traffic and the state of the road, so we set out early, hoping to get to our destination in the afternoon. While we progressed, we heard that the Carretera Central had been closed and there were army units and revolutionary units in the vicinity of some major towns, either fighting or at an impasse. Things were getting serious, but we continued on our journey, mother praying as usual, and I interested in the adventure in which we were engaged. We had no difficulty going through most of the towns until we got to Colón. This is a small town in the province of Las Villas. When we got there, we found the town in turmoil. There was plenty of evidence that some people had already abandoned the town and others were getting ready to do so, but most of the population was staying put. We tried to get information from any authorities we could find, although authorities were few and far between, as the cliché says, and we could not get firm information on whether the road ahead, in the direction we were going, was closed or not.

After some deliberation we decided to go on, but having traveled a few miles we had to stop at a barrier set up by government soldiers. They said that there was some resistance from the insurgents and they could not let us continue; we might get hurt. We explained our situation and the need to proceed, but they insisted that they could not let us go on. So, we had to turn back. By that time, it was late in the day, so mother and I got a room in the only hotel worth the name in the town of Colón and spent the night. Next morning the situation had not changed and we decided to return to Havana.

The following days were full of news, some official and some rumors circulated on the streets. The revolutionaries were coming. But what would happen when they got to Havana? What would Batista's army do? After all, Batista was an army man and the army controlled the country. Those who could stocked up on supplies just in case there were battles and the distribution of food was interrupted. Tanks and bathtubs were filled to the rim with water and in general the population of the city got ready for the worst. In the morning of January first we woke up at the news that Batista and his closest advisers had fled the country and Castro was on his way to Havana.

There was enormous jubilation. Batista had been the strong man in Cuba for decades. He rose to power first through the revolt he led against the authoritarian government of Gerardo Machado in 1933. After his success, he named himself chief of the armed forces and controlled the power under several presidential figureheads until 1940, when he was elected president. After serving a term of four years, he moved to the United States but returned to run for president again. When it became clear that he would not win the elections, he seized power through a coup d'état and ruled by himself or through others until 1958. His regime was thoroughly corrupt and the atrocities that his secret service committed were unpardonable. Cubans were ready for a clean and democratic government.

Castro's entrance into Havana was a triumphant march worthy of a Roman legion, except that the revolutionaries looked nothing like the heroic Romans of ancient times. They drove into Havana in war vehicles of various types, with flags, singing, and proclaiming liberty, dressed in fatigues with rosaries around their necks. Years later, in the early seventies, I was going to see another one of these entries, this time that of Juan Domingo Perón in Buenos Aires, and the similarities were striking. Most interesting was that both initiated periods of governance that were failures and dashed the hopes of large segments of the population.

Castro behaved like a rather modest person during his years of struggle, but when he entered Havana, he transformed himself into an emperor, a Napoleon, although of course of lesser stature. In his mind, I think he thought he was infallible and indispensable, a god, and therefore that Cuba owed him honor and obedience. What followed was tragic for everyone, but particularly so for those who had given everything to the Revolution and found themselves marginalized by the new regime. They had made possible the Revolution, but now it seemed that only some of the revolutionaries owned it. A true revolution belongs to the people, not to a handful of leaders, let alone one supreme leader, as in fact became the case in Cuba. The hurt of those who were marginalized by Castro and his cronies was not so much about what happened to them, but about the course the regime took. Democracy became something different in Castro's lexicon, and eventually, after the complete consolidation of the regime as a result of the failed invasion of the Bay of Pigs, the reality of a communist police state dawned on them.

I have never been gullible about leaders and caudillos. Indeed, I have a positive aversion to authority figures in every area of human experience. I am particularly distrustful of political and army figures. Their claims to authority usually hide a desire for power and control. I am also very distrustful of religious authorities, because apart from a desire for power and what comes with it, some of them are insecure and their only basis for their authority is their own ignorance and the ignorance of those over whom they exert it. Indeed, I am even suspicious of scientists and writers, because often their claims to authority are based on pride, as is often the case with philosophers. The last ones are perhaps the worst of the lot, having no claim to knowledge but nonetheless pontificating about what they know and accosting those who might not be as sharp as they are or seem to be. The moment I saw Castro at the podium of power and start pontificating about things he knew nothing about, while eating-up the adoration of ignorant masses, I said to myself "We are in for a rough ride."

And we were. Imagine someone who will speak for seven hours! Who would say anything sensible in that amount of time in front of adoring multitudes? What purpose could this man have except blow off rubbish to ignorant and subservient crowds? I remember the first and only Castro speech that I attended. It was a 'sermon'. There were thousands of dutiful followers there, bowing to his so-called intelligence. I expected that he would offer something that would make me think, that would realistically explain the Cuban situation, and that would chart a future course that was not dependent on him. But what did he do? He wove a tale, rehashed from other sources and carefully calibrated to make himself appear learned, wise, and indispensable.

I did not stay for the entire peroration. Who would, that had any sense? I actually felt sick. This was the man that overthrew Batista? Unfortunately, the future actions of his government vindicated my negative judgment. I wish I had been wrong. The Revolution turned out to be a front for megalomania. Its true goal was to get Castro to power and crown him as emperor, a divine figure we as Cubans were supposed to adore. Unlike other Cubans who hated him and his message, I did not. It seemed to me that he was in a worse position than I, because he probably believed all the garbage he spewed. He was no better than other dictators and tyrants who despise their victims and love only the manufactured image they have of themselves.

There was no alternative but to wait and see if the government would survive or would fall when large numbers of Cubans realized that they had been sold the London Bridge with another name. But most of them did not realize the game Castro was playing until it was too late. People changed their views when, as they said in Cuba, the Revolution *les pisaba el cayo*, that is, when the Revolution 'stepped on their corn'. We, human beings, are rather predictable. We scream only when we are adversely affected. And so it happened with the Revolution. Everyone was in favor until the revolutionary government did something that went against their interests.

One of the first measures that affected the opinion of the bourgeoisie was the slashing of rents by half. A standard way in which the Cuban middle class supported itself was by buying rental property, and so when Castro cut rents many members of this class turned against him. Even more important were the First Agrarian Reform Law of May 1959, the Urban Reform Law of October 1960, the Nationalization Law of October 1960, and the Nationalization of Education Law of June 1961. Each of these laws divided sections of the population, so that by the end of 1961 a large section of the bourgeoisie felt alienated. By then, however, they could do nothing, because Castro had, like similar figures in history, accumulated enormous power.

In the first week of February, barely five weeks after Castro's march into Havana, I wrote in my diary that there was no hope for the new government or the Cuban people. And everything that followed confirmed it: the condemnation and execution, á la Soviet, and without proper judicial procedures, of people who had presumably committed crimes; the nationalization of industries and lands without proper discussion of the consequences; the confiscation of private property without proper compensation; the death, presumably "by accident," of those in Castro's original group who opposed his views; and many other events indicated a road to a Marxist-Leninist state and a future along the lines of the Soviet Union. On January 1, 1959, I had had hopes for Cuba, but now I was in despair.

Chapter Seventy-Five

The University of Havana

"What do you want to be when you grow up?" I had a hell of a time choosing what I wanted to be, even though picking a profession is surely one of the two or three most important decisions we make in our lives. Sometimes this is a contextual decision, forced on us by circumstances. Children of physicians are pressed to follow on their parents' footsteps, to continue the family tradition perhaps and to profit from its already established connections to a profession. For others the choice is a family business, a trade, or a skill. Children of farmers are pressured to become farmers; of lawyers to become lawyers; of plumbers to become plumbers; and so on. For others the choice is marked by a desire to rebel against something that has been programmed by the family. Children of shopkeepers who made a fortune do not want to be shopkeepers; they want to get away from trade and climb to a higher rung in the social ladder. They'd rather be professionals or artists, even though they cannot change their lower social origin and must suffer social slights for it for the rest of their lives. Even children of well-established lawyers may not want to become lawyers and join the family law firm; they may want to become scientists or dancers. There is also a matter of talent. Some people are good at math and so they drift to careers in which this is essential, such as accounting, economics, or physics. In some cases, a marked interest from an early age in something specific, such as music or acting, makes the choice of a career easy. There are also plenty of career stereotypes, particularly depending on gender. In Cuba, women were steered to certain fields if they were to have careers at all. For most of them, a good espousal match was conceived to be their proper aim: getting married and having children.

    A few of us, however, have no particular talent, being able to do many things fairly well, but nothing extraordinarily well, and there is no context that leads us one way or another. This creates much anxiety and indecision.

Almost every profession or field of human endeavor offers something unique that can captivate the interest of a young person — literature, the arts, philosophy, science, law, medicine, finance, accounting, engineering, theology; baseball, basketball, and hockey; carpentry, electricity, and plumbing; businesses such as farming or commerce; and even the armed forces such as the navy or the air force — all offer something captivating if you go deep enough into them. The fact that people devote their whole lives to these enterprises and are often enthusiastic about what they do constitutes proof of their perceived value and appeal.

Chapter Seventy-Six

Alea Iacta Est

From a very early age I was frequently asked what I wanted to be and for many years the answer was always the same: a physician. I am not sure whether this idea had been deliberately planted in my mind by my family, whether I had come to it because physicians were common in my background and there was a general admiration for them, or because a physician took care of me when I was sick, and this was perhaps something that had impressed my young mind. Father had wanted to be a physician but did not become one because of financial difficulties in his youth. His father had been a physician. And my great-grandfather on the maternal side had also been a physician.

There was no need to make up my mind about a career for many years of course, but when I reached the third year of high school, I had to begin considering seriously what I wanted to be. In two years, I had to make a decision and enter the university in a particular field. Cuba had no colleges of liberal arts, only universities. Whereas college in the U.S. involves a period of general learning rather than specialization, in Cuba post-secondary education was highly specialized and taught in universities. It was necessary to know what one wanted to do when one graduated from high school (called *bachillerato*), and I had to come to terms with that deadline. I needed to choose, but what?

I had read Dickens' *Great Expectations* and had become impressed with the tragic fate of Richard, who had wasted his life waiting for an inheritance that never came and moving from one career choice to another, without ever settling on one to which he devoted all his efforts in order to make it work. Of course, my situation was different than Richard's. He was forever expecting an inheritance, whereas I had already received one. Indeed, the fact that father was dead, and, given to his professional and business successes, I was financially independent put no pressure on a career that would be practical enough to earn me a living. Still, I had to be something, to study something, and I wanted it to be something that satisfied my interests, a challenge that will keep me occupied for the rest of my life. Unfortunately, or perhaps fortunately, depending on the point of view, I liked too many things. Indeed, the list of professions I considered seriously was wild, ranging from extreme opposites.

My greatest fear was not that I would not become something or other. I thought that far I would go. What made me anxious was the possibility that, precisely because I was financially independent and did not need to support myself or my prospective family, I would become a dilettante, never achieving anything. It is pleasant to be a dilettante, to jump from one thing to another, following one's inclination, but never going too deeply into any so that I would have to think and work hard. The idea terrified me, not because I hated to be a dilettante but because it was so attractive when there was no need for me to be serious. Richard's future, with money, not without it, loomed large on my horizon.

My alliances were divided from the very beginning in high school between the natural sciences, the social sciences, and the humanities, but matters got progressively more complicated as I was introduced to new fields in these branches of knowledge. The subjects that had been primary in my mind from the beginning, the ones that excited me, were algebra and geometry in the sciences, and history in the humanities/social sciences. Reading about the Greeks and the Romans was like entering a fantasy world of adventure. But the rigor of algebra and geometry, the beauty of Euclid, whose many theorems I studied in wonder, captivated my attention. Doing the homework in these subjects was nothing like work. It was a delight. I had the particular advantage of a good memory, so that after reading something I could recall the text that I had read, the place on the page, the line, even the order of the words in many cases. And history was perfect for someone with this talent. I read and reread and memorized without difficulty the wonderful tales of adventure and heroism that were part of history. Surely, is there any young man of my age at the time that is not inspired by the heroism of Achilles, by his loyalty to Patroclus, and by the adventures of Odysseus? But Euclid was as enticing, although in a different way. The symmetry of numbers, their predictability, cleanliness, and clarity were miracles. How could one resist wanting to do more of that?

Still, before my third year of high school, I had not yet thought deeply about what to be; I was merely enjoying what was put before me. I confronted this question head on at the beginning of the third year, but by that time I had also been introduced to psychology and physics. I saw physics as the goal of geometry and algebra. This was not just something abstract and beautiful, a kind of fun game, it was knowledge of the world. Now I understood the world better and understood why it worked the way it did. My teacher, Brother Rafael, was wonderful and elicited from me both admiration and affection. He was a model athlete and a fantastic teacher. It was fun to see him playing basketball in his soutane, with his athletic physique and agility. He looked like a Moor, with a very thick beard that showed even when he had just shaved. His hair was very black and his skin a shade of olive. I was one of his favorite students, if not his favorite, because I loved physics as he did and for a while, I also played basketball.

Brother Rafael was an inspiration to me. I wanted to be like him, to know what he knew and I was convinced that he could teach it to me. And he corresponded in kind, because he saw in me an eager pupil who wanted to learn and achieve excellence. I remember many of my teachers but none like Brother Rafael. He was the only one that exemplified the love of knowledge that Socrates so well practiced in Plato's Dialogues.

Physics became a center of my attention, driving me to think that this was the field I wanted to pursue. Was it because of my teacher or because of the field? It is easy to underestimate and overestimate what a teacher means for a young man. Perhaps the affection and sympathy come first and generates the love of the subject matter later, but perhaps it is the other way around. I had several teachers whom I loved and it was not coincidental that I also loved what they taught.

The decision about what to be was not that easy, because in third year I was also introduced to psychology, and that created a storm in my thinking. Here was a field that had to do with the human mind, so close to me and yet so secret and elusive. I was fascinated by psychology and began to think seriously that this was my calling. The idea of combining psychology and the career I had always thought I would pursue, namely medicine, slowly crept into my thinking, challenged, of course, by physics. Physics, medicine, and psychology were all sciences, although they appeared very different from each other. But were they? Besides, becoming a psychiatrist would help me negotiate among at least two of my conflicting alliances.

During the fourth year of high school my interest in psychology deepened, although psychology was not one of the fields studied in that year, but I read on my own. Physics continued to be of great interest to me, although perhaps not as enticing as before—my new teacher at St. Thomas Military Academy was good, but not as good as my old teacher at the Marist School. Brother Rafael had been unique. Slowly, some of the passion for physics faded at the same time that something else made its appearance.

For years I had a true passion for literature, although I generally hated courses on it at school. I believe the reason for the hate was that we did not read literature in them. The object of the courses was to memorize plots about various literary works and information about their authors. Except for poetry, we read selections from famous works, but they were snippets, short paragraphs, too short to give a flavor of the works from which they had been taken. Yet, at home I had been a voracious reader for several years. I read everything available to me, but mostly fiction. French and English fiction were preeminent. Perhaps this was because my family had accumulated a good number of the classics from those languages.

I went along, reading books belonging to father or to aunt Rosario. I read everything and never missed a word, never skipped a passage, no matter how boring and uninteresting. The fear of missing something significant was too strong. I felt this as a kind of moral imperative. I considered it bad, almost a moral transgression, to miss something, to skip what the author had written. I also considered it a sign of disloyalty, a treason, so I worked diligently through impossible passages from Victor Hugo, Alexander Dumas, and Marcel Proust. If there is purgatory and I am supposed to atone for my sins in it, I am sure that all the pain I endured reading endlessly boring prose will count toward reducing my debt and cleaning up my soul. Unfortunately, I did not consider the pain so, and I failed to offer it as atonement. Maybe I missed an opportunity, like so many others I have in my life?

The passion for literature, and particularly fiction, did not diminish, but I was never able to reconcile it with the thought of a career, with one exception: for a while I toyed with the notion of becoming a journalist. Many books I read were written by journalists and novelists were, in a sense, journalists of fictional characters, narrators of the lives of people and the events that had affected them. This is how the idea of becoming a writer grew in me. The power to write well, to communicate the innermost thoughts that I had, and in the process to grasp something almost ineffable, was mesmerizing. Reading fed this flame constantly, but I was timid about writing. I did try, but felt that I was failing. Instead I read and read. The reading, particularly of long and boring books, helped me both to strengthen the discipline I had already developed since fifth grade and to develop a focus. Focusing had been important in my studies. It was what turned me from an indifferent student to a top student when in fourth grade I realized that paying close attention to what my teachers were saying made all the difference when it came to understanding the subject matter and of fixing it in my mind. A well understood lecture and a diligently done homework was all that was needed to perform well in quizzes and exams. The reading outside the curriculum emphasized that focus and expanded the depth of my understanding. But writing was something on the side; it was not really a career. I investigated all the ins and outs of going into journalism school, but eventually gave that up.

Still, when I considered the alternatives for my future, I felt as if I was in a candy store and could not decide what to buy. The move to St. Thomas Military Academy made matters worse, because it exposed me to an entirely different set of possibilities. On the one hand, the enticement of the military.

Remember Achilles and heroism? What young man hasn't wanted at some time or another to be a hero, to fight battles, to wear fancy uniforms, and endure terrible hardships for his country? I had already toyed with the idea of going to sea and spending a year as a sailor in a boat going around the world. (Of course, I had never given a thought to the fact that I had inherited a serious case of motion sickness from *Abuelita Belé*). The lust to visit other places and meet other cultures had in part caused me to consider finishing my schooling in Canada or Switzerland, and eventually ended with the move to St. Thomas. The Academy emphasized the life of the soldier, the hero. And the fact that father had been a cadet helped give, in my eyes, a certain legitimacy to the armed forces that otherwise they would not have had. Nonetheless, I did not ever seriously consider joining the army, but it certainly was a thought that crossed my mind in lighter moments while talking to other cadets. Who would not want to march in splendid uniforms in front of adoring crowds, or die a glorious death, in some field of battle? Isn't that the moral of Borges' *"El Sur"*?

More serious was an interest in art. My family was not particularly focused on art. Mother was quite talented and could draw well, but like everything else with her, it was only a passing interest. And father's interest was in classical music, which mother disparagingly called "funereal." I grew up with very little awareness of arts and artists, but when I moved to St. Thomas Military Academy, one of my classmates was a dilettante who dabbled in many things, one of which was painting. Naturally I was curious about it and started painting myself. But was there an outlet for this? How would my budding interest in art be put together with my other interests? And what about psychology and physics?

To delay further the choice about what to do, to give myself some additional time, I decided to merge two years into one for my final year of high school. In Cuba, the final year of high school was divided into two branches from which students could choose one. One was devoted to the sciences and the other to the humanities and social sciences. Physics, chemistry, mathematics, and biology were studied in one. Sociology, logic, philosophy, the history of the Americas, French, and literature were studied in the other. Almost every student made a decision and chose only one of these paths, but given my predicament I went for both. Matters were further complicated because we had other subjects in addition to these: religion, military training, English, etiquette, manual arts, fencing, and typing.

It was a tough year and the results were not as spectacular as those warranted by my previous record. Still, I got 'A' in every subject, including chemistry, except for mathematics, where I got a 'B+', and my beloved physics, where I got a 'C+'. My excuse was that seventeen subjects in one year were enough to drive someone mad. Still, the low grades in those two subjects were very disappointing to me, although I quite well understood that the sciences in the fifth year were advanced and I just did not have the time to devote to them that I would have liked, particular with the busy social life of a seventeen year old. The previous year I had been awarded "The Most Distinguished Student in the School Medal." In the fifth year I was not able to earn it again because a third-year student had the straight 'A' record I failed to achieve. A small compensation was the promotion to First Officer of Company A.

All in all, I was satisfied that I had done my best and the performance, considering the load, was not embarrassing. In particular I was interested in the new subjects to which I had been introduced. Two I specially loved: logic and philosophy, although neither was taught well. The teacher was a Heideggerian who could not explain clearly anything, perhaps because he was too faithful to Heidegger. Having been trained in the sciences, I found this imprecision and obscurity intolerable. Fortunately, we read Plato's *Apology of Socrates*. The Dialogues of Plato awoke in me passionate debates about justice, duty, and nationality. The bad teacher repelled me but Plato hooked me, as Socrates would say, with a love of wisdom that has never died. Still, like Pontius Pilate, I betrayed that love. I did seriously investigate a career in philosophy, but nothing came of it because it was not clear that one could seriously pursue such a career in Cuba. The subject matter was taught only in one year of high school, and there were not enough universities where one could pursue or teach this subject seriously. The study of philosophy was combined with literature in the university curriculum, and this was not what I had in mind. I hated literature as a profession, equating it with literary criticism. So, I gave up on philosophy and remained where I had been, before I encountered what was ultimately going to be my path in life.

To work through my indecision and choose a "proper" career, in desperation I took a series of psychological tests that were supposed to give me an idea of what I really wanted to do and could do, in spite of my doubts about what to do. It was an elaborate affair, with tests of all kinds, including some that measured my abilities and talents. Unfortunately, the results were inconclusive to this extent: they confirmed that in terms of abilities I was well suited for the sciences, the social sciences, the humanities, and even the arts. And with respect to deep-seated interests they confirmed that I was interested in all the subjects I consciously knew that interested me. The results were therefore a disaster. What to do? After all this work I had not advanced one bit. I was still at my point of departure and would have to decide myself, maybe by throwing the dice? The ghost of Dickens' Richard loomed large, but I was resolved to resist such a future.

OK, so I decided to be scientific about the problem. First, I decided to do something about medicine. Was I suited for this career and would I be happy in it? The way I proceeded was to go to the University of Havana School of Medicine and visit the dissection room. This was stupid, but I figured that if I were not seriously affected by this room, I would have no problem with medicine. The result was decisive. I was repulsed by the dead bodies, but that was not what got me. It was the misery of the bodies and body parts, the remains of what once had been living people that troubled me. The scene was shocking and sad. I became so depressed that I thought I could never get used to becoming a doctor, even if I did not have to deal with dead people on a daily basis. It was just too much for me to live constantly in contact with human misery.

I returned home, and that night I dreamt of death and human frailty, of what we are when life leaves us. It took me some time to get over the experience. I could not get out of my mind the tables with body parts on them, human remains, grim, lifeless, and scattered without order or reason. Where were the original bodies, some beautiful, perfect in some ways, and full of color and life? Where were the experiences of these people, their dreams, their ideas? What happened to their loves and passions, their hates and resentments, their pleas? It was a tough scene, much worse than the craniums that Christian monks kept close by in order to remember that we are nothing, eventually just dust. For me dust was unimpressive; it was the bodies not yet turned to dust that revealed the chasm between life and death. The inert organs, the limbs, the piles of pieces that added up to nothing.

I decided that I could not be happy contemplating human misery. Unlike the Buddha, I tried to turn my back on it by abandoning the idea of a profession that would keep me in constant touch with death and its causes. I kicked psychiatry, and thus medicine, from the field of career possibilities, but that did not affect psychology. Psychology was still of interest and there was a university in Havana that had psychology as a career, the Universidad de Villanueva. This was a private Catholic university located in a plush Havana suburb that I knew well and which I frequently passed by on my way to school. So, I applied to their program. I had a sterling record in school and I knew that I had done very well in tests that measured both verbal and quantitative abilities. I was quite confident that I would have no problem getting in. However, I had a big surprise coming to me. I was rejected. The reason, according to the person that notified me, was that I needed psychological help.

This was a shock because I had always thought that I was quite normal. I got along with others, had many friends of both sexes, and enjoyed the things that young people enjoy. And I had had, some even recently, many psychological tests that had never discovered a problem. But the guy was quite firm, and he went so far as to give me the name of a psychiatrist to check me out. I went to see the doctor and explained what had happened, and he listened at an astronomical fee per hour. I was not impressed the first time I went to talk to him. It seemed to me that he was a charlatan, although most of the time he talked very little. I figured that if I needed help, this guy needed it more. I gave him some time to show me what was wrong with my mind, but after four sessions I decided this was a complete waste of time and money. I still did not know what was wrong with me, or even if there was anything wrong, and this guy seemed not to know himself.

I mulled the matter for a few days and then came to the conclusion that the problem had been the Rorschach tests I took as part of the entrance examinations to the university. Unlike other people who took the tests, I looked at them as an opportunity to have some fun, to show off my creative streak. I wrote pages and pages, inventing all sorts of things that had little to do with what I saw on the ink blots at a first impression. I figured that when the psychologist read all this he thought I was crazy. And maybe I was, as measured by some criteria they used at the time. That did not bother me too much, although I was disappointed that I could not study what I wanted and had to go back to the drawing board about my future. The problem was that future, for the past could not be changed or rectified. I was not crazy enough to believe, as St. Peter Damien held, that the past could be changed, although he thought it could be done only by a supreme divinity. I was stuck with the hand that destiny had given me. What to do?

Surely, I had to forget about psychiatry and psychology, but what else could I do? Time was of the essence. I first decided to go back and consider one of my old interests, science, particularly physics. But that by itself sounded too dry now, I needed something creative, something fanciful, an opportunity to invent. Then it occurred to me that art had to be part of it, although not all of it, the mix had to include science. Which field would do that? The only profession that seemed to fit the requirements was architecture because it combined science and art. So, I registered at the University of Havana, and also at the Escuela de Artes Plásticas San Alejandro which was the school of art.

It was a fortuitous choice, one made in heaven because I loved architecture from the very beginning. Indeed, I could have been very happy as an architect. From the start I excelled both in the science and the art of it. The second was clear from the very first meeting of the design class. It was a very large class, more than two hundred students, and was a required course for all budding architects. Some of the students had been doing art for years and had taken private lessons related to the field. In contrast, I was a complete neophyte and felt like an ignoramus compared to them. But something happened that first day that was to give me confidence in my choice.

In our first meeting, the instructor asked us to take an eleven by eight-inch sheet of white paper and make a design on it. This was preposterous. He gave us no guidance as to what we needed to do. And you can imagine the results. Every student wanted to impress him. And of course, most of them had the tools and experience to do it, whereas I had none. I thought this would be the end of my career as an architect. Yet, I looked at the piece of paper in front of me and at my colors and brushes and I picked one brush, dipped it into bright yellow paint, and did a kind of zig zag on the paper, large, from one corner to the opposite one. Then I picked another brush, dipped it into black paint and painted a line on each of the sides of the yellow zig-zag, and then I stopped. It took me two minutes to do this.

In the meantime, the other students were working feverishly drawing and painting elaborate pictures and furiously trying to get it all done. Well, the time was up, and the main instructor—he had a retinue of assistants—walked through the room looking at the products. Mostly he ignored them, but he picked up one here and another there. And as he passed by my desk, he picked up mine. Wow! He picked up my picture. Was it because it was very bad or very good? The suspense nearly killed me. And my pals did not know what to make of it.

Having finished his tour, the instructor walked to the front of the room. He had picked up half a dozen pictures and then he proceeded to talk about each of them and to explain the principles of design they illustrated and why he had picked them up. About mine he said that it showed a dynamism and movement that was creative, while at the same time it was simple and used colors effectively. Then he proceeded to post the pictures at the front of the classroom. I was elated. Felt to be in high heaven. But, was what I had done really any good? It seemed so simple, so insignificant. After all, what did I know about art, beauty, and architecture? I liked certain things, and disliked others. But I was not clear about the reasons. Perhaps the adage is right: *De gustibus non est disputandum* (there is no accounting for taste). But I wanted to know what made something good, and I had no idea of what did. Did my teacher? Could I trust his judgment? After all, he had picked my picture, and *my* picture could not be any good, since it was *mine,* and what did I know about drawing? Something had to be wrong. The picture was too simple, too elemental. Attractive yes, but really better than the many others that showed a mastery of technique and the history of art and architecture?

I got some reassurances about my work, because from then on, practicably everything I did found a place at the front of the class. I developed a personal style of writing—writing is very important for architects since their blueprints have writing on them. The writing has to be clear and readable, but also beautiful and unique, and I thought the style I developed met the desired criteria. Still, I did not have the answer to the question of what made something plastic good, and this continued to bother me, and still does. I was not satisfied with what my teachers said.

Apart from design and other courses having to do with the creative aspects of architecture, we also had to take courses on calculus and perspective. I had no problem with those courses, although Perspective required a nonintuitive way of looking at spaces and figures that constituted a real challenge. I continued to distinguish myself as one of the best students in first year, and this led me to think that I was on the right track after all, until the unfortunate Bay of Pigs invasion derailed everything, so I had to find a way to flee Cuba.

When I picked architecture as my career, I thought I had made a decision that would shape the course of my life for the rest of it. I felt a bit like Caesar when he passed the Rubicon, the die was cast, and there was no turning back. Little did I know that forces over which I had no control were going to be unleashed shortly and my future would take an entirely different direction. So much for the view that we control our destiny. Obviously, I was not destined to be an architect, although to this day I still take an interest in architecture and follow some of its contemporary developments. I became a philosopher, instead, but that is another story that does not belong in a narrative of my years in Cuba.

Formal training in architecture began later, during the school year at the University of Havana. Instead of copying the work of other artists, we were given casts of famous sculpted torsos for us to draw. We were also given casts of hands and feet that we were supposed to use as models for sculpture. I found out that I could draw pretty well, but to sculpt was beyond me. The hand I had chosen as a model was very simple, but I had extreme difficulty in reproducing it in clay. Indeed, the end product I achieved was hopeless. It did not look like the hand at all, but like a blob of clay, maybe like a paw of a monster. This gave me a great appreciation for what Michelangelo and Canova, among other great sculptors, had done. How could they do it? It was a matter of talent, obviously, and I had none. I was embarrassed by the result of my work, but the teacher told me not to worry. There was plenty of time for me to learn to sculpt, and even if I did not, not every artist is able to do everything. Indeed, most sculptors today do not sculpt at all but instead compose assemblages of ready-made objects that require no sculpting technique. But of course, I did not feel much better because other students had produced fine pieces.

Fall followed summer, and the 1960-61 school year got under way at the University. The nation had been under Castro's iron rule almost two years and things had changed drastically. Cuba had become a communist state, although the official declaration to that effect was not made until a year later. At this time, there were still hopes that things could change, hopes that were shattered after the Bay of Pigs invasion which gave the regime an excuse to crack down and consolidate power, eliminating the few remaining civil liberties that had been still in existence.

I graduated from high school in June and was due to enter university in September. This was the first time that I would go to a public educational institution, and co-educational to boot, so I was apprehensive. The sheltered life of private schools was over. The University of Havana was the only university in Cuba that offered architecture, so there was no other alternative available. What I did not anticipate was that in that year I would have more fun than in all my previous years of schooling taken together, even though that was also the year that changed the course of my life radically and made it impossible for me to remain in Cuba. At the end of the school year the doors to a viable future had closed to those who were not in complete sync with the revolutionary government.

The fact that I had a car made things much easier for me at the University. A car attracted others and facilitated social exchanges. Indeed, the very first day of classes I met a group of young men and women that would become, except for a couple of drop outs, inseparable. We were seven or eight altogether, more or less equally divided between males and females, depending on who showed up. Each of us was as different from the others as we could possibly be, and there were also political and class differences.

One of the young women was slightly older, elegant—lived on a street off Quinta Avenida, in a house full of contemporary art. The house had a large wall bordering a staircase to the second floor which they had filled with contemporary Cuban art. Her father was an architect and she had grown immersed in works of art and architecture. She was very understated, demurring, sophisticated, and perhaps, by pose, an ingenue. Another was a nice, religious, very Catholic girl, and just out of a private school run by nuns. She was pleasant.

The guys were a motley crew. Two of the four had a lower middle class background and were both short. One was very smart, a bit loud but a lot of fun. The other was more self-conscious, and obsessed with everything that looked American. The other two guys were from solid middle class homes. I liked the last guy best and established a good friendship with him which lasted until I left Cuba.

The group clicked on the first day of school, and from then on we were inseparable. If I remember correctly, the entering class had something like two-hundred-fifty students. Given the large number, most classes were divided into smaller sections, except for the class on design and the class on perspective. Our group managed to get into the same section of the class, and we sat together. We compared notes on what we were doing, and sometimes a subgroup of the group studied together for exams. After classes we stayed talking and, whenever there was time, we would eat together, or go to the theater or the movies. My car was the vehicle of choice because I could squeeze as many as six or seven in it, and we seldom were more than that. There was always one or two of us that had to do something else, so we were able to manage. Some of us also paid for private drawing lessons to make sure that we were appropriately primed to do well so we spent even more time together. I managed to continue with my classes at San Alejandro, but I was the only one doing this. It was a very busy year for me.

I had never before experienced anything like the companionship and camaraderie I enjoyed that year. High school was fun at St. Thomas Military Academy. Primary school had been frequently painful, but university was finally a place where I did not just enjoy my subjects but also my mates. This group of people were all interested in similar things. We all wanted to do well in school and to learn. We were serious about what we were doing, and we liked to have fun.

And politics? Occasionally one or another of us would say something disagreeable to some of the others who had a different political affiliation, but this was very seldom and usually it was said in a tone that was not offensive—more like teasing. Most of the time we stayed out of politics. Obviously, we all knew who each of us was, where we came from, and where we stood vis-a-vis the Revolution. This was obvious in the way we behaved, the clothes we wore, the schools to which we had gone before, and the tastes that we had developed. But we never dwelled on the differences among us, and I never uttered a criticism against the government. It was too risky. Those of us who had not bought the 'London Bridge' Castro was selling lived in constant fear.

At the university we were a group of young people, smart, handsome, and with common interests, and that was enough to bind us, in spite of the political chasm that separated us. And we were decent human beings. Unfortunately, the future intended to separate us, and it did so effectively after the Bay of Pigs.

Rumors began to circulate that the Cuban government was going to change the design of paper money and would remove silver coins from circulation. Some people said that we should all save some of the coins for the time when the Revolution came crashing down. I thought that was a good idea and started collecting coins. Soon, I had stashed away a considerable number of coins, which I hid in various places around the house. Eventually I began to feel uneasy about keeping the coins in closets, under beds, and in kitchen cabinets, because the government regarded such hoarding as illegal. So, I thought the best thing was to put them at the bottom of a series of planters we had along the hall that connected all the bedrooms of our apartment. This seemed to work well. I placed them at the bottom of the planters, covered them with dirt, and replaced the plants on top. Who would suspect that there were any coins there? I had not counted on the dangers posed by the unexpected.

Abuelita Belé lived with us and her mind was beginning to go. One day, while I was out, she knocked down one of the planters that was a bit unstable. It fell and the dirt, together with the plant and the coins, spilled all over. What made the situation perilous was that one of the neighbors, known for her Revolutionary zeal, was a member of the block revolutionary committee—the organ used by the government to spy on the population for possible violations of government regulations or tepid revolutionary attitude. She was visiting mother in the living room. The crash of the planter was bad enough to call attention, but it became the least of mother's worries when grandmother proceeded to come into the living room to inform mother, in front of this woman, that there were silver coins all over the hallway, coming out of the planter. Mother got out of the situation as best she could, making signs to the lady that my grandmother's head had gone, which fortunately, was the end of the incident.

That very night we dug up all the coins and put them in bags which my uncle-in-law Fernando was commissioned to take as far as possible from our home and inconspicuously drop them, under the cover of darkness, in the ocean or the river. He was still doing this every few days when I left Cuba.

Chapter Seventy-Seven

The Bay of Pigs and a Police State

The incident of the coins brings to the fore a feature of our daily life in Cuba after Castro took over the nation. Increasingly and surely, the Castro regime put in place measures that turned Cuba into a police state. The idea behind it was clear: to check on everyone so as to prevent counterrevolutionary activity and thus control the population. The most effective of these measures perhaps was the establishment of the feared Committees for the Defense of the Revolution. Their motto was *"¡En cada barrio, Revolución!"* (In every neighborhood, Revolution!). Fidel Castro described it as "a collective system of revolutionary vigilance," that would make sure "everybody knows who lives on every block, what they do on every block, what relations they had with the tyranny, in what activities are they involved, and with whom they met." The committees were very effective, insofar as they kept tabs on what every Cuban was doing.

Everyone in Cuba who questioned the validity of the Revolutionary government, or disagreed with the measures that it adopted, had to keep quiet or suffer the consequences. Since the government was in control of every aspect of Cuban life, including justice and jobs, those who disagreed with it were in a constant state of fear because they had no recourse. Children had to be kept ignorant of their parents' views if they disagreed with the government, so that they might not accidentally reveal something about them that would endanger their wellbeing. Even with adults in the same family, one had to be careful insofar as some of them could be informers. Indeed, some children willingly informed on their parents in reaction to the indoctrination they received in schools, and some members of families informed on other members because of their commitment to the Revolution.

The deadly effectiveness of the block committees was proven without a doubt during the ill-fated Bay of Pigs invasion. The invasion began on April

17, 1961, and ended three days later. The forces of Cuban exiles that the CIA had put together to invade Cuba were easily defeated by the Cuban armed forces and the militia. The irony of this affair was that apparently President Kennedy's administration assumed the entire plan would catch the Cuban government by surprise. That was one of the reasons why they thought the plan would work, encouraged by an incompetent CIA whose intelligence was as far from reality as it often seems to be today, and the optimistic views of Miami Cubans who, like the CIA, seem to live in 'La La Land'. The element of surprise was a key to the entire operation, but it was not the only one. As important, if perhaps not more so, was the belief that the moment the invading troops landed, the Cuban people would rise against Castro's tyranny.

Neither of them had a grain of truth in them. Rumors about an impending invasion of exiled Cubans helped by the CIA were rife in Cuba before the invasion. The question was not whether there would be an invasion but when and where. We were all expecting it at any moment, and as time passed the certainty that it would occur became progressively stronger. There was hardly any conversation among Cubans who did not support Castro's regime that did not, at some point, touch on the impending invasion. And the belief that Cubans would rise the moment invading forces landed was absurd. It not only underestimated the popularity of the Castro regime in Cuba, but it also underestimated the control that the government had established over the population. Furthermore, it ignored the need for weapons and training to mount a resistance against the well-armed Revolutionary forces. Besides, who in his or her right mind would try to do anything without knowing if there were others engaged in a similar effort? Many Cubans hated the Revolutionary regime, but they were not so stupid as to put their lives in danger when they knew nothing about the support they would have from others and the likelihood of success. Indeed, most of the actions of the Cuban counter-revolutionary underground had so far amounted to no more than writing anti-government graffiti on public walls and on posting small pieces of paper with anti-revolutionary propaganda on public places. From this to taking up arms and going on the attack against the well-armed and disciplined forces of the Revolution was a long distance.

The number of forces at the disposal of the government at the time was estimated at 25,000. This was not that many, particularly if one counted on an element of surprise and the counterrevolutionary forces landed at a location that would allow them to establish a base on land and operate from there. But it is estimated that Castro counted with more than 200,000 members of the militia. These were the forces that held the key to the strength of the regime, because most of them were fanatically supportive. By comparison, the invading force amounted to a mere 1,500 men. Was there a chance that the invading force would succeed? It sounds absurd even to consider the possibility, particularly since President Kennedy did not want to give the forces, as it actually turned out, the air support they needed. The whole thing was a joke on Cubans, and a very tragic one for the Cubans who participated. They not only suffered casualties, but some were not able to land and were condemned to be adrift at sea on ill-prepared boats for days before being rescued by the Cuban authorities. One of these, I was told, had been in a grade two years lower than I was at St. Thomas Military Academy. His fate was rather grim because the members of his boat had to eat one of their companions, who died of wounds, in order to survive. The rest ended up in prison.

I remember the day that we learned about the invasion. Some people were euphoric, but the news was not encouraging. I was not a member of any counter revolutionary unit. In fact, although I was clearly not sympathetic to the regime, only one person had approached me to carry out counter revolutionary propaganda. This was someone from the Marist school, not from St. Thomas Military Academy. What he proposed seemed to me so absurd that I declined. If this was what counter revolutionaries were up to, it was clear that the Revolution was quite safe.

The Cuban government was obviously prepared for the invasion. This became clear when they lost no time in rounding-up people suspected of giving support to the invasion. The suspects were picked up and put in large public places, such as theaters or sport arenas so that they could be watched. Rumors about what was happening reached me very quickly and I did not waste any time. Most dangerous for me were the people who lived on my block, and I expected that those associated with the block committee would come for me. So, I took my car, drove it to a safe distance away and then on foot went to the house of friends. There I stayed until things calmed down and I heard from my family that the worst had happened.

Castro had triumphed and celebrations were taking place. Members of the block committee did ask about me and where I was, but because the neighbors were used to our frequent trips to the country and we were known to have family in various places, they did not go further. I do not think anything would have happened if they had found me at home. But I would have been taken and would have had to put up with detention for a while as many other thousands of Cubans did. I am grateful in particular to those friends in the university who, in spite of their political disagreements with me, did not identify me to the revolutionary authorities as a potential danger. Of course, I was not dangerous to the Revolution, since I never took any steps against it. I was merely opposed to a regime that got hold of power under false pretenses and that I saw as nefarious to the nation. Still, some of the members of my university group could have held a grudge against me for politically disagreeing with them. Why they did not, I am not sure. I assume that it was because they did not think that I was involved in any counter revolutionary activity, perhaps they had some regard for me, and they were decent people.

Chapter 77

After the Bay of Pigs, it was clear that I could not go back to the University. It was also clear that my only option was to leave Cuba. In fact, it had been fairly clear since a few months into the Castro regime that this was the only alternative. It had been clear to many families who had children in St. Thomas Military Academy, for after a few months under the new government the exodus of my school mates and their families to the United States had become an avalanche. At the beginning of 1960, no week went by in which one or more students were not pulled out of school because the family had left. Many of them did so legally, but there were some who owned yachts and simply put their valuables in them and sailed to Florida. Tales of the exodus abounded. Some parents, however, delayed their departure to make possible for their children to finish the 1959-60 school year. This was particularly the case in my class, which was the first graduating class in St. Thomas Military Academy and marked an important moment in our lives. One graduates only once from high school, and being a very small class, it was particularly important for us to stay together for graduation. After graduation the exodus was almost universal. Most of my classmates went to the United States, but some went as far away as Canada.

My situation was different. Father had died suddenly and the family had been left without an effective leader. My sister Nena was married and mother did not know what to do, particularly because grandmother was still living. Yet, it was clear that I had no future in Cuba and needed to leave, but how could I do that? It was not as if one could take a plane to Miami or to any other place. No country accepted Cubans except for the United States and Spain. And one could not just go to Miami, because the transportation there was all taken. The number of Cubans who were desperate to leave the island increased by the day, and it was clear that the Bay of Pigs affair had been the last straw.

The Revolution was here to stay and the only way to survive was to leave. Every embassy that gave any hope of granting visas to Cubans was mobbed. The only way to get a visa from a country that was willing to provide one was through some personal or political connection. No country in Latin America, in particular, wanted to be burdened with Cuban refugees. Besides, some countries, like Mexico, were sympathetic to the Castro regime merely because he was anti-American, so there was no possibility of escape through them. The most viable destinations were Spain and Jamaica. Spain because of the ties of Cubans with this country, and Jamaica because it was close to Cuba and also had historical relations to it and there was a good number of Jamaicans in Cuba who came to the island to work.

At St. Thomas Military Academy there had been students whose parents were ambassadors to Cuba, but unfortunately, they were too young to have had any friendly relations with me. The exception was Costa Rica. I had met the son of the ambassador and we had often done things together because we had a common friend. They had a great mansion in a suburb of Havana, which I had visited. So, I asked him whether there was some possibility of a visa for me, and he asked his dad. The ambassador was not encouraging. In the meantime, I had asked a Spanish priest, Father Duran, who was a good friend, whether he could be instrumental in getting me a visa to Spain, and he said that he thought he could and, in fact, he did. That story unfolds in a previous book, "With a Diamond in My Shoe: A Philosopher's Search for Identity in America." (SUNY Press, 2019).

Acknowledgments

My sister, Nena, who enjoyed this project during the last two years of her life.

My maternal grandmother who enjoyed discussing with me what she had not discussed with anyone else.

Aunt Rosario, guardian of the history of the Gracia-Dubié family, whose memory kept me honest.

Grand-Uncle Angelito, keeper of the Otero family dirt, who was neither an angel nor grand, but with whom I had a lot of fun.

Mother Leonila, who, upon reading this, would have shed tears and written a poem.

Father, who would have laughed with gusto reading this memoir.

About the Author

Jorge J. E. Gracia is Distinguished Professor of Philosophy and Comparative Literature at the University at Buffalo, State University of New York. His many books include: *Hispanic/Latino Identity*; *Painting Borges: Philosophy Interpreting Art Interpreting Literature; Images of Thought: Philosophical Interpretations of Carlos Estevez's Art; Identity, Memory, and Diaspora: Voices of Cuban-American Artists, Writers, and Philosophers;* and, *With a Diamond in My Shoe: A Philosopher's Search for Identity in America.*

www.ingramcontent.com/pod-product-compliance
Lightning Source LLC
Chambersburg PA
CBHW020245240426
43672CB00006B/640